SCHOOLS FOR ALL

William Preston Vaughn

SCHOOLS FOR ALL

THE BLACKS & PUBLIC EDUCATION
IN THE SOUTH, 1865-1877

THE UNIVERSITY PRESS OF KENTUCKY

A Phi Alpha Theta Award Book

ISBN: 0-8131-1312-1

Library of Congress Catalog Card Number: 73-86408

Copyright © 1974 by The University Press of Kentucky

A statewide cooperative scholarly publishing agency
serving Berea College, Centre College of Kentucky,
Eastern Kentucky University, Georgetown College,
Kentucky Historical Society, Kentucky State University,
Morehead State University, Murray State University,
Northern Kentucky State College, Transylvania University,
University of Kentucky, University of Louisville, and
Western Kentucky University.

Editorial and Sales Offices: Lexington, Kentucky 40506

For Virginia

Contents

Preface

HISTORIANS have neglected the subject of integration in Southern public schools during Reconstruction despite sweeping revisions of the political and economic history of the period. Progress in education of both races and expansion of public schools were two of the most vital, visible, and lasting achievements of Reconstruction. Many recent studies of Reconstruction, like their predecessors, have treated education in a cursory manner, almost as an afterthought. This book is an attempt to correct this deficiency. The early chapters discuss the process of black education, first by the federal government through the army, Freedmen's Bureau, and the private benevolent societies, and then by the Southern states. The response of Southern whites to black education and their reaction to the active presence of the Bureau and several thousand Yankee teachers is carefully noted. The second phase of the narrative focuses on the most burning educational controversy of the period—that of integration, or "mixed schools." A possibility in all the states undergoing Reconstruction, mixed schools became a reality only in Louisiana and at the University of South Carolina. However, during their few years of existence, these mixed schools worked remarkably well, until a return to Conservative political control produced their destruction.

The chronological period of this study varies with each state, although the general time-span is from 1865 to 1877—from the conclusion of the war to the downfall of Radical Reconstruction in South Carolina and Louisiana. By 1877 all the state governments of the former Confederacy had been reorganized, and segregated schools had been created by either constitutional or statutory provision.

A brief discussion of District of Columbia schools is included because of their importance to the role of Congress in integration, thus illustrating the unwillingness of most congressional Radicals to deal with integration in an honest and forthright manner. No genuine attempt is made to examine the all-black colleges of the South, for during Reconstruction they were either church-related or privately supported institutions, and this monograph is confined to public schools or schools that were absorbed into the Southern public school systems.

I am indebted to the staffs of many libraries and research institutions who helped me in the lengthy preparation of this book, especially those of Ohio State University, North Texas State University, Harvard University, the University of South Carolina, Louisiana State University, the University of Texas, the Library of Congress, and the National Archives. I owe a special debt of gratitude to Henry H. Simms, professor emeritus, Ohio State University, who directed the dissertation upon which this book is based, and to two of my colleagues at North Texas State University, Jack B. Scroggs and William Kamman, who read the manuscript in its entirety and made invaluable suggestions. To my wife, Virginia Meyer Vaughn, who typed many of the earlier drafts and proofread all of them, and to James Maxwell, who typed the final draft, go my sincere thanks for a job well done.

I must give special commendation to William Metz, International Historian of Phi Alpha Theta, for his full cooperation and to the Editorial Board and membership of Phi Alpha Theta who have made possible the publication of this study. I would also like to thank the Faculty Research Committee of North Texas State University, Robert B. Toulouse, chairman, for several grants which gave me substantial assistance for additional research and preparation of the manuscript.

1. *The Entering Wedge*

EVEN before Lincoln's Emancipation Proclamation of January 1863, missionary-minded Yankees with strong antislavery views saw a vast new field of endeavor in the education of several million illiterate blacks in the South. Northerners believed this task required their supervision, for Southern white control over black minds might produce dire consequences. The New England Freedmen's Aid Society warned that unless the North maintained vigilant direction over black education, the victorious nation would waste a golden opportunity for implanting the seeds of liberty in the minds of freedmen. Not only must there be Yankee direction of schooling, but it should be New England inspired, for through the freedmen "the New England leaven, i.e., intelligence and principle . . . [would reduce] the whole lump of Southern ignorance and prejudice."[1]

Some teaching of blacks had actually taken place in the South before the Civil War, usually in violation of state laws. Although every Southern state except Tennessee prohibited the instruction of slaves, many whites ignored these proscriptions until the 1830s. Early advocates of black education included slaveowners who wanted more efficient labor and missionaries who insisted that slaves be able to read the Scriptures. However, following the abortive Denmark Vesey revolt of 1822 and the Nat Turner uprising of 1831, some Southern whites became convinced that it was impossible to cultivate black minds without arousing a spirit of self-assertion and rebellion. Others believed that blacks were incapable of being educated, while still others feared that literate blacks would read and be influenced by abolitionist literature. These whites insisted that a continuation of slavery depended upon keeping the black in a state of ignorance.[2]

Stricter curbs were put on the education of blacks after the Vesey and Turner revolts. South Carolina passed a statute in 1834 that forbade slave instruction and rigidly circumscribed the teaching of free blacks: if a free black taught other free blacks, a white had to be present in the classroom as a restraint. A Georgia law of 1829 provided for punishment by fine and whipping of free blacks who might be caught teaching slaves; whites found guilty of the same offense were to be fined a maximum of $500 and imprisoned at the discretion of the court. Despite the reaction and tighter legislation, education for some blacks was continued by individuals who maintained schools in defiance of public opinion and of the law. Schools for both slaves and free blacks were fairly common throughout the South, especially in urban communities such as Charleston, Savannah, and New Orleans. In Savannah a black woman conducted a school for over thirty years which remained unknown to authorities until Union troops occupied the city during the Civil War.[3]

In addition to attending illegally operated private schools, slaves learned through a variety of other methods: some were taught by their masters or their master's children; others learned through contact with and observation of whites; some learned from other slaves whose achievements were unknown to their masters; and some taught themselves. By 1860 between 5 and 10 percent of the adult black population (both free and slave) in the South was literate, although the level of achievement was low. This probably represented a substantial decline from the period before 1830. It is interesting to note that in both North Carolina and Georgia, influential citizens during the 1850s petitioned their state legislatures to permit education of slaves. The movement was strongest in Georiga, where a Savannah editor advocated the education of slaves as a means of enhancing their value and making them more loyal to their masters. Georgia's representatives to agricultural conventions in 1850 and

1. *Freedmen's Record* 4 (October 1867): 160, quoting *National Anti-Slavery Standard* n.d.; *Freedmen's Record* 3 (April 1867): 61.

2. Horace M. Bond, *The Education of the Negro in the American Social Order* (New York: Prentice-Hall, 1934), p. 21; James R. Buck, "The Education of the Negro in the South prior to 1861" (M.A. thesis, Fisk University, 1938), pp. 111–12, 150–51; Carter G. Woodson, *The Education of the Negro prior to 1861* (New York: G. P. Putnam's Sons, 1915), pp. 2, 223.

3. C. W. Birnie, "The Education of the Negro in Charleston, South Carolina, prior to the Civil War," *Journal of Negro History* 12 (1927): 17–18; Charles H. Walker, "The Attitude of Georgia toward the Education of Negroes, 1865–1935" (M.A. thesis, Atlanta University, 1935), p. 4; Woodson, *Education of the Negro*, pp. 215–16.

1851 debated the question of education of blacks and in 1851 adopted a resolution requesting the legislature to enact a statute permitting the education of slaves. A bill to this effect was introduced during the winter of 1852 and passed Georgia's lower house. The bill would have repealed the restrictive 1829 statute that prohibited slave education. Unfortunately the Georgia senate defeated this bill by a handful of votes.[4]

No progress was made toward the education of Southern blacks until the second year of the Civil War, when Northern religious and philanthropic organizations initiated efforts to educate slaves living within territories occupied by the Union Army. The army itself, and later the federal government's agency of relief, the Freedmen's Bureau, became actively involved in freedmen's education. By 1870, when the bureau was forced to close its schools because of a lack of funds, approximately $6 million in private and federal funds had been donated or appropriated for freedmen's schools in the South and substantial progress toward black literacy had been achieved.[5]

In the early months of the war teachers went to states partially occupied by Union troops, where they established schools for contrabands (escaped slaves). These teachers usually did not finance their own work; generally some church missionary society or nondenominational aid society sponsored them. Public meetings held in 1862 in Boston, New York, and Philadelphia to promote schools for blacks led to the establishment in New York of the Association for the Aid of Freedmen and the Missionary Association and, in Boston, the Committee of Education. Similar associations were formed in Chicago and Cincinnati. These groups collected money and opened schools for blacks. About eighty societies—nonsectarian, denominational, and semi-denominational—were formed during the first

4. Woodson, *Education of the Negro*, pp. 205–7, 226, 228; Joel Williamson, *After Slavery: The Negro in South Carolina during Reconstruction* (Chapel Hill: University of North Carolina Press, 1965), pp. 209–10; "Legal Status of the Colored Population in Respect to Schools and Education in the Different States," *American Journal of Education* 19 (1870): 339.

5. Henry L. Swint, *The Northern Teacher in the South, 1862–1870* (Nashville: Vanderbilt University Press, 1941), p. 3; Edgar W. Knight, *Public School Education in North Carolina* (Boston: Houghton Mifflin, 1916), p. 215; Linda W. Slaughter, *The Freedmen of the South* (Cincinnati: Elm Street Printing Co., 1869), p. 110.

two years of the war. It is impossible to determine the number of the societies because of their usually brief existence, tendency to unite and separate, and the frequency with which they changed titles, officers, and areas of interest.[6]

The American Missionary Association (AMA) was the first Northern group to enter the field of black education. Founded in 1846 to do missionary work in the United States and abroad, the association had a strong antislavery flavor from its inception and directed much of its energy toward emancipation. Although technically nonsectarian, so many leading AMA members were Congregationalists that outsiders often regarded it as a Congregational missionary organization. In 1865 that denomination selected the AMA as its agent for educational and religious work among freedmen. Freewill Baptists, Wesleyan Methodists, and the Dutch Reformed Church also designated the AMA to act for them among freedmen. By 1866 the AMA had 353 teachers working in the South. Four years later, after most of the aid societies had disbanded or discontinued their work, the AMA was still furnishing instruction to over 21,000 pupils.[7]

The Western Freedmen's Aid Commission, established at Cincinnati in January 1863, represented some religious groups in carrying on educational work among freedmen in Tennessee, Georgia, Alabama, Arkansas, Mississippi, and Louisiana. Most of this organization's instructional activities, however, took place in Tennessee where, in 1865, 123 teachers provided manual and domestic training as well as academic instruction.

By 1866 as various aid societies realized that a multiplicity of

6. *House Reports*, 41st Cong., 2d sess., No. 121, p. 21; Swint, *Northern Teacher*, p. 10; Luther P. Jackson, "The Educational Efforts of the Freedmen's Bureau and Freedmen's Aid Societies in South Carolina, 1862–72," *Journal of Negro History* 8 (1922): 15.

7. Richard B. Drake, "The American Missionary Association and the Southern Negro, 1861–1888" (Ph.D. diss., Emory University, 1957), pp. 1–7, 26, 36; Swint, *Northern Teacher*, p. 12; Amory D. Mayo, "The Work of Certain Northern Churches in the Education of the Freedmen, 1861–1900," *Report of the Commissioner of Education for the Year 1901–1902* (Washington: Government Printing Office, 1903), 1:290; Alrutheus A. Taylor, *The Negro in Tennessee, 1865–1880* (Washington: Associated Publishers, 1941), pp. 168–69; E. Merton Coulter, *The South during Reconstruction, 1865–77* (Baton Rouge: Louisiana State University Press, 1947), p. 81.

organizations could not develop an efficient educational program, and as funds became more difficult to obtain, they united into two principal bodies, the AMA and the newly formed but short-lived American Freedmen's Union Commission (AFUC), the latter including most of the nonsectarian groups. The AMA had several advantages over the AFUC and other secular societies: it was an older organization with well-established sources of income; as a missionary society, it could rely on consistent church support, whereas the AFUC had to rely on philanthropy. In addition, the AMA had more cooperation from the Freedmen's Bureau than did the AFUC, perhaps because Oliver Otis Howard, the bureau's commissioner, and John W. Alvord, the bureau's education superintendent, were active Congregationalists and close friends of the AMA secretary, George Whipple.[8]

Historians usually credit the AMA with opening the first black school under Union authority at Fortress Monroe, Virginia, in September 1861. It provided instruction for black refugees from neighboring plantations. Appropriately the first teacher was Mary L. Peake, a free black educated in England.[9] However, the earliest large-scale effort to educate freedmen was made on the islands off the South Carolina coast, an area known as Port Royal. Salmon P. Chase, secretary of the treasury, was responsible for sending Edward L. Pierce, in January 1862, as an agent to the recently captured islands to organize a labor force and to promote the general well-being of approximately 9,000 destitute blacks deserted by their masters. Pierce had already worked with contrabands, having su-

8. James M. McPherson, *The Struggle for Equality: Abolitionists and the Negro in the Civil War and Reconstruction* (Princeton: Princeton University Press, 1964), p. 402. Some teachers such as Salley Holley, who spent over twenty years teaching blacks in Northumberland County, Virginia, were not sponsored by any society and relied upon private gifts to maintain their schools. Salley Holley, *A Life for Liberty*, ed. John White Chadwick (New York: G. P. Putnam's Sons, 1899), pp. 212, 221; Drake, "American Missionary Association," pp. 23–24, 28, 40–42, 58–59, 74–75.

9. Drake, "American Missionary Association," pp. 9–10; Booker T. Washington, *Education of the Negro* (Albany, N.Y.: J. B. Lyon Co., 1900), p. 23; Bond, *The Education of the Negro*, p. 24. Mary Peake had a black mother and white father, the latter described as "an Englishman of rank and culture," Henry A. Bullock, *A History of Negro Education in the South* (Cambridge: Harvard University Press, 1967), p. 26.

pervised their labor when the first ones came through Union lines in Virginia. President Lincoln approved Pierce's recommendation for superintendents and a corps of teachers on February 15, 1862.[10] Before the federal effort in South Carolina could get organized, the Reverend Solomon Peck, acting independently, opened a school at Beaufort in early January for sixteen pupils ranging in age from five to thirty-five years.[11]

A Committee of Education organized in Boston in February 1862 and the Association for Aid to the Freedmen, established two weeks later in New York, volunteered to finance two superintendents and a corps of teachers in the Port Royal area. These groups, subsequently joined by a third from Philadelphia, formed the Port Royal Committee and sent two superintendents and fifty-three teachers, twelve of them women, to South Carolina. They arrived at Beaufort on March 8. This expedition of "clerks, doctors, divinity students, professors and students, underground railroad agents, socialists, Unitarians, free-thinkers, Methodists, the strait-laced, evangelists, young men and old men" worked with the AMA to establish more than thirty schools, in which teachers instructed approximately 2,000 pupils.[12] Among the teachers was the beautiful and accomplished Charlotte Forten, a well-educated free black from a wealthy Philadelphia family. Teaching at the Oaks Plantation, she

10. Edward L. Pierce, "The Freedmen at Port Royal," *Atlantic Monthly* 12 (1863): 296. Pierce was a Boston attorney, politician, and author who studied law in Chase's office in Cincinnati and became his secretary when Chase went to Washington. He was very close to Chase and Sumner and wrote a biography of the latter. Henry L. Swint, "Northern Interest in the Shoeless Southerner," *Journal of Southern History* 16 (1950): 465. See also George W. Smalley to Charles Sumner, December 15, 1861, in Sumner Papers, Houghton Library, Harvard University. For a fascinating and detailed account of the Port Royal experiment, see Willie Lee Rose, *Rehearsal for Reconstruction: The Port Royal Experiment* (Indianapolis: Bobbs Merrill, 1964), pp. 21–22, passim.

11. Ellen Peck to John W. Alvord, February 6, 1868, in Bureau of Refugees, Freedmen and Abandoned Lands, Manuscripts of the Educational Division, National Archives, Washington, D.C.; hereafter cited as BRFAL Ms. Miss Peck quotes from a letter of Solomon Peck dated January 15, 1862.

12. Pierce, "Freedmen at Port Royal," pp. 297–98, 303; William H. Pease, "Three Years among the Freedmen: William C. Gannett and the Port Royal Experiment," *Journal of Negro History* 42 (1957): 98–99; Laura J. Webster, "The Operation of the Freedmen's Bureau in South Carolina," *Smith College Studies in History* 1 (October 1915–July 1916): 80; Rose, *Rehearsal for Reconstruction*, p. 233.

received snubs and shabby treatment from plantation blacks because of her color until they heard her play the piano. White teacher Laura Towne later described Miss Forten as the "pet and belle of the island." Somewhat later, schools modeled after those at Port Royal were started in Union-occupied areas of Florida around Fernandina and Saint Augustine, where about four hundred black children received instruction. Early educational activity was not confined to the Southeast, however, for black schools were opened at Corinth, Mississippi, following its occupation in 1862.[13]

The federal government, through the actions of some Union commanders, became directly involved in black education during the early years of the war. In November 1862 General Ulysses S. Grant, after occupying Grand Junction, Tennessee, was concerned about contrabands who entered occupied territory. Grant believed they should be educated and put to work. To that end, Grant appointed Colonel John Eaton as superintendent of Negro affairs for the military Department of the Tennessee, which included Tennessee and portions of Mississippi and Kentucky. Eaton, a chaplain, was a former school superintendent in Toledo, Ohio, and an excellent organizer. He divided the department's area into school districts, appointed superintendents, helped recruit teachers, and attempted to establish a system for the uniform adoption of textbooks. Eaton also consolidated some schools of the missionary associations into the military's educational system, and by the end of the war, there were 105 teachers and more than 6,200 pupils under his supervision. General Nathaniel P. Banks, a former Speaker of the United States House of Representatives and a former governor of Massachusetts, established a similar educational system in 1863–1864 for his Department of the Gulf—which included Alabama, Louisiana, Mississippi, and Texas—although most of the educational work took place in Louisiana. Banks issued a general order in

13. Rose, *Rehearsal for Reconstruction*, pp. 161–62; Laura M. Towne, *Letters and Diary of Laura M. Towne* (Cambridge: Riverside Press, 1912), p. 97. Laura Towne devoted thirty-eight years to black education. She founded the Penn School on St. Helena Island which existed into this century. The Pennsylvania Branch, AFUC, initially supported Penn School. Martin Abbott, "The Freedmen's Bureau and Negro Schooling in South Carolina," *South Carolina Historical Magazine* 57 (1956): 66–67; James W. Garner, *Reconstruction in Mississippi* (New York: Macmillan, 1901), p. 354.

March 1864 establishing schools for black children under the age of twelve, supported by a tax that was imposed on disloyal whites. He created a three-man board of education to organize at least one school in each district, acquire land, construct buildings, and hire as many teachers as possible from the loyal inhabitants of the state. By May 1864 ninety men and women were teaching over 5,000 black children in forty-nine Louisiana schools. As of January 1865 an estimated 750 teachers were instructing approximately 75,000 blacks in all Union-occupied areas of the South.[14]

General Benjamin Butler instituted an educational program for blacks in the Department of North Carolina and Virginia in December 1863 with the appointment of Lieutenant Colonel J. Burnham Kinsman as chief of black affairs. Kinsman coordinated the educational work of benevolent associations and the government and provided schoolhouses, food, lodging, and transportation for teachers, as was being done in the Department of the Tennessee. Butler, possibly the most devoted of the department commanders to the edification of black soldiers, in December 1864 consolidated thirty-seven black regiments to form the Twenty-fifth Corps. He ordered chaplains in each regiment to conduct instruction, thus offering primary education to almost 30,000 soldiers. Other commanders directed the education of black troops, often to increase the efficiency of the soldiers. One of the greatest incentives for federal black enlisted men to learn to read was the possibility of promotion. Frequently men were not promoted to sergeant until they had made measurable educational progress. By 1865 approximately 20,000 black troops in the Union Army were literate.[15]

Another wartime educational effort for blacks occurred at Charleston on March 4, 1865, when the federal government opened

14. Bond, *The Education of the Negro*, pp. 26–28; George R. Bentley, *A History of the Freedmen's Bureau* (Philadelphia: University of Pennsylvania Press, 1955), pp. 21–23, 169–70; *De Bow's Review* 1 (April 1866): 436; John W. Blassingame, "The Union Army as an Educational Institution for Negroes, 1862–1865," *Journal of Negro Education* 34 (1965): 153–55; Howard A. White, *The Freedmen's Bureau in Louisiana* (Baton Rouge: Louisiana State University Press, 1970), pp. 168–74; "Legal Status of the Colored Population in Respect to Schools and Education in the Different States," *American Journal of Education* 19 (1870): 339.

15. Blassingame, "The Union Army as an Educational Institution for Negroes," pp. 153–59.

schools for freedmen, under the direction of James Redpath, a reporter for Horace Greeley's *New York Tribune* and a longtime abolitionist. Redpath conducted his schools in buildings recently confiscated from the city. Initially about 1,200 blacks and 300 white children attended, with both races in the same buildings, but not in the same classrooms. At recess, however, both races at the Morris Street School played together in the schoolyard. Three months later more than 4,000 pupils were studying in nine day schools and five night schools under thirty-four Northern and sixty-eight Southern teachers, the latter having taken a loyalty oath. Benevolent societies paid the teachers' salaries and supplied textbooks. Redpath returned to the North in June 1865, praised by Charlestonians and abolitionists alike for his efficient reorganization of Charleston's schools. That autumn, however, the schools came under control of local white officials who assigned all black children to the Morris Street School, where the teachers were native whites. The Morris Street School was perhaps the only example of municipal authorities' voluntarily assuming financial support of a black school in South Carolina during this period.[16]

Attempts of the federal government to organize and supervise educational efforts of the aid societies in the occupied areas finally coalesced under one central organization when Congress established the Bureau of Refugees, Freedmen and Abandoned Lands, popularly known as the Freedmen's Bureau, on March 3, 1865. Since the original Freedmen's Bureau Act made no provision for the education of blacks, bureau educational activities were relatively unimportant in 1865–1866. The bureau did help the missionary and benevolent societies with their schools in an indirect fashion, however, taking funds from rental of abandoned property and converting unused government buildings into schoolhouses. It also provided money for books, school furniture, and transportation of teachers. An indirect but important form of assistance was military protection for schools and teachers.[17]

16. Jackson, "Educational Efforts of the Freedmen's Bureau," pp. 18–19; McPherson, *Struggle for Equality*, pp. 388–89; Alrutheus A. Taylor, *The Negro in South Carolina during the Reconstruction* (Washington: Association for the Study of Negro Life and History, 1924), p. 86; *New York Times*, April 16, 1865; Abbott, "The Freedmen's Bureau," p. 74; Williamson, *After Slavery*, p. 216.
17. U.S., *Statutes at Large*, vol. 13, pp. 507–9; Paul S. Peirce, *The Freedmen's*

Demands for specific federal appropriations for black education increased by 1866, when buildings that had been confiscated for school purposes were restored to their original owners. Benevolent associations, at that time without school facilities, pleaded for federal assistance, or "this immense system of education must fail or be greatly crippled unless permanent real estate . . . can be in some way secured."[18] Congress answered these entreaties on July 16, 1866, when it included provisions for education in an act to continue the life of the bureau for two years. The act gave the bureau commissioner, Oliver Otis Howard, the power to seize, hold, use, lease, or sell all buildings formerly held by the Confederacy, and to use the proceeds derived from these transactions for the education of freedmen. Congress sanctioned cooperation with benevolent associations and also directed Howard to hire or lease buildings for purposes of education, whenever private associations supplied teachers and materials without cost to the government. Congress also instructed the commissioner to furnish protection for these schools.

Federal appropriations to finance the bureau, as amended in 1866, included $21,000 for salaries of school superintendents, who were bureau employees, and $500,000 for repairs and rental of schoolhouses and asylums. Although the appropriations bills limited the funds to capital outlay or expenditures, bureau leaders contrived to spend much of this appropriation for current operations. On March 2, 1867, Congress voted an additional $500,000 for bureau schools and asylums. During June 1868, an act prolonging the bureau for an additional year provided that the commissioner, at his discretion, might apply all unspent balances to the education of freedmen.[19]

Bureau (Iowa City: State University of Iowa, 1904), p. 75; "Reports of the Commissioner of the Bureau of Refugees, Freedmen and Abandoned Lands," *House Executive Documents*, 41st Cong., 2d sess., No. 142, p. 11; hereafter cited as "Report of the BRFAL," 1869–1870. The bureau was originally concerned with feeding, distributing land, and regulating labor of freedmen.

18. "Reports of the Assistant Commissioners of the Freedmen's Bureau," *Senate Executive Documents*, 39th Cong., 1st sess., No. 27, p. 108; hereafter cited as "Reports of the Assistant Commissioners."

19. U.S., *Statutes at Large*, vol. 14, pp. 92, 176, 586; ibid., vol. 15, p. 83; Bentley, *Freedmen's Bureau*, p. 171.

Howard was the only commissioner to direct the Freedmen's Bureau. Known as the "Christian general," he was a native of Maine and graduate of Bowdoin College and West Point. Although he had a controversial military career during the Civil War he nevertheless became commander of the Army of the Tennessee. Howard was an intensely devoted Congregationalist and had long been interested in alleviating the condition of Southern blacks. His principal concern, contrary to frequent contemporary accusations, was protecting the rights and interests of freedmen rather than building the Republican (Radical) party in the South.[20]

John W. Alvord, a Congregationalist and former evangelical abolitionist from Oberlin College and Lane Seminary, was appointed general superintendent of the Freedmen's Bureau education division with headquarters at Washington. His duties were to collect information, encourage organization of new schools, find homes for teachers, and supervise the entire operation, which meant, essentially, coordinating association teachers and private educational funds within the bureau's organizational framework. Bureau school superintendents in each state harmonized the societies' work with that of the bureau, secured adequate protection for schools and teachers, collected information, encouraged organization of new schools, and carried out Alvord's duties on the state level.[21] The result was that a Freedmen's Bureau school could have been called an association school with equal accuracy. The bureau did establish schools independently of benevolent associations, which provided teachers, books, maps, and charts. In his autobiography, Howard wrote that so intimate was the cooperation between the associations and the

20. *Dictionary of American Biography,* 9: 279–80; John A. Carpenter, *Sword and Olive Branch: Oliver Otis Howard* (Pittsburgh: University of Pittsburgh Press, 1964), p. 137. For an interesting and sympathetic reevaluation of the Freedmen's Bureau which praises Howard as a skillful and wise administrator, see John and LaWanda Cox, "General O. O. Howard and the 'Misrepresented Bureau,' " *Journal of Southern History* 19 (1953): 427–56. For a negative assessment of Howard as bureau commissioner which describes his virtual abandonment of black interests, see William S. McFeely, *Yankee Stepfather: General O. O. Howard and the Freedmen* (New Haven: Yale University Press, 1968), pp. 126, 315.

21. Paul D. Phillips, "A History of the Freedmen's Bureau in Tennessee" (Ph.D. diss., Vanderbilt University, 1964), p. 191; Jackson, "Educational Efforts of the Freedmen's Bureau," p. 14; "Report of the BRFAL," 1869–1870, p. 11.

bureau that it was often difficult to separate the activities of the two. He stated that in the field of education his purpose had not been to "supersede the benevolent agencies already engaged, but to systematize and facilitate them."[22]

The amount of money spent by the Freedmen's Bureau on education is a matter of conjecture. John Eaton, while he was United States Commissioner of Education, stated in 1876 that the Freedmen's Bureau had spent $3,711,225 on the education of blacks, an amount that did not include the cost of transporting teachers nor of maintaining troops to protect schools, costs not shown on the bureau's balance sheet. One benevolent society publication estimated that all the societies spent $13 million (some $500,000 from freedmen themselves) toward the work, and the bureau spent approximately the same sum.[23]

The methods used by bureau officials to circumvent congressional restrictions on expenditures for education were often ingenious. During the first year of the bureau's existence (1865–1866), when Congress had failed to appropriate funds for education, Howard was able to help the associations by providing money from rental of abandoned property, transforming unused government buildings into schoolhouses, paying transportation for teachers, providing books and school furniture, and paying expenses.[24]

By the summer of 1867 educational work among freedmen began to wane as associations suffered from decreased contributions. The societies had two alternatives: to discharge many of their teachers or to seek aid from the federal government. Although the Freedmen's Bureau Act of 1866 did not authorize payment of teachers' salaries from federal appropriations, this was done in Alabama for about a year until Howard was forced to end the practice in 1867.[25]

22. U.S., *Statutes at Large*, vol. 14, p. 176; *American Freedman* 1 (December 1866): 135; Oliver O. Howard, *Autobiography of Otis Howard* (New York: Baker and Taylor Co., 1908), 2: 221.

23. Bentley, *Freedmen's Bureau*, p. 173; Peirce, *Freedmen's Bureau*, p. 82; Ullin Leavell, *Philanthropy in Negro Education* (Nashville: George Peabody College for Teachers, 1930), p. 48; *Report of the Commissioner of Education for the Year 1875–1876*, p. xvi.

24. "Report of the BRFAL," 1869–1870, p. 11.

25. Oliver Otis Howard to Wager Swayne, September 6, 1866, in BRFAL Ms; Elizabeth Bethel, "The Freedmen's Bureau in Alabama," *Journal of Southern History* 14 (1948): 69. In South Carolina teacher's pay in the bureau-

Salaries ranged from twenty to fifty dollars a month and the estimated cost of maintaining a teacher for a ten-month term averaged five hundred dollars. School terms varied from four to ten months, the average being eight months. The maximum salary never exceeded $500. Howard circumvented the restriction against using federal funds for salaries by transferring numerous bureau-owned school buildings to the benevolent societies which, in turn, leased them to the bureau and used the income for teachers' salaries. In November 1868 Howard authorized schools that were being conducted in buildings still owned or rented by the societies to send a monthly rent bill amounting to ten dollars per teacher. In order to qualify for rental to the bureau, buildings had to be located on sites reserved for education of blacks; and each school collecting rent was required to have at least thirty pupils per teacher.[26]

Determining places of origin and exact number of instructors who taught the freedmen is impossible. According to Howard's report of July 1870 the number of teachers had increased from 972 in January 1867 to 2,948 in January 1868, and from 7,840 in January 1869 to a peak of 9,503 in July 1870. The latter figure included a considerable percentage of native Southerners of both races with probably no more than 5,000 Yankees.[27] The reports and records of the bureau contain numerous requests from native Southern whites, usually impoverished, applying for teaching positions. In 1867 the bureau superintendent of education in Alabama, Charles W. Buckley, reported to Superintendent Alvord that he had experienced no difficulty in attracting competent Southern whites to teach in black schools. Among those Alabamians employed were graduates of the state university and former county school superintendents. Alvord's office received occasional letters from distraught Southerners who

associations schools averaged forty-five dollars a month at Charleston and thirty-five dollars a month in the rest of the state. Abbott, "The Freedmen's Bureau," p. 72.

26. Phillips, "Freedmen's Bureau in Tennessee," pp. 233–34; Julius H. Parmelee, "Freedmen's Aid Societies, 1861–71," U.S., Department of Interior, Bureau of Education, Bulletin No. 38, 1916, p. 288; Bentley, Freedmen's Bureau, pp. 173–74; BRFAL Ms, passim.

27. Report as cited in Swint, Northern Teacher, p. 6; Coulter, The South during Reconstruction, p. 82. Coulter contends that in some areas the entire staff of bureau schools consisted of native whites, and at one time almost half the teachers employed by the bureau were native whites. Ibid., p. 84.

claimed to have remained loyal to the Union during the war, who had suffered for their opinions, and who now needed teaching positions to earn a livelihood.[28]

Many former slaves, educated in normal schools such as Hampton Institute (a bureau-supported institution), became teachers of freedmen. By 1869 about one-half of the bureau-association teachers were black. The New York branch, AFUC, reported in July 1870 that forty-two of its fifty-five teachers in the South were black, fourteen being native Southerners.[29] The percentage of black teachers could not have been large until 1868, however, when they began to emerge from normal schools in appreciable numbers.

Numerous authors have described the joyous and enthusiastic reaction of the freedmen to education. Many former slaves regarded learning as having a miraculous power which would fling open doors of social and political equality with whites. Young and old hurried to enter schools, often expecting with pathetic eagerness that they would become learned within a few weeks. Some grown men tried to study while at work. Black mothers walked miles to towns where they could place their children in school. Lucy Chase, teaching freedmen on Craney Island, Virginia, wrote in 1863 of the black's "greed for letters" and how every progression into the mysteries of letters elevated his spirit like "faith in a brilliant promise."[30]

28. John W. Alvord, *Semi-Annual Reports on Schools for Freedmen* (Washington: Government Printing Office, July 1867), p. 41, hereafter cited as Alvord, *Reports*. See also Fannie Anderson to John W. Alvord, February 11, 1867, in BRFAL Ms; L. Edwin Dudley to Oliver Otis Howard, September 6, 1867, in ibid.

29. Peirce, *Freedmen's Bureau*, p. 79; "A Report of the Continuing Committee for the Year Ending July 1, 1870," p. 1, in the *American Freedman*, 1870. Unfortunately some black communities were reluctant to accept a freedman teacher unless the teacher possessed a light complexion. In Virginia, blacks withheld their children from a bureau school taught by a dark-skinned former slave until the bureau superintendent closed the school for a month. William T. Alderson, "The Freedmen's Bureau in Virginia" (M.A. thesis, Vanderbilt University, 1949), p. 91.

30. Coulter, *The South during Reconstruction*, p. 86; Bond, *The Education of the Negro*, p. 23; Henry L. Swint, ed., *Dear Ones at Home: Letters from Contraband Camps* (Nashville: Vanderbilt University Press, 1966), pp. 41, 157–58. By the summer of 1867 some Virginia freedmen were so enthusiastic concerning education that they believed nine months of school to be insufficient and therefore enrolled their children in private summer schools. Thirty-six summer schools were in operation in Virginia by September 1867. Alderson, "Freedmen's Bureau in Virginia," p. 63.

Alvord observed in 1866 that love of books was universally apparent among black pupils and that a common punishment for misdemeanors was being kept home a day. A threat in most cases was sufficient. Not always, however, did freedmen rush to bureau-association schools. Lieutenant Colonel John R. Lewis, bureau superintendent for Georgia, complained in 1870 that freedmen preferred to attend private schools conducted by "incompetent colored teachers" in uncomfortable, inconvenient schoolrooms and pay tuition of one dollar a month, rather than to go to bureau schools where instructors were qualified and tuition was only twenty-five to fifty cents a month. Lewis blamed this situation on the influence of local black churches, interested in promoting private schools, and solicitation of students by black teachers. The reverse situation was also true, for free or low tuition bureau schools forced many pay schools out of operation.[31]

The learning abilities of black children varied, as with all children, according to the individual. Charlotte Forten reported that the majority of her pupils at Port Royal learned with a "wonderful rapidity," although there were some slow ones. She did admit, as did many teachers, that to keep the minds of her pupils from wandering, it was necessary to hold their interest constantly. One traveler in the South during Reconstruction, who claimed to have heard more than 10,000 black pupils examined in different schools, declared that, when taught by white teachers, these children seemed to progress as fast as white children beginning in school at the same age. A *New York Times* correspondent in South Carolina reported that experienced teachers had found that black children could advance as rapidly as whites and were exceedingly proficient in natural philosophy, history, and mathematics. He also wrote about Charleston's bureau schools, where he saw black pupils working algebra problems, twelve-to-fourteen-year-olds answering questions in ancient and modern history, and many reading with good comprehension. The principal of Charleston's Morris Street School declared that black children learned as readily as whites and that their thirst for knowledge was much greater than that of whites.[32]

31. "Reports of the Assistant Commissioners," p. 107: "Synopsis of School Reports" (unpub.), 2: 168, in BRFAL Ms; Swint, ed., *Dear Ones at Home*, p. 144.
32. Charlotte L. Forten, "Life on the Sea Islands," *Atlantic Monthly* 13

The Freedmen's Bureau and benevolent associations had completed their major educational efforts by 1869. Religious factionalism caused the AFUC to begin to break up almost immediately after its formation in 1866. The Western branches of the AFUC, which required teachers to be practicing Christians, were angered by charges from Eastern branches that they were placing conversion and religious work above general education. The Cincinnati branch withdrew in 1866 and was absorbed into the AMA. Gradually other branches withdrew, until in 1868 the AFUC executive committee decided that the association's activities could be conducted better by individual societies. Formal dissolution of the AFUC was achieved in 1869, and the member societies also rapidly disbanded. A lessening of popular interest in black education by 1867 forced all secular societies to begin a policy of retrenchment. In April 1867 the *American Freedman* lamented that most of the enthusiasm for black education had evaporated and left as supporters only those attached to the cause by unalterable devotion and principle.[33]

The primary reason for a leveling off of educational activities by the bureau and benevolent associations was a shortage of funds. In 1869 and 1870 the bureau was able to authorize only small sums for construction of schoolhouses. Commissioner Howard directed bureau superintendents to travel through their states and advise freedmen to organize their own schools. By July 1869 the bureau had adopted a policy of restricting aid to primary schools in rural areas. Bureau superintendents tried to secure cooperation of state authorities and public school officials and help make public school systems effective agencies of education. Because of the lack of money, the bureau ceased its educational work in April 1870. Alvord resigned as superintendent the following October, and his state superintendents sold the bureau properties and closed their offices.[34]

The benevolent societies had encountered financial difficulties even before the Freedmen's Bureau. By June 1867 the New England

---

(1864): 591–92; Williamson, *After Slavery*, pp. 234–36; *New York Times*, July 3, 1874. See also Phillips, "Freedmen's Bureau in Tennessee," p. 225.

33. McPherson, *Struggle for Equality*, pp. 401–4; *American Freedman* 2 (April 1867): 195.

34. Bentley, *Freedmen's Bureau*, p. 210. The last congressional appropriation was expended in July 1870. Peirce, *Freedmen's Bureau*, p. 82.

branch of the AFUC was having problems raising money. Some former donors thought the time had come for the South and the freedmen to support their own schools; others hoped that the bureau or Peabody Fund trustees would do the financing, for many were worn out by the claims constantly made upon them. By the end of the school year 1868–1869, most societies had ceased their educational work, except in the case of certain normal schools. The New York branch, AFUC, explained that it had laid groundwork that could be taken over by the Southern states. It also admitted that its treasury was dwindling.[35]

Many bureau-association schools continued operation after those organizations had stopped supplying financial assistance and teachers. Some passed into the hands of cities and states and were incorporated into local educational systems; others became private institutions with new sources of support; still others went out of existence. In Tennessee freedmen gave partial or complete financial support to eighty-two of 158 schools in 1868 as association funds decreased rapidly. In Alabama a plan of transition was developed at the end of the 1868 school year whereby the bureau would continue to supply buildings, the societies would recruit teachers, and the state would pay salaries. Unfortunately, a shortage of state funds for educational purposes caused this program to lag. When the bureau concluded its work in 1870, it turned over many of its remaining school buildings in Alabama to the freedmen.[36] In Virginia, the bureau transferred all its schools at Alexandria, Norfolk, Hampton, Petersburg, and Richmond to the state in 1869 and 1870. Richmond incorporated the former bureau schools into its city system in 1869, although benevolent associations continued to pay 50 percent of the teachers' salaries for several years. Ralza M. Manly, the former Virginia bureau superintendent, took a position with the Richmond board of education and remained in charge of black schools.[37]

35. *Freedmen's Record* 3 (June 1867): 101.

36. Phillips, "Freedmen's Bureau in Tennessee," pp. 202–3; Jackson, "Educational Efforts of the Freedmen's Bureau," p. 23; Bethel, "The Freedmen's Bureau in Alabama," pp. 88–89; Robert D. Reid, "The Negro in Alabama during the Civil War," *Journal of Negro History* 35 (1950): 283.

37. *Freedmen's Record* 5 (November 1869): 41; William T. Alderson, Jr., "The Freedmen's Bureau and Negro Education in Virginia," *North Carolina*

In Arkansas the bureau transferred its schools to the state in March 1869, and teachers who so desired became affiliated with the state system. Municipal systems in Louisiana began to take over bureau schools as early as 1867 as cities appropriated funds for black education. The New Orleans board of education, after appropriating $70,000 for black education, added eleven of the bureau's primary schools, with an enrollment of about 1,000, to its system in November 1867 and hired all incumbent teachers, with the stipulation that those instructors who were not certified should take qualifying exams at a later date.[38] New Orleans school superintendent William O. Rogers, complained to the Louisiana bureau superintendent about the condition of the newly acquired black schools, especially the crudeness of the buildings and the problem of officially enrolled students who seldom or never attended. Rogers implied that black children had been allowed to enroll in several institutions to increase the registration.[39] This pattern of transferring bureau schools to local and state control was repeated in all Southern states, and where state funds were available, the schools were valuable additions to new and struggling systems.

The question of how many freedmen actually received instruction in bureau-association schools and the effectiveness of this training is conjectural. Enrollment statistics given by Alvord are unreliable because they include many who were counted twice. A person who attended both a weekday school and a Sunday school, for instance, was recorded as two separate enrollments. Bureau historian Paul Peirce has estimated that in 1869 approximately one-

Historical Review 29 (1952): 79; "Richmond since the War," Scribners Monthly 14 (1877): 312; Parmelee, "Freedmen's Aid Societies," pp. 386–87; Martha W. Owens, "The Development of Public Schools for Negroes in Richmond, Virginia, 1865–1900" (M.S. thesis, Virginia State College, 1947), pp. 55–57; Alderson, "Freedmen's Bureau in Virginia," p. 51.

38. Thomas S. Staples, Reconstruction in Arkansas, 1862–1874 (New York: Columbia University, 1923), pp. 321–22, 373; Annual Report of the State Superintendent of Public Education . . . to the General Assembly of Louisiana, 1867–1868 (New Orleans: n.p., 1869), pp. 10–12, hereafter cited as Annual Report, Louisiana (year); White, Freedmen's Bureau in Louisiana, p. 180; School Board Minutes, Orleans Parish School Board Office, New Orleans, vol. 7, September 11, October 2, 9, November 6, 15, December 4, 1867.

39. William O. Rogers to E. W. Mason, December 29, 1969, in William O. Rogers Correspondence, Orleans Parish School Board Office, New Orleans.

tenth of the 1,700,000 black children of school age were attending school. The New England branch, AFUC, believed that of the total number of school-age blacks in January 1870 only one-thirteenth were in school, and this figure was just one-third larger than that of 1866. Teachers occasionally commented upon the number of black schools in larger towns but pointed out that such schools were nonexistent in many rural areas. Not until 1871 did blacks have a weekday school in Columbia County, Georgia, where there were twice as many blacks residing as in nearby Augusta, which was well supplied with schools and teachers. One benevolent society admitted in 1871 that what had been accomplished was merely a drop in the bucket when compared to the vast number of blacks needing instruction. In 1870, when the federal government withdrew its aid, about 150,000 black pupils were regularly attending 2,677 bureau-association schools throughout the South.[40]

One of the numerous problems that faced the bureau-association schools during their existence was the question of integration. Certain benevolent associations such as the AMA strongly favored racially mixed schools, although some felt that integration would produce an unfavorable reaction in the South. Lyman Abbott, general secretary of the AFUC, set an example for North Carolina and the entire South by promoting integration in the association's North Carolina schools. He believed that establishing segregated schools would merely perpetuate the system, making ultimate and complete integration more difficult. The New England branch, AFUC, staunchly declared that its constitution forbade all racial distinction in schools and that its students ranged "from the blackest negro to pure Anglo Saxon." The *Freedmen's Record* admitted that few white children were enrolled in AFUC schools, but "every one is a

40. Swint, *Northern Teacher*, pp. 6–7; Peirce, *Freedmen's Bureau*, p. 83; *Freedmen's Record* 5 (January 1871): 92; Charles Stearns, *The Black Man of the South and the Rebels* (New York: American News Co., 1872), pp. 477–78. Stearns insisted that three-fourths of the Southern blacks were never affected by bureau-association education. See also Peirce, *Freedmen's Bureau*, p. 535. *Freedmen's Record* 5 (January 1871): 15; Jabez L. M. Curry, *Education of Negroes since 1860* (Baltimore: Trustees of the John F. Slater Fund, 1894), p. 19; Martin Abbott, *The Freedmen's Bureau in South Carolina* (Chapel Hill: University of North Carolina Press, 1967), p. 88. Abbott estimates that of 125,000 school-age black children in South Carolina, only one out of five was in any way involved in education during Reconstruction.

real gain, for he comes into perfectly equal relations with his black schoolmates." The New England branch asserted in August 1866 that its mixed school experiment, when given a fair trial had succeeded in all but one instance. The society's organ, the *American Freedman,* declared that poor whites and blacks would probably not attend the same schools in large towns. In rural areas, however, where one school was sufficient to meet the needs of the entire population, there was good reason to hope that "prejudice of caste can by patience be overcome, and both classes united in a common school."[41]

A number of bureau-association teachers and officials disagreed with their sponsoring organizations over integration policies. In Virginia Ralza M. Manly wrote that whites would not attend mixed schools and the association would lose prestige and influence if it tried to mix both races in the same school. An AFUC superintendent in Georgia told Abbott that there was little probability that poor whites would ever attend such schools with freedmen and that such an experiment would prove both impolitic and inexpedient, for it would raise the "frightful bugbear of *social equality*" against schools, which would impair or destroy their usefulness. Some Yankee teachers admitted that it was futile to persuade whites to attend freedmen's schools, for most would do without education rather than face ridicule resulting from going to a "nigger school."[42]

Racial mixing in bureau-association schools probably did not exceed 3 percent of total enrollment. The New England branch, AFUC, occasionally reported enrollment of whites in its schools. In August 1866 the New York branch stated that in a dozen of its schools there was a ratio of one white to fifty blacks, whites being admitted at the request of their mothers who said they were too poor to give them an education.[43] Alvord's educational division office in Washington compiled suggestive although perhaps inaccurate sta-

41. *American Freedman* 1 (April 1866): 5–6; ibid., 1 (August 1866): 69–70; *Freedmen's Record* 4 (January 1868): 4; ibid., 3 (January 1867): 2. See also Ira V. Brown, "Lyman Abbott and Freedmen's Aid, 1865–1869," *Journal of Southern History* 15 (1949): 22–38.

42. *American Freedman* 1 (August 1866): 73, 76; *American Missionary* 11 (March 1867): 51–52.

43. *Freedmen's Record* 2 (May 1866): 90; *American Freedman* 1 (August 1866): 79.

tistics on the number of whites enrolled in Freedmen's Bureau schools for the years 1867 through 1870:

Month & year	Reported enrolled white pupils	Reported enrolled pupils
January 1867	470	77,998
July 1867	1,348	111,442
January 1868	1,138	81,878
July 1868	1,151	89,466
January 1869	548	61,785
July 1869	953	89,731
January 1870	962	90,616
July 1870	3,169	114,516

At its greatest extent the percentage of whites attending freedmen's schools was under 3 percent,[44] a figure which demonstrates that racial mixing existed only on a small scale, even in schools where teachers and administrators were often determined crusaders for integration.

Three years before the bureau ceased its educational work, the commissioner, Oliver Otis Howard, in 1867 proposed a plan for continuing instructional efforts with the use of federal funds appropriated through the United States Department of Education. He was still convinced in 1869 that federal support was necessary to sustain black education in the South. In a letter to the secretary of war, W. W. Belknap, he proposed a reorganization of the Department of Education which would include the authority and work of the Freedmen's Bureau. He felt that this agency should have the power to establish schools in cooperation with state and local agencies and benevolent societies and to incorporate state superintendents into its organization. Howard pointed out that this new organization might extend benefits to impoverished whites and also to Indians. Realizing that people might attack his plan on grounds of constitutionality and cost, Howard declared that education was

44. John W. Alvord, *Semi-Annual Report on Schools for Freedmen* (Washington: Government Printing Office, January 1867 through July 1870). See especially ibid., January 1, 1868, pp. 12–13, January 1, 1870, pp. 6–7, July 1, 1870, p. 7. See also Paul D. Phillips, "A History of the Freedmen's Bureau in Tennessee" (Ph.D. diss., Vanderbilt University, 1964), pp. 245–46.

the best possible investment that could be made in a government and that general education of the masses procured the "largest liberty consistent with good government," thus counteracting all centralizing tendencies.[45]

Congress failed to act on Howard's farsighted and able suggestion which might have prevented years of educational retrogression for Southern blacks. In 1870 as the bureau closed its schools, Howard lamented there was really nothing to transfer to a federal agency but hoped that the value of education was becoming more apparent to freedmen and other classes in the South. Once again he recommended a congressional appropriation for public education. His proposals received little attention, but in North Carolina the Radical superintendent of education, Samuel S. Ashley, strongly favored it.[46] Ashley asserted that, if all federal aid to education were ended following withdrawal of bureau funds, a combination of Southern poverty and prejudice would deprive blacks of an education "for which they now so ardently thirst." He declared that the Southern states, especially North Carolina, could not possibly raise 50 percent of the funds necessary to continue good schools for even a four-month term each year.[47]

Although by 1870 the Freedmen's Bureau had inaugurated a large-scale educational effort for freedmen, it did not perfect the operation nor assure continuance of the schools. The most permanent evidence of the bureau and associations' work in education

45. *House Executive Documents*, 40th Cong., 2d sess., no. 1, pt. 1, p. 691; Oliver Otis Howard to Secretary of War (William W. Belknap), November 19, 1869, in BRFAL Ms.

46. The terms *Radical* and *Conservative* are used in this study to designate political affiliation in the postbellum South. The Conservatives, sometimes called Conservative-Democrats, were composed mainly of whites—former Confederates, Democrats, Whigs, and Constitutional Unionists. Their fundamental policy was white supremacy, their ultimate goal the destruction of Radical Reconstruction governments. The term Radical has been used with reference to followers of the Republican party in the South, which was composed of Northerners, native Southerners, and blacks. Although Southern Radicals were divided into moderate, conservative, and radical factions and found it difficult to formulate a general policy, a unifying bond was their desire to establish and perpetuate Republican state governments while preventing the return to power of the propertied Conservative minority.

47. *House Executive Documents*, 41st Cong., 3d sess., No. 1, pt. 1, pp. 317–18; Samuel S. Ashley to Charles Sumner, April 7, 1870, in Sumner Papers.

was the establishment and encouragement of numerous institutions of higher learning. The bureau had a part in organizing the National Theological Institute, Saint Martin's School, and Howard University, all in Washington. The bureau and associations also gave financial support to Richmond Normal, Richmond High School, and Hampton Institute in Virginia; Saint Augustine's Normal School and Biddle Memorial Institute in North Carolina; Atlanta University in Georgia; Allen University in South Carolina; and Wesleyan College, Fisk University, and Roberts College in Tennessee.[48] Nevertheless, the Yankee teachers, bureau, and benevolent societies were "evangels" of learning to the freedmen and introduced enough basic education to make literate at least one-quarter of the total Southern black population, while also beginning the training of black teachers who could work with their own people. Undoubtedly, this intangible achievement is their most lasting monument.

48. Coulter, *The South during Reconstruction*, p. 87; Ruth L. Stubblefield, "The Education of the Negro in Tennessee during the Reconstruction" (M.A. thesis, Fisk University, 1943), pp. 58–59.

2. *Southern White Reaction*

THE RESPONSE of Southern whites to the process of black education during and immediately after the Civil War produced two different but related controversies. The first and more intense argument concerned the selection of teachers for what became the bureau-association schools, and whether these schools should be under the jurisdiction of Yankee "missionaries" or native Southern whites. The second controversy, when divested of emotional rhetoric, resolved itself to the more basic question of whether blacks should be educated at all.

Those Northern teachers who came South after 1862 usually possessed strong humanitarian ideals of educating and uplifting a deprived, downtrodden race and elevating blacks to fuller lives as American citizens. Teachers frequently combined humanitarianism with a fervent missionary spirit aimed at converting the unchurched and improving freedmen's moral standards. The AMA actually required that its instructors have true missionary zeal and be persons of fervent piety.[1] Many AFUC teachers, although representing secular organizations, also regarded themselves as missionaries, and occasionally religious fervor seemed to outweigh their desire to educate freedmen.

Many Northern teachers were inspired to introduce the culture, philosophy, and learning of their section to the benighted South. In 1865 the outgoing president of the National Teachers' Association remarked that former slave states would be new missionary ground for the "national schoolmaster," where, without regard to rank, age, or color, he would teach all his pupils that learning and development were the first natural rights of man. Some teachers went South with the attitude of transforming a barbarous land into a civilized area, "free for the travel and settlement of the reddest Republican or the blackest abolitionist." Others came intending to introduce

24

political ideas into freedmen's minds, making them aware of their rights, duties, and new relationships to the white race.[2]

Most Yankee teachers were sincere persons who left their homes determined to do only good works, but they professed such deep sympathy for the black and abiding hatred for the established social order, slavery, and slave owners, that they disregarded traditional customs and feelings of Southern whites. Usually teachers were persons of good character, and most charges of bad behavior against them resulted from local resentment at the presence of these intruders. The teachers' advocacy and practice of social equality, often involving rooming and boarding with blacks, simply intensified efforts by Southern whites to brand the instructors as infamous characters promoting perverted and revolutionary ideas. Dissipation was rare among Yankee teachers, but bureau records indicate that some local blacks hired by the associations were prone to drinking and other "bad" practices.[3]

In contrast to the general pattern, a few bureau-association teachers had strong mercenary motives and regarded black education as simply another business venture by which to defraud the government and benevolent associations. In 1868 Henry R. Pease, bureau superintendent in Mississippi, complained about teachers who presented fraudulent accounts for payment and of others who, although nearly illiterate, started schools with hopes of remuneration and obtained it through connivance of bureau agents. Although

1. Horace M. Bond, *The Education of the Negro in the American Social Order* (New York: Prentice-Hall, 1934), p. 25; Linda W. Slaughter, *The Freedmen of the South* (Cincinnati: Elm Street Printing Co., 1869), p. 110; Henry L. Swint, *The Northern Teacher in the South, 1862–1870* (Nashville: Vanderbilt University Press, 1941), p. 35.

2. Samuel S. Greene, "The Educational Duties of the Hour," National Teachers' Association, *Journal of Proceedings and Lectures* (1865), p. 232; Swint, *Northern Teacher*, p. 58, citing the *Independent*, October 22, 1868; Swint, *Northern Teacher*, p. 88.

3. Bond, *Education of the Negro*, p. 20; Horace M. Bond, *Negro Education in Alabama: A Study in Cotton and Steel* (Washington: Associated Publishers, 1939), p. 117; *Freedmen's Record* 2 (January 1866): 8–9; Henry L. Swint, ed., *Dear Ones at Home: Letters from Contraband Camps* (Nashville: Vanderbilt University Press, 1966), p. 227; "Synopsis of School Reports," 1: 188, in Bureau of Refugees, Freedmen and Abandoned Lands, Manuscripts of the Educational Division, National Archives, Washington, D.C.

few teachers had specific ideas of pecuniary gain for themselves, some (and their sponsoring associations as well) recognized the possible economic implications of their program. Some may have hoped that educated blacks would be better consumers of Northern-manufactured goods and thus create greater markets for Yankee products.[4]

Teachers who came South in many cases endured hardships in living and working conditions and faced unpleasant classroom situations which their Northern colleagues rarely encountered. Occasionally an older student had a drinking problem. For many teachers, maintaining the strict discipline expected in mid nineteenth-century classrooms was impossible because of excessive overcrowding. One teacher complained of attempting to instruct 400 pupils in the alphabet at one time. When 400 seats were full, latecomers were sent away.[5] There were glaring examples of overcrowding in the first black schools; lack of space and inadequate facilities became a characteristic of black classrooms in the South which persisted for generations.

Living conditions for teachers were often crude. Susan Walker at Beaufort, South Carolina, shared an abandoned mansion with eleven other teachers. Since the house had been stripped of most furniture, her bed was a straw-stuffed mattress laid upon a rough board floor, a packing box was her table, a potato became a candlestick, and a marble-top mahogany washstand was the only real piece of furniture. When linens proved unobtainable, she showed her ingenuity by improvising sheets from a white petticoat.[6]

Bureau-association teachers taught in various types of schoolhouses ranging from confiscated mansions to barracks, barns, basements, courthouses, churches, old slave quarters, and sometimes the

4. Henry R. Pease to John W. Alvord, April 24, 1868, in BRFAL Ms; Henry L. Swint, "Northern Interest in the Shoeless Southerner," *Journal of Southern History* 16 (1950): 471.

5. Mary Ames, *From a New England Woman's Diary in Dixie in 1865* (Springfield, Mass.: Plimpton Press, 1906), p. 39; William M. Colby to John W. Alvord, July 15, 1869, in BRFAL Ms; Elizabeth G. Rice, "A Yankee Teacher in the South," *Century Magazine* 62 (1901): 152.

6. Swint, *Northern Teacher*, p. 77; Susan Walker, "Journal of Miss Susan Walker," ed. Henry M. Sherwood, *Quarterly Publication of the Historical and Philosophical Society of Ohio* 7 (1912): 15.

great outdoors. An AMA teacher at Savannah, Georgia, conducted school under an awning stretched upon a pine pole framework, which she described as a "very rude, though cool and pleasant arrangement." In Richmond an AFUC school met in the former Confederate naval arsenal, where seats were shell boxes and study tables were ammunition cases.[7]

Aside from occasional threats of burning down schools and residences and of whipping male teachers by disgruntled whites, the most serious danger that Northern teachers faced was disease. Some came South hoping that the balmy climate, as was then commonly believed, would cure consumption. Many were accustomed to the brisk weather of New England and proved ready victims for tropical diseases such as malaria, especially on the sea islands of South Carolina, in the Mississippi River delta country, and in southeast Texas.[8]

Although environmental and climatic hardships were difficult to overcome, they were not as serious as another problem that faced the teachers—the bitter and determined opposition of Southern whites. Much of this opposition arose because teachers believed that freedmen were entitled to equal opportunities and were not to be treated, even socially, as inferior. Most Southern whites categorically refused to accept this concept and despised those trying to promote it. Some antagonism was a direct result of teachers' attitudes toward the South, local whites, and their way of life. On rare occasions sponsors advised prospective teachers to achieve cooperation with the Southern gentry. The *American Freedman*, edited by Lyman Abbott, warned that a teacher might enter a city, secure his location without consulting the authorities, make his acquaintances and friends solely among blacks, ignore the whites, disregard local customs and lifelong prejudices, and thus give the appearance of another invasion. If a teacher did this, according to Abbott, he could expect no cooperation from former Confederates. He should instead seek advice from leading politicians and clergy and conform to their suggestions as much as possible. He should be "courteous,

7. Swint, *Northern Teacher*, p. 79.
8. Laura M. Towne, *Letters and Diary of Laura M. Towne*, ed. Rupert S. Holland (Cambridge, Mass.: Riverside Press, 1912), pp. 14–15, 117; Lt. Charles Garretson to John W. Alvord, September 30, 1867, in BRFAL Ms.

frank and kind to all."[9] Probably few teachers would have followed these suggestions even if they had been permitted to do so by the local inhabitants.

An obsession with many Yankee teachers, and one that made them thoroughly hated wherever they went, was their preoccupation with reconstructing the South along New England lines. The *Freedmen's Journal*, published by the American Tract Society, asserted "New England can furnish teachers enough to make a New England out of the whole South, and, God helping, we will not pause in our work until the free school system . . . has been established from Maryland to Florida and along the shores of the Gulf." A bureau official and teacher wrote from North Carolina that the New England free school had commenced its march through the South and that its progress would be irresistible.[10]

Some teachers made themselves unpopular by expressing strong abolitionist sentiments. Laura M. Towne at Saint Helena's Island, South Carolina, complained as early as 1862 about the overly cautious spirit prevailing among other teachers regarding emancipation and asked, since they already had acquired the odium of out-and-out abolitionists, "Why not take the credit?" The wide use of Lydia M. Child's antislavery reader, *The Freedmen's Book*, in AMA schools aroused the ire of many whites. Its readings included a poem by William Lloyd Garrison called "The Hour of Freedom," an essay on Toussaint L'Ouverture, the Haitian black revolutionary, and a poem by Lydia Child about John Brown, in which she referred to him as "that kind old man."[11]

Many teachers derived their knowledge of Southern social customs from abolitionist literature and war propaganda from which they deduced that all Southerners who had ever owned slaves and rebelled against the Union had sinned. A Port Royal teacher, Mrs. Austa M. French, asserted that slavery forever doomed the slaveholder, making him a traitor and an heir of perdition. Any former

9. *American Freedman* 1 (November 1866): 114–15.

10. As quoted in Luther P. Jackson, "The Educational Efforts of the Freedmen's Bureau and the Freedmen's Aid Societies in South Carolina, 1862–72," *Journal of Negro History* 8 (1923): 28; *American Missionary* 11 (March 1867): 51.

11. *Letters and Diary of Laura M. Towne*, p. 8; Lydia M. Child, *The Freedmen's Book* (Boston: Ticknor and Fields, 1865), p. 242, passim.

slave owner gained "certain condemnation in the Millennium." Mrs. French was one of the first teachers to arrive on the sea islands in March 1862, an area that she described as "a land of horrid visions of cruelty and sin." A Georgia teacher was certain that it would not be many years before "all intelligent Southerners will bless those who have thus endeavoured to remove from their midst these heavy burdens of crime and woe."[12]

Perhaps more upsetting to Southern whites than antislavery remarks were the patronizing comments which women teachers were prone to make, comments that revealed contempt and disdain for the Southern way of life. They constantly complained about dirt and grime which they found in the frequently long-abandoned houses requisitioned for their use. One instructor sarcastically commented that her new quarters "must be thoroughly cleaned for the 'chivalry' look not to corners and cupboards. They leave this to the poor despised 'mudsie' of the North."[13] Some teachers and school officials could find nothing favorable about the region where they taught. The bureau superintendent in Louisiana, Henry H. Pierce, pictured local whites as possessing no law, order, or intelligence and being at least two hundred years behind in everything. He promised to use "every endeavor to throw a ray of light here and there, among this benighted race of ruffians, rebels by nature." Some teachers attempted to break down racial barriers in bureau-association schools by admitting a few white children, but this was rarely successful.[14] Such interference with the social order caused further deterioration of relations between Northern teachers and local whites.

When Yankee teachers reached their destination and began to work, they usually had no contacts with local whites. Sponsoring organizations urged teachers to conduct extracurricular activities for freedmen after school. The Pennsylvania Freedman's Relief Association sent a letter of instruction to its staff, asking them to visit

12. Mrs. Austa M. French, *Slavery in South Carolina and the Ex-Slaves, or the Port Royal Mission* (New York: W. M. French, 1862), pp. 32–33, 172–73; Charles Stearns, *The Black Man of the South and the Rebels* (New York: American News Co., 1872), p. 133.

13. Walker, "Journal," p. 14.

14. *Letters and Diary of Laura M. Towne*, p. 178; "Synopsis of School Reports," 1: 284, in BRFAL Ms; *American Missionary* 11 (September 1867): 195.

blacks in their homes, instruct women and girls in sewing and domestic economy, and take part in religious meetings and Sunday
schools. These activities, combined with regular classroom work,
gave the teacher little time to socialize with white neighbors, had they
allowed her to do so. A few teachers refused to associate with any
local whites, but lived and boarded with blacks and made no calls
on persons of their own race. On occasion black pupils lived in
white teachers' homes. As late as 1876 Laura M. Towne could coldly
reject the pleasant overtures of an amiable young member of the
Rhett family in South Carolina, when he apologized for not calling
on her. She squelched whatever good intentions he might have had
by replying that it was just as well, for "our ways are not their
ways, and it is troublesome to know them."[15]

The use of patriotic, anti-Southern songs in the classroom was
another point of contention. In September 1865 New Orleans school
officials dismissed pro-Union teachers who had entered the school
system during the occupation, for leading pupils in such songs as
"Hail Columbia," "The Star-Spangled Banner," and "John Brown's
Body." In the minds of local whites, singing these songs was a con-
tentious act, but even worse was the use of the hated *Harper's
Weekly* in teaching freedmen to read.[16]

In bureau schools pupils spent most of the day on the "three
R's" and practical skills. The curriculum might also include some
religious instruction, geography, history, and, in a few of the more
advanced schools, physiology, natural philosophy, Latin, and classi-
cal literature. Teachers also devoted time to citizenship, which
sometimes meant making the freedman aware of politics and voting
procedures that he might become the social and political equal of
whites. James H. Clanton of Alabama, chairman of the Conservative
state executive committee, testified before a congressional investi-

15. Quoted from the *Pennsylvania Freedmen's Bureau*, October 1866, p. 1,
in Jackson, "Educational Efforts of the Freedmen's Bureau," p. 29; Willie Lee
Rose, *Rehearsal for Reconstruction: The Port Royal Experiment* (Indianapolis:
Bobbs Merrill, 1964), p. 399; Henry A. Bullock, *A History of Negro Education
in the South from 1619 to the Present* (Cambridge: Harvard University Press,
1967), p. 30.

16. *House Reports*, 39th Cong., 2d sess., No. 16, pp. 239–399; Slaughter,
Freedmen of the South, p. 134; Oliver Otis Howard, *Autobiography of Oliver
Otis Howard* (New York: Baker and Taylor Co., 1907), 2: 275.

gating committee that it was understood among whites in Alabama that the teachers had come as political emissaries and were instructing black children to look with distrust upon the white people of the South. One benevolent association journal lent credence to this claim: "In the coming struggle with the spirit of rebellion and slavery . . . we must have the freedmen on our side. As we stand by him, so may we expect him to stand by us. Every teacher you send to the field is a pledge to the freedmen of your determination to see justice done him; it is a pledge to the disloyal rebel that you will not yield to him in the future. A teacher costs less than a soldier."[17]

Just as most teachers inherently disliked local whites, so did Southerners hate and distrust Yankee teachers as the personification of Reconstruction. When teachers associated only with freedmen and urged blacks to assert their individuality and political power, they were identified by Southern whites with their worst enemies, the Radicals. *De Bow's Review* expressed a widely held opinion when it accused Northern teachers of having the most bitter feelings against everything associated with whites and of fostering breaches between the two races. Clanton visited a freedmen's school which he believed to be under Radical control, taught by strangers and a "political nursery to prejudice the Negro race against us."[18]

Southern whites frequently contended that it was the missionary teachers they wished to eliminate, not black schools. Testifying before the congressional joint committee on Reconstruction, a North Carolina carpetbag publisher stated that local whites hated the teachers because they fancied "that these missionaries interfere with other matters, in the relations between the servant and the employer." Teachers usually found Southern white women more antagonistic than men. A Milledgeville, Georgia, instructor said that

17. "Report of the Joint Select Committee Appointed to Inquire into the Condition of Affairs in the Late Insurrectionary States . . . ," *House Reports*, 42d Cong., 2d sess., No. 22, Alabama, 1: 252, hereafter cited as "KKK Reports"; *Freedmen's Record* 2 (September 1866): 158. For an indictment of the bureau school curriculum because it included subjects foreign to the experience and needs of black children and failed to recognize that, in society, economy, and cultural tradition, South Carolina was not the counterpart of Massachusetts, see Martin Abbott, *The Freedmen's Bureau in South Carolina* (Chapel Hill: University of North Carolina Press, 1967), p. 91.

18. Swint, *Northern Teacher*, p. 94; *De Bow's Review* 3 (March 1867): 310; "KKK Reports," vol. 8, Alabama, pt. 1, p. 236.

she wished the ladies had treated her and her fellow teachers with as much respect as had the men, for the women "shrink from contact with us in the streets, point us out, and stare at us in church, evidently desiring to annoy, and make us uncomfortable."[19]

In Alabama citizens manifested so much opposition to teachers in 1865 that John W. Alvord wrote to Oliver Otis Howard requesting military protection if the associations wished to send more instructors to that state. The bureau superintendent in Florida wrote in January 1866 that in no case had local citizens shown a willingness to render educators any assistance, including provision of room and board. At this time the Florida legislature passed a law attempting to drive Yankee teachers from the state. It provided for education of blacks on a tuition basis of one dollar per month per child and stated that no person could teach in a black school without a license costing five dollars a year, which the state superintendent might issue or withhold at his discretion. Although violation of this statute could lead to a fine of between $100 and $500, or imprisonment of thirty to sixty days, Union troops and the Freedmen's Bureau prevented its enforcement. White reaction to teachers in Georgia was so strong that Alvord admitted in his January 1866 report that the bureau and associations were unable to establish schools in the interior because of a fear of violence to unprotected teachers. He asserted that a military police force was needed everywhere.[20]

On occasion teachers themselves admitted that most of the opposition encountered was directed at them and not at black education. One AMA teacher wrote that alleged friends of freedmen had begun to promote black schooling in public meetings, "but the question with them is not so much *how they shall secure the education of the blacks,* as how they can get rid of the *Yankee teachers.*"[21]

In Virginia Yankee teachers were as much despised as they were in the lower South. Ralza M. Manly, bureau superintendent,

19. "Report of the Joint Committee on Reconstruction," *House Reports,* 39th Cong., 1st sess., No. 30, pt. 2, p. 278, hereafter cited as "Reconstruction Committee"; Slaughter, *Freedmen of the South,* p. 119.

20. "Reports of the Assistant Commissioners of the Freedmen's Bureau," *Senate Executive Documents,* 39th Cong., 1st sess., No. 27, p. 110; *National Freedman* 2 (January 15, 1866): 35; Howard, *Autobiography,* 2: 337.

21. *American Missionary* 10 (October 1866): 218; *Freedmen's Record* 2 (February 1866): 30.

remarked that the Northern teacher was intensely hated, his work was "despised and derided," and that only the presence of federal troops permitted continuation of educational work.[22] The conservative Virginia press in 1866 launched a vicious attack on Northern teachers, obviously intended to force them from the state. In January the *Richmond Times* facetiously editorialized: "White cravatted gentlemen from Andover, with a nasal twang and pretty Yankee girls, with the smallest hands and feet, have flocked to the South as missionary ground and are communicating a healthy moral tone to the 'colored folks' besides instructing them in chemistry, botany and natural philosophy, teaching them to speak French, sing Italian, and talk Spanish. So that in time we are bound to have intelligent and probably intellectual labor." Five months later the same paper reported that a dreadful calamity had befallen Petersburg—the Yankee teachers had gone home. The *Times* facetiously commented that Petersburg citizens were bearing the loss of "these attractive and interesting females with philosophic if not with Christian resignation." It hoped the teachers' sense of duty would not induce them to remain a moment longer than necessary to complete their "magnificent mission," for there was a splendid mission field available to New England females in Africa, where the teachers might become a gastronomic if not an educational success![23]

The opposition to Northern teachers, which ranged from passive to violent, took many forms. Probably the most common means of showing displeasure, especially on the part of Southern women, was social ostracism which male teachers usually disregarded but which bothered female instructors more than they cared to admit. The assistant bureau commissioner in North Carolina, Colonel Eliphalet Whittlesey, reported that he had never known of one instance of a respectable white person's inviting a teacher into his home. In Georgia even Radical families excluded teachers from society, fearing social exile if they entertained them. A teacher near Augusta said that he knew of no social relations between female teachers and townsmen, and one teacher told him of being spat upon in the streets. *De Bow's Review* remarked that in some Southern communities the only ones to speak to teachers were small boys who

22. *New York Tribune*, February 3, 1866.
23. *Richmond Times*, January 16, 1866; ibid., May 10, 1866.

told them to "go to the Devil" and that local whites ignored the teachers more than they did Union officers.[24]

The AMA bewailed the cold treatment that its personnel received, declaring that they encountered silent contempt, profanity, "or that feminine accomplishment, peculiar to Southern gentility, of 'gathering up their skirts,' that in passing, their dresses shall escape the hated contact." A North Carolina teacher indicated the extent of social exclusion by relating that she had not been in the house of a white person for two months, nor had she been spoken to except by four or five white women during the same period. Only one white woman had entered her house in seventeen months. As late as 1875 a Radical school official and former teacher in Louisiana related that after ten years in that state, no Southern lady Democrat dared call on his wife, unless "secretly and stealthily lest her friends may know that she calls on a Yankee." The teachers' reaction to this treatment was usually one of quiet resignation; they had little choice to do otherwise.[25]

Local whites either insulted or ignored teachers when they attended services at white churches. Julia Sherman visited a Presbyterian church in Lexington, Virginia, where a sexton directed her and a friend to an empty pew. After they returned home he delivered a message from the pew owners requesting that the two women never again occupy their pew. At Brandon, Mississippi, a newspaper editor warned AMA instructor May Close that if she attended church, white children sitting near her pew would leave. She retorted that "children of well-bred Christian parents never left the pew when I entered, in this or any other town."[26]

One of the most pressing problems for Northern teachers, es-

24. "Reconstruction Committee," pt. 2, p. 183; "KKK Reports," Georgia, 2: 1133; Stearns, *The Black Man of the South*, p. 132; *De Bow's Review* 2 (July 1866): 94–95.

25. *American Missionary* 12 (June 1868): 126; ibid., 10 (August 1866): 173; John W. Alvord, *Semi-Annual Reports on Schools for Freedmen* (Washington: Government Printing Office, July 1, 1869), p. 28; "Notes on the Mixed School Imbroglio," Ephraim S. Stoddard Diary for 1874–75, in Ephraim S. Stoddard Collection, Howard-Tilton Memorial Library, Tulane University; *National Freedman* 1 (December 1865): 347; "Synopsis of School Reports," 1: 434, in BRFAL Ms.

26. *American Missionary* 10 (March 1866): 50; ibid., 10 (September 1866): 200.

pecially those in the rural deep South, was securing room and board. Most Southern whites were reluctant to rent teachers a room or house or provide meals. John W. Alvord somewhat overstated the situation when he remarked that if it had not been for the loyal Germans in Texas, there would have been few places in that state for teachers to board. One method of preventing them from securing lodgings was to increase rents to ridiculous amounts, as was done in Raleigh, North Carolina, where houses renting for $350 a year in 1861, by 1865 rented for $1,900 a year in gold, or $3,000 in currency. May Close shut down her school and left Mississippi because she could not find room or board with local whites, who also refused to allow blacks to rent her a room or lease a building for school purposes. Community pressure often discouraged Southerners who might have been willing to lodge teachers. Tactics aimed at denying teachers room and board sometimes culminated in refusal by whites to sell food, and local blacks lacked sufficient surplus to supply the teachers' needs.[27]

After Congress established its initial Reconstruction program in 1867, tensions increased noticeably in the South and teachers who heretofore had been ignored or simply denounced were now subjected to physical violence to force a hasty departure. Although rumors of brutality, murder, and incendiarism were widespread, it is difficult to determine the number of violent acts which Southern whites directed at teachers during this period. Usually threats by the Ku Klux Klan were sufficient to drive a teacher away, as in the case of an AMA teacher in Lewisburg, Arkansas, who had taught only one week when the Klan notified him to quit teaching "niggers" and leave, or be killed.[28]

Harassment of teachers was most common in outlying areas of the South, including northeastern Texas and Louisiana and the remote rural regions of Georgia and Arkansas. In October 1868 the assistant bureau commissioner in Texas, General Joseph J. Reynolds, wrote Howard that it would not be advisable for young female teach-

---

27. Alvord, *Reports*, July 1, 1867, p. 53; *Nation* 1 (November 30, 1865): 674; *Freedmen's Record* 2 (June 1866): 121; *National Freedman* 2 (January 15, 1866): 3; Stearns, *The Black Man of the South*, p. 132; *American Missionary* 10 (March 1866): 44; ibid., 10 (August 1866): 173.

28. Alvord, *Reports*, July 1, 1870, p. 41.

ers to apply for jobs in Texas, since it was impossible to assure their safety from "outrage or insult." He concluded that he was unwilling to assume responsibility of placing them in a position of so much exposure, "thus tempting what we most dread." Although most women teachers faced bitter, intense hatred from local whites, rarely did this take the form of open insult. On occasion, however, female instructors faced physical attack. Margaret Thorpe, while teaching at Williamsburg, Virginia, during 1867–1868, reported that she had been hit by a stone which a white man had hurled at her. Later unknown assailants sicced a bulldog on her horse (she rode away unharmed), and on another occasion she was almost knocked off her horse by a board protruding from a house window in a narrow passageway. What bothered this teacher more than attacks on her person was overhearing a conversation between two young women who stopped in front of her, one asking if she [Margaret Thorpe] were pretty–the companion replying, "good heavens, no!"[29]

While some teachers heeded Klan warnings and left, others remained and found the threats were not idle. Whites severely whipped and hanged a Georgia teacher by the neck until almost dead and told him to leave within five days, which he did. Occasionally a teacher lost his life. Persons reputed to be Klansmen hanged William Luke, an AMA teacher near Talladega, Alabama, in 1869. In this case, leading white citizens of the area attended the funeral and expressed regrets over the murder. In rare instances a teacher's punishment was the result of alleged questionable personal conduct. A group of white boys in Russell County, Alabama, attacked a teacher named Few. Few was allegedly notorious for drinking and mistreating his wife; he had a knife and pistol fight with his brother-in-law; and he continually insulted local Conservatives.[30]

Not all treatment of Northern teachers consisted of insults, ostracism, and outrages; there were instances of cordiality. The bureau superintendent in Louisiana wrote in 1867 that some planters were offering hospitality to white teachers, such as "seats at the

29. Joseph J. Reynolds to Oliver Otis Howard, October 23, 1868, in BRFAL Ms; Swint, ed., *Dear Ones at Home*, p. 193; Richard L. Morton, ed., "Life in Virginia by a 'Yankee Teacher,' Margaret Newbold Thorpe," *Virginia Magazine of History and Biography* 64 (1956): 201.

30. *American Missionary* 14 (January 1870): 12; ibid., 14 (October 1870): 235–37; "KKK Reports," Alabama, 2: 1147.

family table, and treating them with that kindness which teachers receive at the South, even employing them to give private lessons to their own children." The people of Camden, South Carolina, apparently were pleasant to Yankee instructors, for a teacher wrote that white people seemed well disposed and that she had met with nothing but courtesy on their part. When Mrs. Abbie Winsor, a teacher at Oxford, North Carolina, died, the local minister and several white women showed much kindness to the other teachers, and about thirty prominent men in town, but no women, attended the funeral.[31]

The presence of black teachers in freedmen's schools generally aroused less hostility among Southern whites than that of Yankee instructors. The bureau superintendent in North Carolina, when asked whether black teachers were treated respectfully by local whites, replied, "They are not very often insulted in any way, but they are entirely passed by and looked upon with contempt, that is certain." Native white teachers of freedmen received some of the same treatment as their Yankee counterparts, but it usually took the form of social ostracism rather than physical violence. In 1866 John W. Alvord indicated his admiration for Southern whites who were willing to endure jeers, the contempt of friends, and virtual exclusion from society in order to carry on their educational work.[32]

The Yankee teachers thus frequently created a storm of controversy when they conducted schools for freedmen. This was undoubtedly motivated by a great fear among many Southern whites that these unwanted missionaries were emphasizing social and political equality over basic academic subjects. It is remarkable that so few of these teachers actually faced violence and physical attack. Many probably had anticipated social ostracism in the South, and

31. "Synopsis of School Reports," 2: 14, in BRFAL Ms; *American Missionary* 11 (August 1867): 8; *American Freedman* 2 (January 1868): 349.

32. Paul S. Peirce, *The Freedmen's Bureau* (Iowa City: State University of Iowa, 1904), p. 79; "Reconstruction Committee," pt. 2, p. 183; "Reports of the Assistant Commissioners," p. 112. In South Carolina by 1867 the white community evidently attached no social stigma to teaching of freedmen by local whites. See Abbott, *The Freedmen's Bureau in South Carolina*, p. 95. This observation contrasts with that of Vernon Lane Wharton, *The Negro in Mississippi, 1865–90* (Chapel Hill: University of North Carolina Press, 1947), p. 243, who says that in some Mississippi counties attacks on native white teachers of freedmen were more bitter than those on Yankee missionary instructors.

when they encountered it, often regarded such treatment as an occupational hazard. It must be admitted that many teachers did little or nothing to foster good relations with local whites and at times seemed to wear their martyr's crown with grim enjoyment. This should not detract from the realization that it was the creative, courageous, and determined efforts of the Yankee teachers which produced most of the initial learning experiences for freedmen in the postwar South.

The controversy that related to the need for black schools produced a more varied response from Southern whites than that concerning the Yankee teachers. Postwar white reaction to the principle of black education included all shades of opinion, from violent and persistent opposition to moral and material assistance. John W. Alvord, bureau superintendent of education, in 1866 reported an improved outlook among better classes of the South toward black schools and believed many planters concurred that such schools would provide valuable and contented labor. Alvord admitted, however, "that multitudes usually of the lower and baser classes, still bitterly oppose our schools. . . . Nothing, therefore, but military force for sometime to come, ever on the alert and instantly available, will prevent the outbreak of every form of violence."[33]

Upper classes of Southern whites advanced numerous reasons for their approval of freedmen's schools. One commonly discussed reason was that such instruction would promote citizenship and produce better members of society. At a June 1866 public meeting in Oxford, Mississippi, local whites declared that it was bad policy to keep freedmen ignorant because suffrage would be given to blacks someday, and "if we do not teach them someone else will, and whoever benefits them will win an influence over them which will control their votes."[34] Delegates at the annual Mississippi Methodist conference in 1865 concluded that freedmen needed far more knowledge than slaves, for they now had to read laws as well as the Bible. These Methodists believed that if left without education, freedmen would sink deeper into ignorance, superstition, and fa-

33. Alvord, *Reports,* July 1866, p. 2.
34. *De Bow's Review* 2 (September 1866): 310; ibid., 1 (May 1866): 560. See also Paul D. Phillips, "A History of the Freedmen's Bureau in Tennessee" (Ph.D. diss., Vanderbilt University, 1964), pp. 254–55.

naticism, and possibly into careers of crime. The former secretary of the Confederate navy, Stephen R. Mallory, in 1867 told an integrated audience at Pensacola, Florida, that since the black was entitled to vote he must be educated and that it would be in the best interests of Florida to aid freedmen in "education, elevation, and enjoyment of all rights which follow their new condition." James De Bow, an editor, testified before a congressional committee that better-informed whites in the South believed that black education was in the best interests of the entire region, although the majority scoffed at the idea of blacks learning.[35]

In addition to humanitarian motives were those of an economic nature, most pronounced among planters who reasoned that a literate, informed group of laborers would do better work than a group that was not. They viewed the plantation school as an asset and as an inducement for blacks to remain on one plantation and work rather than roam aimlessly through the countryside. Some planters favored black education at public expense only as long as it could be controlled and directed to maintain established master-servant relationships. This element largely dominated Southern state governments until the advent of congressional Reconstruction. The bureau superintendent in Arkansas, William M. Colby, wrote in 1867 that he noticed a more agreeable attitude among higher classes of planters toward black schooling, but he felt that economic motives of self-interest were all-important.[36]

Most Southerners supporting black education usually qualified their views by insisting that only native whites be allowed to teach the "three R's," thus hopefully avoiding any attempt to remake the social order or encourage racial antagonisms. Well-known

35. Hunter D. Farish, *The Circuit Rider Dismounts: A Social History of Southern Methodism, 1865–1900* (Richmond: Dietz Press, 1938), pp. 177–78; *American Freedman,* "Fifth Annual Report" (1867), p. 23; "Reconstruction Committee," pt. 4, p. 135.

36. Horace M. Bond, *Negro Education in Alabama: A Study in Cotton and Steel* (Washington: Associated Publishers, 1939), p. 114, citing *Montgomery Alabama State Journal,* May 1, 1869; *De Bow's Review* 8 (April–May 1870): 338–39; Marjorie H. Parker, "Some Educational Aspects of the Freedmen's Bureau," *Journal of Negro Education* 23 (1954): 17; William M. Colby to Bvt. Maj. Gen'l Edward O. Ord, March 1, 1867, in Bureau of Refugees, Freedmen and Abandoned Lands, Manuscripts of the Educational Division, National Archives, Washington, D.C.

Southerners taking this position included Governor James L. Orr of South Carolina, ex-Governor Andrew B. Moore of Alabama, Jabez L. M. Curry, and Methodist Bishop Holland N. McTyeire. At times even blacks demanded that teachers be chosen from among the local citizenry. In December 1865 a group of blacks at Selma, Alabama, requested that local whites, principally well-educated widows and crippled veterans, be hired to teach their children. They warned, "If you stand back, strangers will come in and take the money from under your hands and carry it away to build up their own country."[37]

Southern clergy were active in campaigning for native instruction of freedmen. A Northern teacher at Columbus, Georgia, was upset by news that a local pastor had recently admonished black ministers of the area to promote the hiring of only Southern teachers, because Yankees would continue to foster racial prejudice. Episcopal Bishop of Tennessee Charles T. Quintard appealed in 1867 for capable Southern teachers of freedmen, warning that the alternative would be "such as chance or fanaticism may send." Stephen Elliot, Episcopal Bishop of Georgia, remarked in December 1866 that it was his sincere conviction that if any future good or blessing were to come to the freedmen, it must be of Southern origin because every person imported to teach the blacks was an influence, however unintentional, to widen the breach between the races.[38]

Southern approval of black education varied in consistency and intensity from year to year and from one area to another. Visits by newspaper editors and other leading citizens often resulted in favorable descriptions of school activities, but the number of white visitors to freedmen's schools was small, and the resulting commentaries were usually those of an enlightened minority. In the spring of 1866 the editor of the *Savannah* (Ga.) *Republican* visited the Bryan Free School final recitation examination in which 350 children participated. He thought the examination went well and commented

37. E. Merton Coulter, *The South during Reconstruction, 1865–77* (Baton Rouge: Louisiana State University Press, 1947), p. 83; Walter L. Fleming, *Documentary History of Reconstruction, Political, Military, Social, Religious, Educational and Industrial, 1865 to the Present Time* (Cleveland: A. H. Clark, 1906–1907), 2: 83.

38. *Freedmen's Record* 2 (July 1866): 132; *Nashville Republican Banner*, January 27, 1867; *De Bow's Review* 2 (September 1866): 313.

upon the quiet, orderly behavior of the pupils, and hoped the federal government would continue operation of the bureau-association schools: "The salvation of both races [in the] South depend [sic] altogether upon their rapid intellectual advancement, and the humane policy will sanction free schools everywhere." A Savannah reporter, visiting a final examination at Bethlehem High School, witnessed the "universal astonishment . . . experienced by all present at the extraordinary intelligence revealed by the scholars."[39]

By 1866 public opinion in Alabama was becoming more favorable to black education. The Methodist conference, meeting at Montgomery in January, recommended that fellow churchmen approve and encourage day schools for black children, operated under proper regulations by trustworthy teachers. Public opinion in North Carolina regarding freedmen's instruction appeared apathetic in 1866, according to the assistant bureau commissioner, who believed that in some instances Tarheel citizens had no objection to establishing schools on their farms if teachers could be found and routine farm work would not be interrupted. In South Carolina benevolent association and bureau personnel noticed a marked change in local attitudes; a teacher at Marion noted that several former slaveholders in his area were becoming strong advocates of black schools and were materially encouraging them.[40]

By 1867 numerous whites were carrying out promises of assistance to black schools. In Dallas County, Alabama, whites helped build forty schoolhouses for blacks, and at Montgomery they donated money to a black college and paid tuition for black students at private schools. The superintendent of an Arkansas plantation belonging to former Confederate General Gideon J. Pillow established a school on the grounds and, surprisingly, employed a teacher from Keokuk, Iowa. This school provided instruction to more than

39. *National Freedman* 2 (July 1866): 197–98, citing *Savannah Republican*, July 12, 1866. Quoted in *De Bow's Review* 1 (May 1866): 560.

40. *New York Daily Tribune*, February 3, 1866; Farish, *The Circuit Rider Dismounts*, p. 177; "Report of the Joint Select Committee Appointed to Inquire into the Condition of Affairs in the Late Insurrectionary States . . . ," *House Reports*, 42d Cong., 2d sess., Alabama, 1: 234; ibid., 3: 1548; *Freedmen's Record* 2 (July 1866): 135; ibid., 2 (August 1866): 148; *American Missionary* 10 (May 1866): 114; "Reconstruction Committee," pt. 2, p. 183; *National Freedman* 2 (February 1866): 43.

one hundred freedmen from two plantations. A country doctor at Barton, Georgia, wrote to Howard requesting bureau aid to establish a school for blacks on his property. He promised to organize the school if the bureau would supply teachers and hopefully noted that "we have hundreds—hundreds—of smart little colored children and youths, who are burning with anxiety to learn."[41]

Despite impoverished conditions, Mississippi whites worked hard in 1867 to further black education. John M. Langston, a black inspector of schools for the bureau, reported to Howard that he was treated with great civility everywhere in Mississippi and believed former slaveholders were adjusting to the idea that black education was inevitable. At Columbus whites gave blacks about $1,000 to rebuild a recently burned schoolhouse. A citizen of Meridian donated two churches and a school site worth over $500. At Canton, Corinth, Jackson, and Artesia, whites helped blacks by contributing money to purchase school sites. However, when the two carpetbagger brothers living at Yazoo City offered carpentry assistance to a local black school-church project, they were threatened with violence until the Freedmen's Bureau agent warned that he would bring in federal troops. Six mill hands, all Union veterans and employees of Albert T. and Charles Morgan, then proceeded to construct the building without incident.[42]

Donations of land and labor by whites for black schoolhouses were not uncommon in Virginia. In some areas, planters built schools on their property, and upper-class white women gave free lessons during the week. A few planters provided board and lodging for teachers. By 1867 Reuben Tomlinson, bureau superintendent in South Carolina, could declare that only half a dozen men of intelligence in any major up-country town would deem it in the public interest to discontinue black schools. He cautioned, how-

41. Walter L. Fleming, *Civil War and Reconstruction in Alabama* (New York: Columbia University Press, 1905), p. 626; P. S. Wright to Oliver Otis Howard, March 13, 1867, in BRFAL Ms; William Houser to Oliver Otis Howard, April 30, 1867, in BRFAL Ms.

42. Edgar W. Knight, *Public Education in the South* (Boston: Ginn and Co., 1922), p. 315; Howard, *Autobiography*, 2: 341. John M. Langston to Oliver Otis Howard, July 10, 1867, in BRFAL Ms; John M. Langston to John W. Alvord, July 25, 1867, in BRFAL Ms; *American Missionary* 11 (September 1867): 210; Albert T. Morgan, *Yazoo: or, on the Picket Line of Freedom in the South* (Washington: Rufus H. Darby Press, 1884), pp. 102–6.

ever, that this did not presume their active support and cooperation. Even the most liberal South Carolinians who favored schooling for blacks usually did so with two reservations: that it be confined to the rudimentary level and that there be no integration.[43] Fear was ever-present that any education of blacks, even if carried on by private associations in segregated schools, would eventually lead to mixed schools. Edmund A. Ware, bureau superintendent in Georgia, attended the first meeting of the Georgia Education Association in 1867 and learned that the delegates believed blacks must be educated immediately but were hostile to Yankee teachers and especially to the possibility of integrated schools.[44]

Certain Southern whites believed it was absurd to educate blacks. Dr. Josiah C. Nott of Mobile, Alabama, noted for his studies of black "inferiority," believed blacks were physically incapable of benefiting from academic instruction. Nott declared that a black's brain was nine cubic inches smaller than that of a white man, and "the idea that the brain of the Negro or any other race can be enlarged and the intellect developed by education has no foundation of truth, or any semblance of support from history."[45]

Those opposing black education often made frequent use of pseudo-psychological and economic theories. At Doctortown, Georgia, General Charles H. Howard (brother to Oliver Otis Howard) found that most local whites believed that instructing freedmen would result in a loss of labor output, and some believed that book learning was injurious to all working classes. A bureau agent in Tennessee reported similar sentiments, i.e., "the more ignorant they [the freedmen] are the better they work; that in proportion as they increase in intelligence the more insolent, lazy and worthless they become."[46]

43. "Synopsis of School Reports," 1: 13, 116–17, in the manuscripts of the Educational Division, Bureau of Refugees, Freedmen and Abandoned Lands, National Archives, Washington, D.C.; *American Missionary* 11 (November 1867): 245; Bullock, *Negro Education in the South*, p. 27; Joel Williamson, *After Slavery: The Negro in South Carolina during Reconstruction, 1861–1877* (Chapel Hill: University of North Carolina Press, 1965), pp. 214–15.

44. "Synopsis of School Reports," 1: 121, in BRFAL Ms.

45. *New York Times*, December 25, 1868; *De Bow's Review* 2 (March 1866): 282.

46. "Reconstruction Committee," pt. 3, p. 43; Alvord, *Reports*, July 1, 1868, pp. 46–47.

Some Southern whites feared that freedmen's schools would produce a new generation of overly intelligent and aggressive blacks. A reporter for the *Norfolk Journal*, impressed and perhaps somewhat stunned by the quality of recitations at a local freedmen's school, warned that "more encouragement must be given by our councils to our public schools, to prevent our white children from being outstripped in the race for intelligence by their sable competitors." A more pressing worry among whites than being surpassed intellectually was the realization that educated blacks would intensify their demands for social and political privileges. In 1866, Oliver Otis Howard stated that opposition to freedmen's schools arose largely from the belief that bureau-association teachers were fostering social equality.[47]

By 1866 a variety of federal and private agencies were involved in the Reconstruction process: the Freedmen's Bureau, the Union League, the Union Army, and a multiplicity of benevolent and missionary societies. As actions of these groups began to affect numerous aspects of Southern life, local whites more and more looked upon freedmen's schools as symbols of Yankee meddling and interference. Any effort made to educate blacks was another source of irritation on which to vent wrath and indignation. Frequently whites directed their anger as much against the presence of federal troops, the bureau, or carpetbag politicians holding forth at local courthouses, as at the idea of black education. Burning a schoolhouse or harassing a teacher often symbolized resentment against the whole process of Reconstruction. It is evident that many whites often viewed the burning of a school or the cessation of black education as an indirect victory over the hated Yankees. Outrages against schools and teachers are a barometer for judging public opinion concerning bureau-association schools.

Opposition to bureau schools became more aggressive in 1866. At Columbus, Georgia, outsiders interrupted several schools' sessions by throwing rocks through windows and hitting pupils. In

47. *National Freedman* 1 (September 1865): 269; Linda W. Slaughter, *The Freedmen of the South* (Cincinnati: Elm Street Printing Co., 1869), p. 147, citing the *Norfolk Journal*, June 1, 1867; *House Executive Documents*, 39th Cong., 1st sess., No. 11, p. 13; John A. Carpenter, *Sword and Olive Branch: Oliver Otis Howard* (Pittsburgh: University of Pittsburgh Press, 1964), p. 165; Phillips, "Freedmen's Bureau in Tennessee," p. 258.

Mississippi John W. Alvord reported hardened opposition to black schools. The reaction in North Carolina was less violent than in other states but just as determined. In Tennessee the bitterest opponents of black education were poor whites of the mountain areas, many of whom had been Union loyalists. Norfolk, Virginia, became the scene of violence in January 1866 when unknown attackers burned and pillaged a concert hall used to accommodate black schools. Teachers were certain that whites had set the blaze "for the express purpose of breaking up the 'nigger schools.' " In some areas, it must be admitted, whites attacked teachers and burned schools primarily because of their hatred and fear of black education.[48]

Assistant commissioners of the Freedmen's Bureau by 1867 felt that white reaction to bureau schools was so strong that military protection was required in all areas of the South and should be strengthened in many places where it already existed. The assistant commissioner in Louisiana remarked that if military power were withdrawn, the bureau-association schools would cease to exist. John W. Alvord declared that military force alone would save many schools, and "where, as yet there have been no atrocities attempted against the schools, protecting power is called for to give that sense of quiet and consciousness of security which the calm duties of both teacher and pupil always require."[49] In their final two years of operation (1868–1870), bureau schools continued to have difficulties, even though many whites had begun to accept the idea of black education. Although the situation in the South as a whole was more critical in 1868 than during the previous year, it still varied considerably within a given state. On one page of a monthly report the bureau superintendent of Arkansas could describe public sentiment toward bureau schools in such diverse terms as "dormant," "against," "less opposition," "favorable," "improving," and "bitter opposition." The bureau superintendent in Louisiana quoted a Clai-

48. Stearns, *The Black Man of the South*, p. 132; "Reconstruction Committee," pt. 2, p. 183; Peirce, *Freedmen's Bureau*, p. 80; *Freedmen's Record* 2 (January 1866): 25; Bond, *Education of the Negro*, p. 31. For an excellent discussion of violence against schools and teachers in Virginia, see William T. Alderson, "The Freedmen's Bureau in Virginia" (M.A. thesis, Vanderbilt University, 1949), pp. 55–56.
49. "Reports of the Assistant Commissioners," pp. 112, 120.

borne Parish official who said that he could organize schools only with the help of troops, because whites used every means possible to retard his efforts, including threatening his life and intimidating freedmen with promises of violent death if they should attend school.[50]

The presidential contest between Horatio Seymour and Ulysses S. Grant in 1868 and the accompanying campaign, which found Radicals determined to deliver the South to Grant, greatly increased tensions and resulted in more resentment and violence against bureau schools. In July Alvord alluded to the political canvass which had diverted the freedmen's interest from education and enticed them to spend money on political meetings instead of schools. After the election, he remarked that "bitter opposition and frequent violence were manifested up to the eve of the late presidential election. For a time it became doubtful whether schools in such localities could go on at all." Oliver Otis Howard reported in October that public feeling since August had become so bitter against freedmen's schools that teachers and bureau agents found it difficult to perform their duties as a result of the animosities fostered during the recent elections. At Yazoo City, Mississippi, conservative whites contributed from fifty cents to two dollars a month to establish a school for children of members of the local "Colored Conservative Club." This brazen attempt to gain black votes for Seymour was a failure, and the school closed shortly after the election. The bureau superintendent in Louisiana stated that during the recent campaign "downright anarchy" had prevailed in many localities. "The past month, with its horrors and excitements, has been a season of terror to the freedmen—he has been driven from the schoolhouse, the church, the fireside, and the Ballot-box." Political unrest also distracted freedmen to the extent that they temporarily lost some of their interest in education, being too busy with election rallies to attend school or see that their children did.[51]

50. "Synopsis of School Reports," 1: 277, in BRFAL Ms; *American Missionary* 12 (July 1868): 150; Frank R. Chase to Capt. Lusius H. Warren, May 11, 1868, in BRFAL Ms; Alvord, *Reports*, July 1, 1868, p. 38.

51. Alvord, *Reports*, January 1, 1869, p. 4; ibid., July 1, 1868, p. 1; Slaughter, *The Freedmen of the South*, pp. 181–83; "Synopsis of School Reports," 1: 267, in BRFAL Ms; Phillips, "Freedmen's Bureau in Tennessee," pp. 258–59; Morgan,

Following Grant's victory, the situation temporarily improved and a period of false calm ensued for several months. Accounts by bureau superintendents for the first six months of 1869 still varied considerably. Arkansas reported little open opposition to black schools, but the superintendent in Alabama wrote in September 1869, after visiting several parts of the state, that he found the attitude of whites toward bureau schools and teachers had worsened. A bureau inspector at Gardner, Tennessee, noted a great deal of Klan activity by January 1869. In July 1869, sixty-three Tennessee counties reported that thirty-seven schoolhouses had been burned since the first of the year, teachers had been mobbed and whipped, and "ropes were put around their necks accompanied with threats of hanging." Five months later the bureau superintendent of North Carolina wrote that in many sections teachers were frightened and threats of violence had nearly disbanded numerous schools. Assaults upon teachers were frequent, and black parents feared sending their children to school. Northwestern Louisiana and northern Texas were so hostile in 1869 that bureau superintendent Captain James McCleery wrote that irate citizens often drove him from communities when they discovered he had come to organize a school for black children. Consequently he had to handle much of his business secretly and travel in disguise. Someone attempted to assassinate McCleery's clerk, other assailants attacked his messenger on several occasions, and McCleery himself received threatening letters, was pelted with bricks, and found dead cats in his cistern.[52]

The erroneous impression has sometimes been given that, after the 1868 election, opposition to black education declined until there was little outward manifestation of antagonism by 1870. Even Oliver Otis Howard, who was either optimistic or desirous of creating a more favorable impression than actually existed, indicated that violence against freedmen's schools and teachers tended to evaporate after 1869. Reports of the bureau's educational division and

Yazoo, pp. 218–21; Alvord, *Reports*, January 1, 1870, p. 35; "Synopsis of School Reports," 1: 224, in BRFAL Ms.

52. Alvord, *Reports*, January 1, 1869, p. 4; ibid., July 1, 1869, p. 59; "Synopsis of School Reports," 2: 146, 178–79, in BRFAL Ms; Alvord, *Reports*, January 1, 1869, pp. 42–43; Alrutheus A. Taylor, *The Negro in Tennessee, 1865–1880* (Washington: Associated Publishers, 1941), p. 180.

other available materials do not support this judgment.[53] Opposition to freedmen's schools and teachers in the Gulf states of Louisiana, Mississippi, and Texas continued into the next decade. School burnings, destruction of textbooks, and threats upon lives of teachers were commonplace in Bossier, Winn, DeSoto, and Ouachita parishes in Louisiana, eight northern Mississippi counties, and in Bastrop County, Texas. In 1870 McCleery tried to overcome animosity by sending letters to 1,000 white ministers, hoping that they would help restore order and stability. Most of the letters went unanswered. A few of those replying gave assurances of sympathy and understanding, but others warned McCleery and all bureau agents to stay away if they valued their lives. Numerous incidents of incendiarism, violence, and abuse against bureau teachers and schools persisted through 1870 and remained a problem after education of blacks was taken over by the state governments.[54]

Contrary to the almost universal hatred of Northern teachers, attitudes of Southern whites toward black education displayed great variance. Many upper-class whites, motivated by economic or humanitarian reasons, favored freedmen's schools, but most preferred that these schools be taught by native Southerners. The poorer classes often indicated a strong opposition to "nigger schools" which intensified as their hatred of Reconstruction increased. This led to violent outrages against schools and teachers which reached a climax during the presidential campaign of 1868, especially in remote and sparsely settled areas of Georgia, Alabama, Mississippi, Texas, and Louisiana. By 1870, when the bureau closed its schools,

53. Swint, *Northern Teacher*, pp. 132–33. In a speech given before the National Education Association in August 1869, Howard stated that opposition to the bureau's educational work had almost ceased, teachers were no longer mobbed, and "for a long time" he had not heard of "an instance of abuse of a teacher." Oliver Otis Howard, "Education in the South," National Teachers' Association, *Journal of Proceedings and Lectures* (1869), p. 99.

54. Wharton, *The Negro in Mississippi*, p. 245; Capt. James McCleery to John W. Alvord, April 25, 1870, in BRFAL Ms; Alvord, *Reports*, July 1, 1870, p. 33; "KKK Reports," Mississippi, 1: 82–95, 281, 416–20; ibid., 2: 777–79; *Report of the Commissioner of Education . . . for the Year 1870–1871* (Washington: Government Printing Office, 1872), p. 350; Stearns, *The Black Man of the South*, p. 482; *Annual Report of the State Superintendent of Education . . . to the General Assembly of Louisiana, 1873* (New Orleans: n.p., 1874), p. 209; ibid., 1874, p. 233: *House Reports*, 43d Cong., 2d sess., No. 261, pp. 320–21.

some Southern whites were at least willing to assume the materialistic outlook that the *Richmond Times* had advocated in 1867. The paper then condemned as preposterous two prevailing attitudes toward black education: first, that a "nigger is a nigger, and you can't make anything out of him," and second, "that he is a Christian, a scholar, a gentleman and a philosopher by intuition." The *Times* believed both ideas to be "equally false and ridiculous" because "the Negro is but an ignorant laborer, who undoubtedly can be improved and rendered more serviceable and valuable by education."[55] The concept that education of blacks would produce intelligent, law-abiding, productive citizens and voters was almost a century away.

55. January 16, 1867.

3. *Southern Public Schools & Integration*

ALTHOUGH there were no tax-supported schools for slaves or free blacks in the South before 1860, some public schools existed for whites. By that year all Southern states except South Carolina had enacted constitutional provisions for public education, often optional rather than mandatory, and all made at least token efforts toward educating some white children at public expense. North Carolina and Louisiana organized the most comprehensive school systems, but these fell apart during the war.

Perhaps because of its urban character, its long-standing commercial ties with the Northeast, and the high percentage of white citizens who had migrated from the North, New Orleans outshone all antebellum Southern cities with respect to schools and gave Louisiana its good reputation in education. In 1841 a group of New Orleans lawyers and merchants, most of them Northern-born, secured passage of a state law that permitted the establishment of independent school districts in municipalities and that received a small subsidy from the state government. Public-spirited men consulted Horace Mann, eminent Massachusetts educator, about the formation of a tax-supported school system. At Mann's suggestion, a New Orleans administrative division, the second municipality, appointed an experienced school administrator, John A. Shaw of Bridgewater, Massachusetts, to organize schools along lines of those in New England. Shaw recruited teachers from the North, mainly from New England, to work with the Massachusetts-patterned teaching techniques, division of elementary schools into primary and intermediate divisions, rules governing the lives of pupils, and curriculum. Textbooks, usually of New England authorship, were purchased in Boston, and most school equipment, furniture, and library books came from New England. By the 1850s Yankee visitors to New Orleans' schools made favorable comments, one observer reporting that "with few exceptions, the teachers are natives of New England." Samuel R. Goodrich, Connecticut-born author of the Peter Parley stories for children, told a New Orleans audience that some of the city's schools would be deemed excellent in any part of New England, even Boston. He concluded, "Your schools declare that the wise and philanthropic social principles of the Pilgrims have taken root in the midst of a city signalized over the world by the extent and activity of its commerce."[1]

North Carolina undoubtedly had the most vigorous prewar state school system in the South. The state legislature created this system in January 1839, giving each county the right to establish schools. Calvin H. Wiley became North Carolina's first state superintendent in 1853 and served until 1866. He was largely responsible for strengthening the system. At the beginning of Wiley's tenure there were approximately 2,500 public schools in North Carolina with an enrollment of almost 95,000 out of an estimated school-aged population of 195,000 white children. In 1860 approximately 150,-000 children attended the more than 3,000 public schools. School expenditures that year included more than $100,000 of local taxes and $280,000 from state funds. The average salary for teachers was $28.00 a month.[2]

South Carolina was unique among Southern states in that it had no constitutional provision for education until Reconstruction and the adoption of a new constitution in 1868. The General Assembly of South Carolina, however, in 1811 established free schools for whites, but if more children applied than could be accepted, preference was given to poor orphans and children of indigent parents. This provision had an unhealthy effect; the schools acquired the stigma of being pauper schools, and white parents of property and social standing avoided them. There was no state superintendent nor any form of supervision for the schools. Their

1. William W. Chenault and Robert C. Reinders, "The Northern-Born Community of New Orleans in the 1850's," *Journal of American History* 51 (1964): 233; Robert C. Reinders, *End of an Era: New Orleans, 1850–1860* (New Orleans: Pelican Publishing Co., 1964), pp. 131–32; "The Schools of New Orleans," *Common School Journal* 13 (June 1, 1851): 170–71; Samuel R. Goodrich, *Recollections of a Lifetime or Men and Things I Have Seen* (New York: Miller, Orton and Mulligan, 1857), 2: 329–30.

2. Edgar W. Knight, *Public School Education in North Carolina* (Boston: Houghton Mifflin, 1916), pp. 140, 164–86.

financial support came, in the main, from a state allotment of $300 per year for each representative that the school district or county had in the legislature. Charleston in 1856 established a municipal system of primary schools for both rich and poor white children, followed a few years later by a secondary school and a normal school.[3]

While Southern advocates of public education made some progress before 1860, they met bitter opposition from groups favoring private schools, and public schools often were in reality private, being only partially supported by state funds. In 1868 *De Bow's Review* summarized the beliefs that caused the South's alleged prewar reluctance to support public schools: it was unnecessary to educate white laborers; it was undesirable to teach slaves; school costs rested upon slave property owned by a minority of whites, an expensive and unequal form of taxation; the sparseness of population made the establishment of public schools impractical in many areas.[4] In addition, many whites were able to afford tutors or private academies and seminaries and usually had little concern for public education.

During the Civil War the rudimentary Southern school systems disintegrated: buildings were destroyed; others were used as hospitals; male teachers entered military service; and states diverted school funds to other purposes. Several states invested their school funds in state and Confederate bonds which became worthless after April 1865. When the war was over, practically nothing remained of these systems.

The constitutions ratified by the former Confederate states during the preliminary phases of Reconstruction, 1864–1866, paid little attention to education. Alabama's constitution of 1865 contained a vague statement about legislative encouragement of schools and education with no regard to race. Some school officers were appointed, but only a few schools were organized in Alabama before the constitutional convention of 1868. In 1864 Arkansas ratified

3. *Report of the Commissioner of Education for the Year 1875–1876* (Washington: Government Printing Office, 1876), pp. 362–63; Edgar W. Knight, *The Influence of Reconstruction on Education in the South* (New York: Teachers College, Columbia University, 1913), p. 61.

4. *De Bow's Review* 5 (1868): 1107–8.

a constitution that merely incorporated the educational provision of the previous constitution of 1836. This state did nothing to further public education until 1868–1869. Florida's constitution of 1865 was indefinite concerning schools, and the section on education did not lead to the creation of a system. An 1865 constitution authorized the General Assembly of Georgia to provide education for "the people," but the legislature remained unresponsive.[5]

Of all the constitutions passed by Southern states in the period 1864–1866, Louisiana's, ratified in 1864, had the most specific provision concerning public schools: "The legislature shall provide for the education of all children between the ages of six and eighteen years, by maintenance of free public schools by taxation or otherwise." There was no mention of mixed (racially integrated) schools, but such might be inferred from the phrase "education of all children." However, a new school system did not begin until the adoption of another constitution and election of a new state superintendent in 1868. Mississippi did not ratify a constitution before 1868, but did add some amendments to the constitution of 1832, none of which dealt with schools. North Carolina's proposed constitution was rejected in 1866 by the electorate, and another was not drafted until the advent of Radical Reconstruction. Tennessee also continued to operate under a prewar constitution, which had created a system of common schools that were partially supported by local tax levies and which a minority of students attended at public expense. South Carolina ratified a new constitution in 1865, but it contained no provision concerning education or establishment of schools. In the wartime constitution drawn up in 1864 by the Union-sponsored Pierpont government in Alexandria, Virginia, there was no specific reference to public schools for either race. Virginia ratified no other constitution until 1870 and, until then, retained a school system in which most students paid tuition.[6]

Texas was one of the two Southern states during the moderate

5. Benjamin Perley Poore, comp., *The Federal and State Constitutions, Colonial Charters, and Other Organic Laws of the United States* (Washington: Government Printing Office, 1878), 1: 54, 131, 343, 406; *Report of the Commissioner of Education for the Year 1875–1876*, p. 6.

6. Poore, *Federal and State Constitutions*, 1: 753; ibid., 2: 1079–80, 1637–45, 1937–53.

first years of Reconstruction that provided (on paper) for a system of black education. Its 1866 constitution authorized the legislature to establish a system of schools for blacks, but only taxes collected from "Africans" were to be used for the support of those schools. The Texas legislature continued the prewar practice of selecting private schools for instruction of public-fund pupils. Before any action could be taken, however, the federal government nullified the constitution and voided all plans for reorganization. In January 1866 Florida's legislature passed a law that created a separate school system for blacks. The state's plan for financing these schools was to impose a $1.00 state tax upon all black males between twenty-one and forty-five years of age and to charge each pupil fifty cents tuition. This law stimulated the establishment of about twenty-five black schools by 1866, schools that were soon united with the Freedmen's Bureau system. Florida's dual school system continued, at least in theory, until the constitution of 1868 went into effect.[7]

Forces that gained political control in the South after 1867 stressed the necessity of educating both freedmen and whites, and, therefore, new educational systems were developed. Although these schools were sometimes deprived of funds by unscrupulous politicians, and at times provided sinecures for the politically faithful, they were far superior to their antebellum predecessors and gave a measure of basic education to some blacks and many whites who previously had received none. Public schools in the South were not an innovation of Reconstruction, but their reestablishment, revitalization, and provisions for both races were among the most important achievements of this period. These educational accomplishments included specific constitutional and legal provisions for education; schools for both races; and financial support from state and local taxes. Atticus G. Haywood of Georgia, bishop of the Methodist Episcopal Church, South, referred to the Reconstruction schools as "one of the best issues of the revolution. . . . So much

7. Ibid., pp. 1799–1800; Frederick Eby, *The Development of Education in Texas* (New York; Macmillan, 1925), p. 156; Guy H. Wheeler, Jr., "The History of Education in Texas during the Reconstruction Period" (M.A. thesis, North Texas State University, 1953), p. 49; William W. Davis, *The Civil War and Reconstruction in Florida* (New York: Columbia University, 1913), pp. 387–88; George G. Bush, *History of Education in Florida* (Washington: Government Printing Office, 1889), p. 24.

the South owes to the carpetbag governments; they did not give to the Southern people common schools, but they began them."[8]

As the Reconstruction constitutional conventions of 1867–1868 pondered the establishment of tax-supported public schools for both races, an immediate point of issue was whether these schools should be integrated or mixed. Principal advocates of mixed schools in the South included carpetbag politicians of varying degrees of sincerity, well-meaning reformers such as bureau-association personnel, and well-known crusaders such as Charles Sumner and William Lloyd Garrison. Most white Southerners convinced themselves that blacks did not favor integration; whether a majority supported it is a moot point. Many blacks seemed more interested in equal educational opportunities than in encouraging integration, especially on the elementary level. Those courageous enough to express pro-integration opinions preferred mixed schools for a variety of reasons: they believed that any racial discrimination violated principles of democracy and the Fourteenth Amendment; they knew that separate facilities would result in black schools receiving a smaller share of school funds; and many realized that segregated schools would be inferior in every respect.[9]

Although the Southern states had Northern examples for constitutional reforms, racially integrated schools were not common in the North at this time. Some Northern states provided separate schools for each race, others permitted both mixed and separate schools. Indiana's 1869 school law required trustees to supply adequate schools for white students only, and by 1873 less than 1 percent of Hoosier school districts provided any facilities for blacks. Until 1874 Illinois law failed to protect black children adequately in their rights to attend public schools. In Kansas an 1868 statute allowed cities over 150,000 population to maintain separate schools until 1871 when the legislature made them illegal on the basis of an

8. Knight, *The Influence of Reconstruction*, p. 99; Atticus G. Haygood, "The South and the School Problem," *Harper's Monthly* 79 (1889): 225.

9. John Hope Franklin, *Reconstruction after the Civil War* (Chicago: University of Chicago Press, 1961), pp. 110–11; Horace M. Bond, *The Education of the Negro in the American Social Order* (New York: Prentice-Hall, 1934), p. 56; Joel Williamson, *After Slavery: The Negro in South Carolina during Reconstruction, 1861–1877* (Chapel Hill: University of North Carolina Press, 1965), pp. 222–23.

1869 state supreme court ruling. Ohio's school law, as amended in 1864 and left intact in the 1880 code, permitted separate schools for blacks in districts with thirty or more black pupils. New York's 1864 law, repassed in 1873, provided separate-but-equal schools for blacks in towns and villages and was still in effect by 1882. Some Northern states attempted to outlaw school segregation. Rhode Island did so in 1866, and between 1867 and 1874 the legislatures or courts of Michigan, Connecticut, Minnesota, and Iowa took similar action. Other states maintained various degrees of segregated schooling for many years.[10]

Although the subject of mixed schools created controversy throughout the South after 1867, in many states a final reckoning was avoided by legal and legislative maneuverings. The school systems established by the Reconstruction constitutional conventions and legislatures were far more the work of white delegates than black. Most white delegates were scalawags who desired to establish free schools for all children, although not necessarily on an integrated basis. Yankee delegates emphasized the value of free tax-supported schools and centralized administrations; black delegates stressed education as the only way to achieve full emancipation. Only in South Carolina did blacks predominate in the constitutional convention (seventy-six blacks, forty-eight whites). Of 133 members of the North Carolina convention, only fifteen were blacks—110 were native whites. In Mississippi eighty-four of 100 delegates were whites, sixty-seven of them natives.[11] With one ex-

10. Francis E. Bonar, "The Civil Rights Act of 1875" (M.A. thesis, Ohio State University, 1940), p. 13; *Code of Iowa, 1873*, secs. 1793–94, pp. 329–30; *Report of the Commissioner of Education for the Year 1869–70* (Washington: Government Printing Office, 1870), p. 127; *Statutes of Indiana, 1876*, 1: 779; *Statutes of Illinois, 1818–1874, 1874*, 3: 397; *Chicago Daily Inter-Ocean*, January 23, 1875; *Statutes of Kansas, 1868*, chapt. 18, art. 5, sec. 75; *Acts of Michigan, 1871*, 1: 274; *Laws of Ohio, 1852–53*, 51: 429–41; *Revised Statutes of Ohio, 1880*, p. 1005; *Revised Statutes of New York, 1882*, 2: 1184; New York, *Statutes at Large, 1872*, 11: 583–84; James M. McPherson, *The Struggle for Equality: Abolitionists and the Negro in the Civil War and Reconstruction* (Princeton: Princeton University Press, 1964), pp. 228–29; *Acts of Rhode Island, 1866*, p. 225; Irving H. Bartlett, *From Slavery to Citizen: The Story of the Negro in Rhode Island* (Providence: Urban League of Greater Providence, 1954), pp. 25–29.

11. Bond, *Education of the Negro*, pp. 75–77; Vernon L. Wharton, *The*

ception therefore, blacks possessed insufficient power by themselves to achieve mixed schools in their states. In that one exception, South Carolina, schools were not integrated on the elementary and secondary level, although such was permitted by the state's new constitution.

At Alabama's constitutional convention in 1867 black delegates demanded mixed schools, but some white conservatives and scalawags protested. There was an attempt to amend the education article and specifically provide for education of black and white pupils in separate schools, but delegates killed the motion by tabling it, 47–26. On the same day, December 5, 1867, delegate John Carraway of Mobile proposed an amendment stating that if it should prove expedient to have separate schools, the board of education would equally divide school funds in districts where residents demanded such division. This motion never came to a vote, and when delegates adopted section 6 of article XI, it was a vague statement with no reference to requiring either separate or mixed schools.[12] Foes of mixed schools in Alabama gained a victory during the following year when the legislature passed a law stating that it was unlawful to unite both races in the same school unless the board obtained unanimous consent of parents or guardians involved. In 1868, as ninety years later, this act virtually insured a segregated school system. After Conservatives regained political control of the state in 1874 they framed a new constitution which specifically stated that separate schools be provided for the children of citizens of African descent.[13]

Arkansas made no provision in an 1865 education law for instruction of black children, but this act also prohibited the collection of school taxes from blacks. A law passed in 1867 prevented

Negro in Mississippi, 1865–1890 (Chapel Hill: University of North Carolina Press, 1947), pp. 146–47.

12. Walter L. Fleming, *Civil War and Reconstruction in Alabama* (New York: Columbia University Press, 1905), p. 607; *Official Journal of the Constitutional Convention of the State of Alabama . . . 1867* (Montgomery: Barrett and Brown, 1868), pp. 237–38. The official debates and proceedings of the 1867 convention were either not recorded or not preserved. The *Journal* is all that remains. See also Poore, *Federal and State Constitutions*, 1: 73.

13. *Acts of Alabama*, 1868, p. 148; Poore, *Federal and State Constitutions*, 1: 93; Franklin, *Reconstruction*, p. 110.

blacks or mulattoes from attending any public school in the state except those established exclusively for members of their race.[14] In Arkansas's Reconstruction constitutional convention of 1868, the question of mixed schools was a minor one at best, as none of the forty-eight Radical delegates (out of a total of seventy present), including eight blacks, seemed willing to push it. The convention avoided a direct confrontation over this problem by passing an education article providing for maintenance of free public schools for all persons between five and twenty-one years of age. There was no reference either to segregated or integrated facilities. White delegate John M. Bradley, a former Confederate officer and one of the sixteen Conservatives attending the convention, feared the education article would create mixed schools and thus thrust "social inferiors" into school with white children. Nine white delegates ultimately opposed the proposed constitution for twelve reasons, one being that it would compel whites to support public schools from which their children, in effect, would be excluded. The *Arkansas Gazette* interpreted the constitution as establishing mixed schools for both races and urged its defeat by the voters. The constitution containing the enigmatic education article was ratified, however, by a narrow margin of 1,316 votes.[15]

It was not until 1873 that Arkansas explicitly established separate schools for white and black children, but in the same year, section 6 of the state civil rights act made it unlawful for any public school officer or teacher to refuse to provide equal and identical ac-

14. Hoy Taylor, *An Interpretation of the Early Administration of the Peabody Education Fund* (Nashville: George Peabody College for Teachers, 1933), p. 44; Gilbert T. Stephenson, *Race Distinction in American Law* (New York: D. Appleton, 1910), p. 170, citing *Acts of Arkansas, 1866–1867*, p. 100.

15. Martha Skeeters, "The Negro and the Arkansas State Constitution of 1868: A Change in Political Emphasis," *Trinity Valley Historical Review* 1 (Spring 1969): 59–60; *Debates and Proceedings of the Convention Which Assembled at Little Rock, January 7th, 1868 . . . To Form a Constitution for the State of Arkansas* (Little Rock: J. G. Price, 1868), pp. 8, 601, 645, 660–61, 666; *Little Rock Arkansas Gazette*, February 12, 15, 1868; Richard L. Hume, "The Arkansas Constitutional Convention of 1868: A Case Study in the Politics of Reconstruction," *Journal of Southern History* 39 (1973): 188, 204, 206; Martha Ann Ellenburg, "Carpetbagger Policies during Reconstruction in Arkansas" (M.A. thesis, North Texas State University, 1963), p. 47; Poore, *Federal and State Constitutions*, 1: 146–47.

commodations for every school-age child. This clause, which could have led to agitation over integration, failed to impede the creation of separate schools for both races. Nevertheless, by contemporary standards for Southern states, Arkansas developed a reasonably successful public school system with the proportion of whites in attendance increasing from 42 to 63 percent during 1869–1870, while the proportion of black pupils increased from 28 to 50 percent during the same period.[16]

Florida also held its Reconstruction constitutional convention during the winter of 1868, and although the delegates were more evenly balanced as to race (twenty-seven whites, eighteen blacks) than in other conventions, black rights was not the major issue. Many sessions were held in secret, without a quorum; and the official *Journal* gives virtually no indication of what transpired. One of the more able delegates was Jonathan C. Gibbs, a black Presbyterian clergyman, who was a graduate of Dartmouth College and Princeton Seminary and who would later (1873) serve as state superintendent of education. Article VII, section 1, of the constitution produced by this convention avoided the integration question altogether, declaring, "It is the paramount duty of the State to make ample provision for the education of all children residing within its borders, without distinction or preference."[17]

A school law passed the following year avoided all references to race. Florida thus began a tacit policy of separate educational facilities which continued despite a state civil rights act of 1873 forbidding any racial discrimination in public schools, cemeteries, hotels, and benevolent institutions supported by general taxation. There are no references to integrated schools in any reports of the state superintendent of education from 1869 through 1873, although there are numerous allusions to black and white schools in

16. *Acts of Arkansas, 1873*, pp. 17–18, 423; Henry A. Bullock, *A History of Negro Education in the South from 1619 to the Present* (Cambridge: Harvard University Press, 1967), p. 54.

17. *Constitution of the State of Florida . . . 1868* (Jacksonville: Edw. M. Cheney, 1868), p. 17; *Journal of the Proceedings of the Constitutional Convention of the State of Florida . . . , 1868* (Tallahassee: Edw. M. Cheney, 1868), pp. 69–70; *New York Tribune*, February 5, 7, 20, 1868; Rembert W. Patrick, *The Reconstruction of the Nation* (New York: Oxford University Press, 1967), p. 149.

the same counties. The brief history of the public school system presented in the report of the United States Commissioner of Education for 1876 does not mention racial mixing in Florida schools. Northern journalist Edward King, writing in 1873, referred to a strong prejudice against public schools in Florida "because of the lurking fear of the whites that someday mixed schools may be insisted upon by the black masters of the situation." Regardless of a *de facto* segregation policy, it was not until 1877 that Florida established a constitutional basis for legal separation of races in public schools.[18]

Georgia was slow to start its public school system after the Civil War. The Reconstruction constitution of 1868 merely provided for free schools for all children of the state, thus ignoring any distinction between separate or mixed schools. The first school law of the state (1870) rectified this omission with a specific and emphatic provision for separate-but-equal facilities. However, the statute, as amended in 1872, provided a basis for discrimination in distribution of funds.[19]

Only sixteen blacks served as delegates to Mississippi's constitutional convention in 1868, and little is known of them or the part they played in the proceedings. Had they wished to promote mixed schools, they might have done so in coalition with the carpetbag and resident white Radicals who dominated the convention. Black delegates were successful on two occasions when they prevented Conservatives from inserting a separate school clause into the proposed constitution, although one maverick black, William T.

18. George G. Bush, *History of Education in Florida* (Washington: Government Printing Office, 1889), pp. 24–25; Thomas E. Cochran, *History of Public-School Education in Florida* (Lancaster, Pa.: New Era Printing Co., 1921), pp. 28–33; Stephenson, *Race Distinctions*, pp. 115–16, citing *Laws of Florida*, 1873, No. 13, chapt. 1947, p. 25; *Report of the Superintendent of Public Instruction for the State of Florida* (Tallahassee: n.p., 1869–1875), passim; *Report of the Commissioner of Education for the Year 1876*, p. 63; Edward King, *The Southern States of North America* (London: Blackie and Son, 1875), p. 420; Stephenson, *Race Distinctions*, p. 170.

19. *Constitution, Ordinances and Resolutions of the Georgia Convention* ... (Atlanta: New Era Job Office, 1868), p. 18; *Journal of the Proceedings of the Constitutional Convention of the People of Georgia* ... *1867–1868* (Augusta: E. H. Pughe, 1868), pp. 151, 477–80, 482–83; *New York Tribune*, March 6, 1868; *Acts and Resolutions of Georgia, 1870*, p. 57; Charles H. Walker, "The Attitude of Georgia toward the Education of Negroes" (M.A. thesis, Atlanta University, 1935), pp. 12–13.

Combash, for some unknown reason voted against tabling the separate school amendment. The school provision adopted by the convention said nothing about race, merely declaring it the duty of the legislature to establish free public schools for all children between five and twenty-one years of age, and the decision of mixed schools was thus left to that body. Fifteen black delegates, however, refused to support their colleague, Charles W. Fitzhugh, member of a leading free-black family from Wilkinson County, who resolved that although the question of school integration had been left to the legislature, "that it is the sense of this Convention that separate schools for the races ought not to be established." Fitzhugh's resolution was tabled by a vote of 58–1.[20]

The *Jackson Clarion*, a Conservative organ, viewed with disgust the absence of a constitutional sanction requiring separate schools and believed that the delegates had "sown the seeds of discord" between the two races by leaving a loophole for integrated schools. Three weeks later, the *Clarion* predicted, prophetically, that it would require a standing army to enforce integrated schools in Mississippi.[21]

In the spring of 1870 James L. Alcorn, a Southern Whig who turned Radical to serve best what he believed to be the interests of Mississippi, became governor. Shortly after his inauguration he outlined plans for the organization of a school system based upon separate schools for both races. Alcorn's advice went unheeded, for that year the legislature passed a school law which, in the eyes of many whites, opened the way for mixed schools by allowing all children between the ages of five and twenty-one to have "in all respects, equal advantages in the public schools." In the opinion of some citizens, equal advantages meant identical advantages, and a few integrated schools opened in Mississippi, but state officials made no efforts to integrate the entire system. There is evidence of

20. Wharton, *The Negro in Mississippi*, pp. 146–47; *Journal of the Proceedings in the Constitutional Convention of the State of Mississippi, 1868* (Jackson: E. Stafford, 1871), pp. 316, 359–60, 506; *Constitution and Ordinances of the State of Mississippi . . . 1868* (Jackson: State Journal Office, 1868), p. 18; *New York Tribune*, March 11, 1868.

21. James W. Garner, *Reconstruction in Mississippi* (New York: Macmillan, 1901), p. 363; ibid., citing the *Jackson* (Miss.) *Clarion*, February 21 and March 11, 1868.

only two mixed schools and those during the year 1870–1871. A newspaper editor from Pontotoc County told a congressional committee that the 1870 education law really permitted separate schools because of one clause allowing county directors to establish new schools upon application of parents or guardians of twenty-five children, thus creating separate schools when desired. The controlling element in Mississippi's Radical party had no intention of establishing mixed schools. Superintendent of Education Thomas W. Cardoza, himself a black, told Edward King that he had insisted upon an integrated school only in one county where white teachers had refused to instruct black pupils. Cardoza then informed the teachers that they must not stop black children from attending white schools, if this were the only way that they could receive instruction. The first legal prohibition of racial mixing in Mississippi schools did not come until after Reconstruction when an 1878 statute forbade teaching of white and black pupils in the same school building.[22]

The 120 delegates to North Carolina's constitutional convention in 1868, of whom only thirteen were Conservatives, bitterly argued the question of mixed schools with little success for either side. An education committee, organized in January and consisting of two Conservatives and eleven Radicals with the Reverend Samuel S. Ashley, an AMA missionary formerly of Massachusetts, as chairman, made its first report on March 6. Since it contained no provision for separate schools, Plato Durham, leading Conservative from Cleveland County (and later a Klan chieftain), offered an amendment directing the general assembly to provide separate schools for black and white children. Ashley (soon to be elected state superintendent of education under the Holden administration)

22. Stuart G. Noble, *Forty Years of the Public Schools in Mississippi* (New York: Teachers College, Columbia University, 1918), pp. 29–30; *Laws of Mississippi*, 1870, p. 17; Noble, *Forty Years*, p. 39; "KKK Reports," Mississippi, 1: 89; King, *The Southern States*, p. 316; Stephenson, *Race Distinctions*, p. 173: Wharton, *The Negro in Mississippi*, pp. 244–45. According to one historian the Mississippi legislature actually intended to establish mixed schools through the 1870 law but failed to do so because "of the good sense of the mass of Negroes of the state" who were opposed to mixed schools. Jesse T. Wallace, *A History of the Negroes of Mississippi from 1865 to 1890* (Clinton, Miss.: by author, 1927), p. 133.

fought back, and the convention overwhelmingly defeated Durham's amendment. Conservatives continued their efforts as John W. Graham proposed separate and distinct schools and colleges for whites and blacks. This was quickly followed by a substitute amendment from Radical Albion W. Tourgée stating that wherever officials established separate schools, they would also provide ample and equal facilities and funds to each race. Delegates rejected both amendments and the original section passed. The convention approved the entire report 88–12, and it became section IX of the constitution. It was an innocuous statement, reflecting Radical unwillingness to attack segregation, and merely said that the general assembly at its first meeting should provide a free and uniform system of public schools to all North Carolina children between the ages of six and twenty-one. There was no reference to either separate or mixed schools.[23]

In the North Carolina convention it was clear that white Radicals and Conservatives both opposed mixed schools. Near the end of their session, delegates adopted a resolution declaring that the happiness and best interests of both races could be realized through the establishment of separate schools. Although this was a statement of Radical policy and not part of the constitution, Conservatives attempted to transform the resolution into an admission of the inevitability of mixed schools. They advanced three major arguments regarding education in attempting to defeat ratification of the proposed constitution: insistence that the resolution implied mixed schools; assertions that the compulsory attendance clause would force poor whites to send their children to mixed schools; and emphasis on the high tax burden that all whites would have to bear. Nevertheless, voters (117,428 whites and 79,444 blacks were registered in North Carolina) approved the constitution in April 1868 by a margin of 93,084 to 74,015.[24]

23. Richard B. Drake, "The American Missionary Association and the Southern Negro, 1861–1898" (Ph.D. diss., Emory University, 1957), p. 190; *Journal of Constitutional Convention of the State of North Carolina at Its Session of 1868* (Raleigh: J. W. Holden, 1868), pp. 342–43; Otto H. Olsen, *Carpetbagger's Crusade: The Life of Albion Winegar Tourgée* (Baltimore: Johns Hopkins Press, 1965), pp. 95–97; Poore, *Federal and State Constitutions*, 2: 1432–33.

24. Daniel J. Whitener, "Public Education in North Carolina during Recon-

The North Carolina legislature convened in November 1868, and one of the crucial items on its agenda was passage of an education bill. Radical Governor William W. Holden answered those who had predicted mixed schools when he called for a general and uniform system of free schools but requested separate facilities for both races. Conservatives in the senate proposed a number of school-related measures aimed at prohibiting the teaching of abolition sentiments and preventing black teachers from instructing white pupils. These bills were rejected. The North Carolina senate was not interested in mixed schools, however, for it passed an amendment creating separate schools, 24–6, on March 17, 1869, and the house concurred, with minor changes, on the same day. This law declared that "the school authorities of each and every township shall establish a separate school or separate schools for the instruction of children and youth of each race resident therein, and over six and under twenty-one years of age." After North Carolina returned to Conservative control in 1870, a new convention amended the constitution to provide for separate schools. Several delegates offered proposals to this effect. The one ultimately approved established separate schools for both races, with "no discrimination made in favor or to the prejudice, of either race." This provision became article IX, section 2, of the 1876 constitution.[25]

The Reconstruction of South Carolina was a disturbing experience for most of its white citizens. Although small in area, the state contained the largest percentage of blacks of any in the South, having a population of 415,814 blacks and 289,667 whites in 1870. In 1867 the state came under the political control of an alliance of native whites, blacks, and carpetbaggers. The coalition governed South Carolina until the compromise of 1876 led to removal of federal troops by President Rutherford B. Hayes in 1877. Many teach-

---

struction, 1865–1876," in *Essays in Southern History Presented to Joseph Gregoire de Roulhac Hamilton*, ed. Fletcher M. Green (Chapel Hill: University of North Carolina Press, 1949), pp. 75–79.

25. Knight, *The Influence of Reconstruction*, pp. 23, 25; Knight, *Public School Education in North Carolina*, pp. 232, 234; *Public Laws of North Carolina, 1868–69*, p. 471; *Journal of Constitutional Convention of the State of North Carolina Held in 1875* (Raleigh: J. Turner, 1875), p. 130; Poore, *Federal and State Constitutions*, 2: 1447; Whitener, "Public Education in North Carolina," p. 79.

ers who had come to Port Royal during the war remained and were joined by others who aided in establishing schools for freedmen. In looking ahead to creation of a public school system, some teachers and bureau officials hoped that it would be integrated. Benjamin F. Whittemore, the assistant bureau superintendent, stated in June 1867 that blacks who were to be members of the forthcoming legislature would be pledged to a uniform system of public schools without distinction of race, color, or previous condition of servitude.[26]

When the constitutional convention met at Charleston in January 1868 a primary task was to establish a public school system. For many delegates education seemed as important as universal male suffrage, for the latter could not successfully exist without the former. After the education committee made its report, there was heated discussion over a section requiring compulsory attendance of all children between the ages of six and sixteen. Benjamin Byas, a black from Berkeley County, objected to the word *compulsory* because he considered compulsion alien to a republican form of government. Conservatives disliked the fines and imprisonment that would result from parents' failure to send children to school, for, to them, this clause implied compulsory attendance at mixed schools. The chairman of the education committee, Francis L. Cardozo, a highly educated black representing Charleston, said this section would merely give those black children who desired to go to white schools the privilege of doing so.[27]

Justus K. Jillson, originally from Massachusetts and later state superintendent of education, favored the compulsory clause as a means of encouraging school attendance, while Cardozo insisted

26. *American Annual Cyclopaedia*, 1871, 11: 702; *Ninth Census of the United States*, 1870, 1: 3–4; *Freedmen's Record* 3 (July 1867): 122.

27. *Proceedings of the Constitutional Convention of South Carolina, 1868* (Charleston: Denny and Perry, 1868), p. 691; Francis L. Cardozo, who later became secretary of state and state treasurer, was the son of J. N. Cardozo, economist and newspaper editor, and a half-Indian, half-black mother. Francis L. Cardozo was educated at Glasgow and London and pastored a Congregational church in New Haven, Connecticut, before the war. After the war he became principal of the Avery Institute, an AMA school at Charleston. Franklin, *Reconstruction*, pp. 88, 109–10, 133; Williamson, *After Slavery*, pp. 210–11; James R. Buck, "The Education of the Negro in the South prior to 1861" (M.A. thesis, Fisk University, 1938), p. 128; Drake, "American Missionary Association," p. 189.

that charges inferring this clause would lead to mixed schools were ungentlemanly and untrue. Referring to another section of the education article which provided free open public schools to all children, Cardozo declared that this did not preclude separate facilities. He believed that blacks in most localities preferred separate schools until current race prejudices lessened. He reconciled differences over the compulsory education controversy by proposing an amendment, subsequently adopted, that no law compelling attendance in public schools would be passed until a system of schools had been "thoroughly and completely organized, and facilities afforded to all inhabitants of the State for free education of their children."[28] The last clause of this amendment provided a loophole stating that attendance would not be compulsory until "facilities," meaning separate facilities where so desired, were established throughout the state.

Delegates at the South Carolina convention then became embroiled over section 11 of the education article which declared that all educational institutions supported by public funds should be free and open to all children "without regard to race, color or previous condition." Cardozo tried to avoid another impasse by attempting to send the section back to committee for further consideration, but other black delegates, feeling this would lead to removal of the words "race, color or previous condition," demanded an immediate vote. Cardozo's wishes prevailed, however, and the section was referred to committee. A few days later when this subject came up for debate, B. O. Duncan, scalawag from Newberry, asserted his desire to see all children educated without distinction of race, but "if the attempt is made to enforce a mixture in this way, I have no idea that [but] fifty white children in the state would attend the public schools." Believing that no white children attended the Freedmen's Bureau schools, which were open to all, he warned that this would be the situation if public schools adopted integration. Poor whites would be deprived of any chance for education and whites of means would continue sending their children to private schools with the result that those who paid nine-tenths of the taxes would regard themselves as being excluded from the schools. Duncan

28. *Proceedings of the Constitutional Convention of South Carolina, 1868,* pp. 704, 706, 708.

feared that integration would bring continual strife to South Carolina, for "these extreme measures are fraught with danger to the peace and welfare of our country, and should be defeated at all hazards." To avoid such dangers he suggested eliminating the integration clause altogether, leaving the problem to the legislature which could establish mixed schools and, if found unworkable, alter its decision more easily than a state could change its constitution.[29]

Jonathan J. Wright, a black delegate, answered Duncan by declaring that the section should be adopted because it did not specifically require attendance at mixed schools and that separate schools would be established anyway. He believed that blacks did not want to force social equality, for that was a matter which would regulate itself. He favored inclusion of the "race, color or previous condition" clause because it allowed white and black children to attend the same school if they wished, although he did not believe that this was the desire of either race. Although J. M. Runion (white) of Greenville, claiming to be a true Republican, warned that voting for this measure would be detrimental to the Radical party, section 10 passed, 98–4, with fourteen delegates absent. As it appeared in the ratified constitution of 1868, this controversial passage (article X, section 10) stated: "All the public schools, colleges and universities of this State, supported in whole or in part by the public funds, shall be free and open to all the children and youths of the State, without regard to race and color."[30]

None of South Carolina's Reconstruction governors wished to promote mixed schools. James L. Orr, former Confederate senator who served as his state's chief executive from 1865 until 1868 and the adoption of the new Radical constitution, frequently warned against integration. Shortly before the end of his term in June 1868, Orr recommended to the newly elected assembly creation of separate schools for white and black pupils. He declared the education article of the new constitution was "an authority for making a most reckless experiment," which, if enforced, would only increase racial disharmony. Orr's successor, Robert K. Scott, Pennsylvania-born and Ohio-reared, a former Union Army colonel and assistant bureau commissioner, did not want to make mixed schools a crucial

29. Ibid., pp. 748–50, 889–92.
30. Ibid., pp. 894, 900–902; Poore, *Federal and State Constitutions*, 2: 1661.

issue of his administration. On July 9, 1868, Scott asked the legislature to create a school system with at least two schools in every district, one for each race. He warned that integrated schools would discourage and repel whites from securing desperately needed instruction and would virtually give blacks sole benefit of the public schools. In proclaiming what came to be official Radical policy in South Carolina, Scott urged the assembly to rely upon time and the "elevating influence of popular education" to dispel unjust racial prejudice until such a time when segregated schools could be abolished.[31]

When state superintendent Justus K. Jillson began to formulate plans for an educational system after passage of an education law in February 1870, he received numerous reports from county commissioners urging creation of separate schools. A Clarendon County commissioner wrote that both races opposed mixed schools, and whites, fearing this, had refused to register their children. Blacks were equally against interracial schooling but would submit if necessary in order to educate their children. William B. Peake of Fairfield County said that blacks feared "the natural antagonism resulting from birth and caste, on the one hand, and a sense of equality, on the other, will produce discord and strife in such a school." A commissioner from Kershaw County wrote that blacks did not desire the explicit equality of a mixed school but claimed a fair and equal apportionment of the school fund for the education of their children. Commissioners in Marlboro, Pickens, Union, and Spartanburg counties voiced similar sentiments. Only one commissioner, according to Jillson's 1869 report, actually favored mixed schools. James A. Bowley of Georgetown County believed that mixed schools would promote racial harmony. He admitted, however, that none existed in his county, which was heavily black.[32]

31. *Journal of the House of Representatives . . . of South Carolina*, special session of 1868 (Columbia: J. W. Denny, 1868), p. 30; ibid., p. 62; Knight, *The Influence of Reconstruction*, pp. 71–72; Williamson, *After Slavery*, p. 221.

32. *Reports and Resolutions of the General Assembly of the State of South Carolina, 1869* [containing the reports of the state superintendent of education] (Columbia: J. W. Denny, 1870), pp. 406, 467–69, 471, 476, 480–86. The education bill, passed in February 1870, reestablished the public school system but ignored the race question completely with regard to mixed or separate schools; *Acts of South Carolina, 1869–70*, pp. 339–48. For an indication that South

With the exception of the University of South Carolina during the years 1873–1877, there were apparently no mixed schools in the state during this period. An earnest attempt was made in 1873 to integrate the school for the deaf, dumb, and blind, located in Spartanburg County. In that year the governing board of the institution directed the opening of a building on the school grounds as a separate department for black students. On September 17, 1873, Jillson, acting both as state superintendent and as a member of the board of directors, wrote to the superintendent of the school ordering that blacks not only be admitted upon application but also be encouraged to apply for admission. Jillson demanded that black pupils, when admitted, be housed, fed, and taught in the same dormitories and classrooms and receive identical care and consideration as whites. After the superintendent transmitted this message to his faculty, all but two resigned. These mass resignations forced the school to close on September 30. In his annual report for 1873 Jillson tersely remarked, "The Institution is now without officers, and its exercises have been, for the present, suspended." The *Charleston News and Courier*, furious over the attempted integration of the deaf, dumb, and blind school, complained about the demagogism which had driven the staff from the institution. Political leaders of South Carolina, unable to decide what to do about the school, did nothing. Efforts to recruit a new faculty proved futile. Radical Governor Daniel H. Chamberlain, in his 1875 message to the legislature, merely recommended reopening the school but made no suggestion as to the segregation or integration of future pupils. It reopened in September 1876 with separate departments for each race.[33]

Segregation on the primary and secondary levels continued to prevail throughout Reconstruction in South Carolina. In 1875 Richard Cain, a black minister originally from Ohio and now

Carolina blacks were hesitant to push for mixed schools, see the *New York Times*, July 3, 1874.

33. As cited in John S. Reynolds, *Reconstruction in South Carolina, 1865–1877* (Columbia, S. C.: State Co., 1905), p. 237; *Reports and Resolutions of the General Assembly of the State of South Carolina, 1873*, p. 399; *Charleston News and Courier*, December 19, 1873; Reynolds, *Reconstruction in South Carolina*, pp. 237–38; Richard T. Williams, "History of Public Education and Charitable Institutions in South Carolina during the Reconstruction Period" (M.A. thesis, Atlanta University, 1933), pp. 60–61, 114.

representing the Columbia district, told the United States House of Representatives that in South Carolina where blacks controlled the entire state system of education, there was not a mixed school except for the university. There were a few isolated cases in Charleston and Columbia where white and black children attended classes in the same school building but not in the same room. In 1876 commissioner of education John Eaton commented on the apparent failure to establish mixed schools in the Palmetto State: "Separate schools for white and colored children, though not apparently made obligatory by law, have yet been the rule, under the influence of a general public sentiment." When Radical control of South Carolina ended in 1877, Conservatives failed to repeal the mixed school clause of the 1868 constitution although they passed a law (1877) establishing segregated schools in violation of the state constitution. Not until 1896 were integrated schools specifically prohibited by constitutional statute in South Carolina.[34]

Delegates in most Southern constitutional conventions, realizing that segregation would probably cause Radicals in Congress to reject the state's application for admission, tabled specific proposals for separate schools. Tennessee, having ratified the Fourteenth Amendment, was not subject to congressional Reconstruction and could get away with such legislation. The legislature passed an act in February 1867 explicitly establishing separate schools for children of both races between six and twenty years of age. Although Fisk professor John Ogden denounced this as pandering to wicked prejudices and encouraging caste and racial prejudice, forces desiring integration were not strong enough to secure their objective, for Tennessee's act of 1867 was later enforced by a provision in article XI of the 1870 constitution which stated that "no school established or aided under this section shall allow white and negro children to be received as scholars together in the same school." Whether or not Tennessee's public schools were integrated made

34. *Congressional Record*, 43d Cong., 2d sess., p. 997; Francis B. Simkins and Robert H. Woody, *South Carolina during Reconstruction* (Chapel Hill: University of North Carolina Press, 1932), p. 439; Bond, *The Education of the Negro*, p. 51; Truman Pierce and others, *White and Negro Schools in the South: An Analysis of Bi-Racial Education* (Englewood Cliffs, N.J.: Prentice-Hall, 1955), p. 42; *Report of the Commissioner of Education for the Year 1876*, p. 364; *Acts and Resolutions of South Carolina*, 1896, p. 171.

little difference, for in 1869 conservative Republicans had joined Democrats to control the state government and repealed the compulsory school law which led to the closing of most black public schools. For all purposes, the remainder of Tennessee's schools were destroyed in a bitter fight over taxation, and each county resumed authority and responsibility for its schools until 1873, when the state laid foundations for its present system.[35]

Texas was late in establishing its school system and, when it did, provided separate schools for blacks. The Reconstruction constitution of 1868 made no reference to integration or segregation of schools, and by 1873 Edward King reported little apparent interest in mixed schools in the Lone Star State. Texas also had its problems with the youthful Jacob C. DeGress. DeGress, born in Prussia and a Union Army veteran, was appointed state superintendent of education in May 1871 by Radical Governor Edmund J. Davis. Trying to run the school system along military lines and without taking into consideration the general poverty of postwar Texas, DeGress brought about his own downfall and that of the public schools. After Conservatives regained political control (1873), they held a constitutional convention in 1875 in which there was consensus for including a separate school clause in the education article. The constitution, ratified in 1876, not only contained a segregation clause (article VII, section 7) but virtually destroyed the public schools by abolishing the office of state superintendent, eliminating compulsory attendance, and returning land to counties which had produced revenue for the state.[36]

35. Franklin, *Reconstruction*, p. 111; *Report of the Commissioner of Education for the Year 1870*, p. 364; James W. Patton, *Unionism and Reconstruction in Tennessee, 1860–69* (Chapel Hill: University of North Carolina Press, 1934), p. 101, quoting the *Nashville Daily Press and Times*, November 15, 1867; Phillips, "Freedmen's Bureau in Tennessee," pp. 243–44; *Journal of the Proceedings of the Convention Elected . . . to Amend, Revise, Form and Make a New Constitution for the State of Tennessee . . .* (Nashville: Jones and Purvis, 1870), pp. 190, 221–22, 304, 307–9, 351, 386; *Nashville Republican Banner*, February 15, 23, 1870; *The New Constitution of the State of Tennessee . . . 1870* (Nashville: Jones and Purvis, 1870), p. 27; James M. McPherson, "Grant or Greeley? The Abolitionist Dilemma in the Election of 1872," *American Historical Review* 81 (1965): 45; Pauline L. Sneed, "Education of the Negro in Tennessee during the Reconstruction Period" (M. A. thesis, Fisk University, 1935), pp. 66, 115–17.

36. King, *The Southern States*, p. 135; Poore, *Federal and State Constitutions*, 2: 1841; *Journal of the Reconstruction Convention Which Met at Austin,*

Virginia's constitutional convention, meeting at Richmond in December 1867, contained thirty-three Conservatives and seventy-two Radicals, twenty-four of the latter being blacks. The education committee contained about the same proportion of Conservatives and Radicals. A fight over mixed schools began in January and lasted until April 1868. Near the end of January the committee submitted an education article which omitted any reference to separate or mixed schools. Early in the debates, Conservative delegate James M. French introduced a separate school amendment. Black delegates, realizing that separate schools would doom their educational rights and opportunities, heatedly opposed the French amendment which was never voted upon. Later another Conservative proposed a more explicitly worded separate school provision which also divided poll tax receipts on a racial basis, i.e., the tax from black polls would be used only for black schools. After delegates tabled this motion, Thomas Bayne of Norfolk, a former slave who had learned dentistry and later escaped to practice in Massachusetts, moved that public schools accept all races and no pupil be removed on account of race or any distinction.[37]

Although a motion to table Bayne's proposition failed, black delegates sensed and feared that white members of their own party would not support them fully in this matter. Willis A. Hodges warned white Radicals that without black support, the Radical party in Virginia "would hardly be a skeleton." Another black noted that not a single white had spoken in favor of mixed schools. A proposal from white Radical William J. Parr would have permitted school

---

Texas, Dec. 7, A.D., 1868 (Austin: Tracy, Siemering and Co., 1870), pp. 80, 146, 229; Eby, *Education in Texas*, p. 161; *Journal of the Constitutional Convention of the State of Texas, Begun and Held at the City of Austin, September 6th, 1875* (Galveston: News Office, 1875), pp. 45, 57, 518, 523; Wheeler, "The History of Education in Texas during the Reconstruction Period," pp. 106, 117–18.

37. Cornelius J. Heatwole, *A History of Education in Virginia* (New York: Macmillan, 1916), p. 214; Edgar W. Knight, "Reconstruction and Education in Virginia," *South Atlantic Quarterly* 15 (1916): 5; *Richmond Daily Dispatch*, March 31, April 8, 1868; *Journal of the Virginia Constitutional Convention of 1867–68* (Richmond: New Nation, 1868), pp. 121, 299, 301; *The Debates and Proceedings of the Constitutional Convention of the State of Virginia, 1868* (Richmond: New Nation, 1868), 1: 704; Richard G. Lowe, "Republicans, Rebellion and Reconstruction: The Republican Party in Virginia, 1858–1870" (Ph.D. diss., University of Virginia, 1968), p. 252.

integration with the unanimous consent of all parents involved. The delegates tabled this motion and then returned to Bayne's mixed school motion which they killed, 67–21. To the distress of black delegates, mixed schools had failed largely because white Radicals refused to support them. The section of the 1868 constitution which had provoked such furor emerged as a nebulous statement (article VIII, section 3) with no reference to race.[38]

In Virginia's legislative session of 1869–1870, controversy again arose over mixed schools when state superintendent William H. Ruffner prepared an education bill which stipulated that whites and blacks be taught in separate schools. Black senator William Mosely, a farmer and owner of considerable property, moved to delete the separate school clause, thereby initiating debate similar to that in the recent constitutional convention. Once again blacks alone favored mixed schools, but with less fervor than in the convention. Delegates defeated Mosely's motion, 6–23, (three whites and three blacks voting aye). The bill with a separate school provision passed the senate on June 13, 1870, by a wide margin. Afterwards Mosely entered a formal protest, declaring this bill would only continue caste and prejudice and was subversive of "good order, justice, and harmony." He later accused white Radicals of turning their backs on him. The bill encountered some opposition in Virginia's lower house, where Radicals made futile attempts to strike out the separate school clause and add an amendment prohibiting racial distinctions in the hiring of school trustees. The bill passed the house on July 1, 1870, and after a few changes by the senate, became law on July 11. The disputed section stated that schools were to be free and open to all children between five and twenty-one years of age whose fathers had paid the head tax, but there would be separate schools for each race.[39]

38. *Richmond Daily Dispatch*, April 8, 1868; *Journal of the Virginia Constitutional Convention of 1867–68*, pp. 336–37, 340; Poore, *Federal and State Constitutions*, 2: 1968; Lowe, "Republicans, Rebellion and Reconstruction," p. 253; Luther P. Jackson, *Negro Office-Holders in Virginia, 1865–1895* (Norfolk: Guide Quality Press, 1945), pp. 28–29. See also James D. Smith, "The Virginia Constitutional Convention of 1867–1868" (M.A. thesis, University of Virginia, 1956).

39. Knight, "Reconstruction and Education in Virginia," pp. 16–17; *Acts of Virginia, 1869–1870*, p. 413.

While discussions over mixed schools in state conventions and legislatures created much interest in Congress and throughout the nation, the segregated school system which Congress established in the District of Columbia went virtually unnoticed. In April 1862 Congress emancipated all slaves in the District and a month later made efforts to provide schools for some 3,000 black children. Senator James W. Grimes of Iowa sponsored a measure which provided that 10 percent of the property taxes paid by blacks would be used exclusively for primary education of black children. President Lincoln signed the Grimes bill on May 21, and in July Congress created a separate board of trustees to administer the black schools of Washington and Georgetown. Two years later Congress established separate schools for all blacks living in the county of Washington. Three sections of the law (17, 18, 19) contained specific references to separate schools for blacks. Another section repealed the 10 percent feature of the 1862 statute, stating that the school fund would now be divided according to the proportion of each race between the ages of six and seventeen. Blacks received little monetary satisfaction from the law because of the authorities' reluctance to turn over a just share of funds to trustees of black schools.[40] During the two-year interim (1862–1864) before black public schools actually opened, benevolent associations established and operated schools for freedmen. Ultimately twenty-six associations established 254 schools, many of which continued to operate after public schools began to function.[41]

The early history of Washington's black public schools was characterized by deep resentment of the black population over segregation and failure of the city council to appropriate a fair share of funds. In November 1867 Alonzo Newton, superintendent of black schools, bitterly complained that as a result of the authorities' obstinacy, black schools in the District had received no money for over a year and would have to suspend operations unless revenue

40. Henry Wilson, *Anti-Slavery Measures of the 37th and 38th United States Congress, 1861–1865* (Boston: Walker, Fuller and Co., 1865), p. 184; *Congressional Globe*, 37th Cong., 2d sess., pp. 1854, 2020, 2037, 2879; ibid., 38th Cong., 1st sess., pp. 725, 2813; U.S., *Statutes at Large*, vol. 13, p. 191; Lillian G. Dabney, *The History of Schools for Negroes in the District of Columbia, 1807–1947* (Washington: Catholic University of America, 1949), p. 113.

41. Dabney, *Schools for Negroes in D.C.*, pp. 24, 99, 114.

was forthcoming. In reality, as late as 1866–1867 the school trustees hired and paid only seven of eighty-two teachers in black schools; benevolent associations employed the remainder. Between 1867 and 1869 the District incorporated most of the association schools into its system and the remainder by 1872.[42]

Although most members of Congress were content to allow the District's segregated school system to continue unchanged, many black residents were infuriated by the arrangement. Some mixing had taken place in bureau-association schools, for bureau superintendent John Kimball was a strong advocate of integration. At a meeting of trustees for white schools in August 1869, citizens presented a petition signed by thirty whites and thirty-two blacks requesting establishment of an integrated school in the northeast section of the fourth ward. In September the committee assigned to study the petition (and others similar to it) reported in favor of a mixed school in that ward. The committee also requested that the word *white* be deleted from an 1858 law which specified that all white children between the ages of six and seventeen be admitted into public schools. After much discussion, during which a black trustee of the white schools complained that his children could not enter the schools he helped supervise, the board passed a resolution calling for reference of all questions concerning establishment of mixed schools to the board of aldermen. The trustees, voting 11–2, thus transferred responsibility to the aldermen, who proceeded to ignore the many demands for mixed schools and pigeonholed all petitions.[43]

The cause of mixed schools in the District was championed from 1870 to 1872 by Senator Charles Sumner of Massachusetts, who simultaneously was attempting to secure passage of his civil rights bill containing a mixed school provision. On January 10, 1870, Sumner introduced a bill to secure equal rights in the public schools of Washington and Georgetown. The bill reached the Senate calendar but was left among unfinished business. This inaction caused

42. John W. Alvord, *Semi-Annual Reports on Schools for Freedmen* (Washington: Government Printing Office, July 1, 1867), p. 7; *American Freedman* 2 (December 1867): 332; ibid., 3 (July-August 1868): 444; Dabney, *Schools for Negroes in D.C.*, pp. 115–16; Alvord, *Reports*, January 1, 1869, pp. 9–10.

43. Dabney, *Schools for Negroes in D.C.*, p. 86; *Washington Chronicle*, August 31, 1869; ibid., September 15, 1869; ibid., September 29, 1869.

two trustees of Washington's black schools to send a report to the secretary of the interior pleading for abolition of separate schools which "recognize and tend to perpetuate a cruel, unreasonable and unchristian prejudice."[44]

Senator James W. Patterson (R.-N.H.), chairman of the committee on the District of Columbia, in February 1871 introduced a bill to establish a single, integrated public school system for the District under a common board of trustees. Patterson complained that a majority of the committee had added a mixed school clause over his objections, and he urged its deletion. This suggestion infuriated Sumner and other Republican Radicals including Hiram Revels (a black) of Mississippi. But most Republican senators remained silent and the Senate took no action at this time. Charles M. Hamilton, a Florida Radical (originally from Pennsylvania), introduced a similar bill to the House. After the committee reported the measure and unanimously recommended deletion of the mixed school clause, the entire measure was killed by a vote to reconsider. Advocates of mixed schools, too weak to defend retention of the controversial clause, were not interested in the bill without it; Conservatives were happy to let the entire question die.[45]

Charles Sumner, never daunted by opposition, on December 12, 1871, reintroduced his bill to desegregate District schools. The Senate briefly debated the bill in April 1872 but adjourned without voting. On two occasions in early May, Sumner attempted to bring the measure to a vote, but without success. On May 6 Orris Ferry of Connecticut complained that Sumner's bill proposed a "tyrannical rule from without, without considering the sentiments of those within." The black-owned New National Era, edited by Frederick Douglass, prompted by congressional inaction and a recent proposal to submit the school integration question to a popular vote, declared that suggestion of a referendum was pure cowardice. The paper pointed out that as Congress had abolished slavery against the wishes of the District's white inhabitants, why should it not also

44. *Congressional Globe*, 41st Cong., 2d sess., p. 323; *Senate Executive Documents*, 41st Cong., 3d sess., No. 20, pp. 7–8, 10.

45. *Congressional Globe*, 41st Cong., 3d sess., pp. 1053–60, 1365–67; Alfred H. Kelly, "The Congressional Controversy over School Segregation, 1867–75," *American Historical Review* 64 (1959): 546.

abolish the "teaching of caste" whether the local citizens liked it or not.[46]

Although constitutional and statutory provisions for school integration were proposed in several Southern states and the District of Columbia, in nearly all cases the decision concerning mixed schools was avoided in the final documents. The difficulty of securing tax-financed public education for blacks would have been an impossibility in most states if accompanied by strong demands for integration. Most whites, who paid the great majority of property taxes, simply would not tolerate mixed schools, nor would they pay taxes for integrated schools which they believed would, in effect, exclude white children. Therefore, school segregation, usually with Radical sanction, was general practice in the South during Reconstruction.[47] Most states quickly passed segregation statutes after returning to Conservative control. Although South Carolina emerged with a mixed school provision in the 1868 constitution, it was not enforced except at the state university and the school for the deaf, dumb, and blind. It remained for Louisiana, among all Southern states, to experiment with school integration on a reasonably extensive basis. This experiment, fraught with hostile and violent emotions, warrants separate consideration and treatment.

46. *Congressional Globe*, 42d Cong., 2d sess., pp. 68, 2484, 2539–42, 3057–58, 3099–100, 3124–25, 3174; *Washington New National Era*, May 9, 1872.

47. C. Vann Woodward, *The Strange Career of Jim Crow*, 2d ed. (New York: Oxford University Press, 1957), p. 15. Woodward admits the school question counters his general hypothesis that segregation came with the Populist era, but he gives no evidence or explanation of this.

4. Desegregation of Schools in Louisiana

ALTHOUGH all Southern states and the District of Columbia debated the mixed school issue during Reconstruction, only one state—Louisiana—went beyond token integration on the primary and secondary levels. Louisiana's constitutional convention in February 1868, by a vote of 71–6, passed an education article (title VII, article 135) which provided that all children between six and twenty-one years of age be admitted to public schools without distinction of race, color, or previous condition of servitude. It emphasized that "there shall be no separate schools or institutions of learning established exclusively for any race by the state of Louisiana."[1]

The emergence of an active school integration policy in Louisiana was due not so much to the constitutional provision of 1868 or the education laws of 1869–1870 which reinforced it, but to the impetus of an unyielding state official determined to prevent racial segregation. Only twenty-eight years of age at the time, Thomas W. Conway was elected state superintendent of education in 1868 on a Radical ticket headed by Henry C. Warmoth, who became governor. Conway was born in County Clare, Ireland, in 1840 and came to the United States as a child. After working his way through Madison University, he was ordained a Baptist minister at twenty-one. He served a church on Staten Island, New York, until the Civil War when he became a Union Army chaplain, ultimately serving in Louisiana. In January 1863 General Nathaniel P. Banks appointed Conway to head a Bureau of Free Labor, which included black schools among its projects. When Congress created the Freedmen's Bureau in 1865, Conway became an assistant commissioner and Oliver Otis Howard placed him in charge of Louisiana. Conway's advocacy of black suffrage and equality angered President Johnson and his appointed governor, J. Madison Wells. The president finally forced Howard to remove Conway from bureau service in the autumn of 1865.[2]

After his dismissal Conway led a political faction composed primarily of army officers who urged freedmen to disregard a New Orleans law providing for segregation on streetcars. Little is known of Conway's activities for late 1866 and 1867 except that he toured Louisiana and Mississippi as spokesman of the Union League, promoting membership and addressing bureau agents with the aim of consolidating the work of the two organizations. During these tours he established a following and gained the approval of Radical leaders. By January 1868 Conway, anticipating his nomination as state superintendent by the Radical state convention, believed he was destined by the Almighty to further black education and promote racial equality.[3]

Conway's election was virtually assured when his predecessor as state superintendent, Conservative segregationist Robert M. Lusher, declined to run, seeing that federal Reconstruction legislation would soon place Louisiana under Radical control. As soon as Conway became superintendent, he asked the state legislature to

1. *Official Journal of the Proceedings of the Convention for Framing a Constitution for the State of Louisiana* (New Orleans: J. B. Rouandez and Co., 1867–1868), pp. 94, 240, 268, 306; *New Orleans Picayune*, March 21, 1868; John Hope Franklin, *Reconstruction: After the Civil War* (Chicago: University of Chicago Press, 1961), pp. 112–13; Benjamin Perley Poore, Comp., *The Federal and State Constitutions, Colonial Charters and Other Organic Laws of the United States* (Washington: Government Printing Office, 1878), 1: 768; Roger A. Fischer's "The Segregation Struggle in Louisiana, 1850–1890" (Ph. D. diss., Tulane University, 1967) contains two chapters on school desegregation in Louisiana, one dealing with the rural parishes, the other with New Orleans. Unfortunately, the entire dissertation is marred by a strong racist bias which belies its fairly recent completion date. See especially pages 103 and 110 for examples of Fischer's segregationist leanings.

2. *Appleton's Annual Cyclopedia for 1887*, n.s., 12: 578; Willie M. Caskey, *Secession and Restoration in Louisiana* (Baton Rouge: Louisiana State University Press, 1938), p. 193; Walter L. Fleming, *Louisiana State University, 1860–1896* (Baton Rouge: Louisiana State University Press, 1936), p. 154; George R. Bentley, *A History of the Freedmen's Bureau* (Philadelphia: University of Pennsylvania Press, 1955), pp. 57, 70–71.

3. Bentley, *Freedmen's Bureau*, pp. 106, 187; John A. Carpenter, *Sword and Olive Branch: Oliver Otis Howard* (Pittsburgh: University of Pittsburgh Press, 1964), p. 142; Leon O. Beasley, "A History of Education in Louisiana during the Reconstruction Period, 1862–1877" (Ph.D. diss., Louisiana State University, 1957), p. 129; Fischer, "Segregation Struggle," p. 100; Martin Abbott, ed., "Reconstruction in Louisiana: Three Letters," *Louisiana History* 1 (1960): 153, citing letter from Thomas W. Conway to Oliver Otis Howard, January 5, 1868.

pass education laws which would "meet the expectations of the waiting public, [and] secure free schools to all, regardless of color, condition, or station, and give us light where darkness reigns." Before the legislative session of 1868 convened, Conway drew up an education bill incorporating most of his ideas. It placed all state-established institutions or those incorporated by the legislature under state control. Schools were opened to both races and, to insure that white parents would not boycott them, the bill required all children between eight and fourteen years of age to attend school for at least six months a year. If children did not attend, parents would be fined $25.00 for the first offense and $50.00 for subsequent violations. If, after imposition of three fines, the children were still not in school, the state board of education would give them instruction for at least five months a year "in such [a] school or place of correction as shall be provided by the board for that purpose, at the expense of the parents, if they are able to bear it."[4]

The Conservative *New Orleans Picayune*, attacking this bill, called the fine and seizure provision "inquisitorial and impertinent, oppressive and full of outrage" and warned that if passed, it would result in civil war. The paper advised Conway that Louisiana whites would never submit to the social equality required by the mixed school clause, "or at least not until the blood of the white man turns to water, and he consents to accept what the white race of all countries and all ages has, by common consent, regarded as a social impossibility." An Alexandria paper declared that few white parents would listen with patience to any such proposition. News of the revolutionary education bill reached New York, where the *Herald* referred to it as "one of the most atrocious measures ever conceived of by any of the Jacobin carpetbag governments of the Southern States," for not only did it propose to mix blacks and whites, it also made attendance compulsory. The *Herald* did not think "radical miscegenators" would be able to carry out this legal despotism, for the pride and instincts of Southern whites would revolt

4. Robert M. Lusher, Autobiography Ms of May 31, 1889, p. 15, in Robert M. Lusher Papers, Department of Archives and Manuscripts of Louisiana State University; *Annual Report of the State Superintendent of Public Education . . . to the General Assembly of Louisiana*, 1867–1868 (New Orleans: n.p., 1868), p. 22; *New Orleans Picayune*, August 11, 1868.

at this proposition as would Northern whites if confronted with similar legislation.[5]

Legislators fiercely debated Conway's bill during August and September, but it was buried in committee, and the General Assembly did not pass any education law during its session of June–December 1868. By this time Louisiana whites were reacting violently to the mixed school provision of the 1868 constitution.[6] Especially opposed to admission of blacks to a white school was David F. Boyd, president of Louisiana State University. Boyd, along with J. C. Egan, representative of the Twentieth Senatorial District, persuaded Hugh J. Campbell, prominent and accomplished "carpetbag" lawyer and member of the General Assembly's education committee, to draw up a section which he inserted into education bills in 1869 and 1870. The 1869 bill made it a misdemeanor, punishable by a $100–$500 fine and imprisonment, for any municipality, parish, or state school officer or public teacher to refuse admission of any child of lawful age. Offenders were also liable for damages by the parent or guardian of the child thus refused. Boyd's addition stated, however, "that in each sub-district there shall be taught one or more schools for the instruction of youths between the ages of six and twenty-one years." Both the 1869 and 1870 bills passed with the votes of black legislators lured by promises of financial aid to a university for blacks.[7]

The clause of the 1869 and 1870 statutes (as drawn up by Boyd and introduced by Campbell) allowing one or more schools to be established in each district was a distinct concession to segregationists, for there was an alleged understanding at the time that in a given district one school would be for whites, the other for blacks. Many whites were able to avoid the mixed school provision of the 1868 constitution while conforming to the laws of 1869 and 1870.

5. *New Orleans Picayune*, August 11, 1868; ibid., August 13, 1868; *Alexandria* (La.) *Democrat*, August 19, 1868; *New York Herald*, August 17, 1868.

6. Fischer, "Segregation Struggle," p. 103; *New Orleans Picayune*, August 22, September 3, 1868; Fleming, *Louisiana State University*, p. 154. See also *Acts of Louisiana*, 1868; *Report of the Commissioner of Education . . . for the Year 1875–1876* (Washington: Government Printing Office, 1876), p. 146.

7. Fleming, *Louisiana State University*, pp. 155–57; *Acts of Louisiana*, 1869, pp. 178, 188; ibid., 1870, p. 21. In 1870, $35,000 was appropriated to support Straight University for blacks.

In districts where two schools existed, white and black parents would often agree among themselves, sometimes under pressure, that black children would attend one school and white children, another. If only one school existed in a community, whites would not patronize it, and those who could afford to do so would send their children to private schools. Occasionally, separate rooms were provided in the same school building for both races.[8]

Nonetheless, Conway was not deterred in his objective of a completely integrated educational system for Louisiana. The state board of education at its April 1870 meeting adopted a rule to govern all public schools. It stated that every school was open to all children of educable age without distinction of color or race. A new education act, passed the previous month, tightened state control over the local schools by dividing Louisiana into six divisions with New Orleans ultimately becoming the sixth division. A superintendent appointed by the governor upon recommendation of the state superintendent and board of education headed each division. New Orleans and other towns and parishes lost control of their schools, since the state board now had the power to appoint all local boards. Each local board member was required to swear an oath accepting the equality of all men and agreeing not to deprive any person of an education because of race or color.[9]

Conway admitted in his report for 1869 that no subject connected with public education in Louisiana had evoked stronger feelings than mixed schools. He insisted, however, that the constitution and laws of the state left no discretion in this matter, for if schools were to exist under the constitution, they "must be open,

8. Fleming, *Louisiana State University*, p. 157; Thomas H. Harris, *The Story of Public Education in Louisiana* (New Orleans: by author, 1924), pp. 30–31. Harris, state superintendent of education in Louisiana for some thirty years, knew many educators of the Reconstruction era. His book, however, is a highly prejudiced and undocumented account based largely on hearsay evidence. See also Louisiana State Board of Education, Proceedings and Minutes, April 7–8, 1870, microfilm, Louisiana State University Library; Germaine M. Reed, "David Boyd, Southern Educator" (Ph.D. diss., Louisiana State University, 1970), p. 145 n.

9. *Annual Report*, Louisiana, 1870, pp. 7, 15; Ella Lonn, *Reconstruction in Louisiana* (New York: G. P. Putnam's, 1918), pp. 55–56; Louisiana State Department of Education Archives, Miscellaneous Records, January 1870, Department of Archives and Manuscripts of Louisiana State University.

impartially, to all citizens." Conway realized that the mixed school requirement made the education act obnoxious to thousands in Louisiana, but he believed that "a republican State can make no distinction between those who are equally citizens, nor can any humiliating conditions be made in the bestowment of benefits to which all have an equal claim." In one of his more candid moments, Conway conceded that for the present, the mixed school question would, in most localities, adjust itself, "if left to the unconstrained choice of those immediately interested; and it is doubtful that liberty of choice should be interfered with by a forcible attempt to mix the schools in localities where such action is undesired by any." Although keeping the schools open, even on a separate basis, was his paramount objective, Conway also declared paradoxically that he must enforce the laws and see that no public schools be allowed to exist which excluded any children because of race. In an 1870 letter to John W. Alvord, Conway even decried the existence of Freedmen's Bureau schools in Louisiana, for "their continuance aids in the perpetuating of a spirit of caste."[10]

Thus in one breath Conway declared that mixed schools could not be forced upon hostile citizens while in the next utterance he asserted his avowed intention of carrying out the integration provisions of the 1868 constitution and 1869 law. His annual reports from 1968 to 1872 are equally confusing on the extent of mixed schools but do indicate a few instances of racial integration. In 1871 the school board secretary of Assumption Parish referred to certain localities where children of both races attended classes together, and he attributed improvement of pupils in these classes to "the constant emulation between the two races." However, teachers' monthly reports from the same parish for 1872 indicate no integration and an all-black enrollment. Ephraim Stoddard, superintendent of the second division including Jefferson, Saint Charles, Saint James, Saint John the Baptist, Lafourche, and Terrebonne parishes, indicated a small amount of integration in 1871. By 1874 Stoddard stated that of 5,695 children in his division attending public schools (out of a possible 28,000), 4,890 were blacks and 805 were whites

10. *Annual Report, Louisiana*, 1869, pp. 11–13; Thomas W. Conway to John W. Alvord, September 19, 1870, in BRFAL Ms.

of whom forty-seven attended integrated schools. Such specific statistics were a rarity in Louisiana education reports of the Reconstruction period. Most of the reports of division and state superintendents from 1869 through 1875 do not separate attendance of white and black children nor do they indicate the total number of integrated schools.[11]

R. K. Diossy, superintendent of the third division in southwestern Louisiana, related that in his district most schools were separate by the choice of children and parents of both races, but in some localities children of both races attended in common, and "sometimes a colored teacher has in his school numbers of white children." In 1871 Conway made several claims about the extent of integration throughout the state which simply are not corroborated by reports of his division superintendents nor by some of his own admissions. For example, he asserted that mixed schools existed in every division but admitted that few whites attended integrated schools. Available evidence indicates that integration was almost unknown in rural parishes where the wealthy educated their children abroad or at private schools. In these areas poor whites refused to attend school with blacks, and, thus, except in Cajun areas where few blacks lived, public schools were virtually abandoned to blacks. Conway liked to boast that in instances where integration had occurred, "no difficulty had been experienced." He declared that the right of every child in Louisiana to attend school regardless of race *"has been vindicated with such prudent firmness as to be no longer questioned."* Although most children still attended separate schools, Conway pointed out that in integrated classrooms pupils of both races might be found learning together, whites treating blacks with greater kindness than would be seen in most Northern cities.[12]

New Orleans, the South's largest and most cosmopolitan city

11. *Annual Report, Louisiana*, 1871, p. 120; ibid., 1874, pp. 269–70; Teachers' Reports, Assumption Parish, 1863–1866, Louisiana State Department of Education Archives, Miscellaneous Records.

12. *Annual Report, Louisiana*, 1871, pp. 46, 119–21, 134, 189; Beasley, "History of Education in Louisiana," p. 169; for a detailed account of the school segregation problem in rural Louisiana, see Fischer, "Segregation Struggle," pp. 105–8, 115–17, 130. Fischer insists that the few examples of integration in the rural parishes "reflected more the realities of local racial accommodation than the ideal of the equality of all peoples." Ibid., p. 117. *Congressional Globe*, 41st Cong., 3d sess., p. 1055.

in 1870, witnessed, despite great opposition, the most successful Southern school integration during Reconstruction.[13] Integration took place only after three years of resistance and evasion which began before the constitutional convention. In the autumn of 1867 the city established its first black schools on a separate-but-equal basis by incorporating bureau-association schools into the city system. Bureau officials opposed to mixed schools hastened to transfer their facilities to the city in November and December 1867 at a time when these would still remain all-black schools. White Radicals in the city government now cooperated with the school board to resist Conway's integration efforts. In June 1868 the city board established a pupil placement system and ordered all principals of white schools to transfer any black children in their schools who might have been admitted by mistake. The following September city superintendent William O. Rogers directed all principals of white schools to refuse admission to black applicants and inform them they would be admitted only to all-black schools.[14]

The city used every legal resource available to evade or block integration, and a bewildering succession of suits and injunctions were filed in several courts as the board tested loopholes of all school laws. At one time five school cases were simultaneously on the dockets, all technically involving distribution of school funds but actually relating to integration. Finally in December 1870 Judge Henry C. Dibble of the Eighth District Court issued a decision taking financial power away from the city board and giving it to boards

13. For a detailed and favorable account of Reconstruction school integration in the Crescent City, see Louis R. Harlan, "Desegregation in New Orleans Public Schools during Reconstruction," *American Historical Review* 67 (1961): 663–75. Harlan's research voids traditional accounts which pictured New Orleans school integration as a dismal failure, e.g., Alcée Fortier, *Louisiana Studies* (New Orleans: F. F. Hansell and Bro., 1894), pp. 267–68; and John S. Kendall, *History of New Orleans*, (Chicago: Lewis Publishing Co., 1922), 1:331.

14. Harlan, "Desegregation in New Orleans Schools," pp. 664–65; School Board Minutes, vol. 7, September 11, 1867, pp. 203–14, Orleans Parish School Board Office, New Orleans; ibid., October 9, 1867, pp. 219–23; ibid., October 9, 1867, pp. 223–26; ibid., November 6, 1876, pp. 235–37; ibid., December 4, 1867, pp. 251–53; ibid., May 24, 1868, pp. 327–28; ibid., June 3, 1868, pp. 336–37; New Orleans Board of Education to all Principals, September 4, 1869, in William O. Rogers Correspondence, 1865–70, Orleans Parish School Board Office, New Orleans.

within the various wards. This meant that funds for integrated schools could no longer be blocked at city hall, and desegregation began within a month. The state education law of 1870 replaced the New Orleans board with a state-appointed board, which was allowed to estimate its annual expenses and require collection of local taxes sufficient to meet its needs.[15]

During these three years of frustration and evasion the conservative New Orleans press, creating an atmosphere of fear and distrust, advocated a white exodus from the schools as well as refusal to pay school taxes and predicted the destruction of public schools and racial conflict if integration took place. In 1867 the *Picayune*, reacting to demands for mixed schools by the black-operated *Tribune*, asserted that if whites declined to send their children to mixed schools they should send them to private schools or keep them at home. Only the "lowest and most depraved" whites would send their children to mixed schools. Besides, blacks should be satisfied with having their children educated at white expense without demanding integration. The *New Orleans Times* vigorously opposed integration, declaring the only white children to attend mixed schools would be those of the Radicals.[16]

Proposal of Conway's extreme education bill with the fine and seizure clause in August 1868 gave most of the New Orleans newspapers an ideal opportunity to increase their opposition. The *Picayune* predicted the bill would establish a nursery for propagation of Radicalism. If the people permitted Conway and his teachers to seize white children from their parents and force them into "miscegenating schoolhouses," it "will surely be at the cost of blood," for the white males of Louisiana would resist this attempt "to degrade their mothers, sisters, wives and daughters to the level of the Negro race." The *Times* declared that it was not within the realm of human power to compel racial mixing in schools while public opinion condemned it. A letter to the *Times* of February 1870, signed by "Pacificus," declared that the true purpose of mixed schools was to promote black equality.[17]

15. *Annual Report, Louisiana*, 1870, pp. 17–27; ibid., pp. 200, 205; Fischer, "Segregation Struggle," p. 135; Harlan, "Desegregation in New Orleans Schools," pp. 665–66.

16. *New Orleans Picayune*, October 22, 1867; *New Orleans Times*, May 2, 1868.

While New Orleans whites were battling integration in the courts, former state superintendent Robert M. Lusher organized a special committee including himself as chairman, along with William O. Rogers, former city superintendent, and several prominent citizens to formulate a plan for opening special schools for whites only, free from Radical interference. Failure of the committee to obtain sufficient funds for what probably would have been a system of all-white private schools similar to those established in Prince Edward County, Virginia, ninety years later, led to abandonment of Lusher's scheme. One observant Radical who remained after Reconstruction to become a respected public figure, Ephraim S. Stoddard, pointed out in 1874 that New Orleans citizens should not be upset by mixed schools, since the schools had been integrated for years. Before the Civil War, said Stoddard, illegitimate children, fathered by prominent white citizens of their black mistresses, were enrolled in schools as whites "and no objections made."[18]

During the years 1871–1874 New Orleans learned to tolerate mixed schools if not to accept them. This tacit acceptance may have resulted from the skill with which school officials administered desegregation. More important, thousands of New Orleans whites and leading newspapers attempted to win the black's vote by recognizing his civil rights. In addition, Thomas W. Conway, his black successor William G. Brown, and New Orleans superintendent Charles W. Boothby pursued a firm but moderate course and administered a system good enough to win loyalty from teachers and even occasional compliments from Conservatives. Other factors making school desegregation in New Orleans more feasible in comparison to other Southern cities were the city's cosmopolitan nature, the desegregation of local Roman Catholic churches, and the relatively small black

---

17. *New Orleans Picayune*, August 13, 1868; *New Orleans Times*, August 13, 1868; ibid., February 17, 1870.

18. Lusher, Autobiography Ms of May 31, 1889, pp. 16–17, in Lusher Papers; "Notes of the Mixed School Imbroglio," Ephraim S. Stoddard Diary for 1874–75 in Emphraim S. Stoddard Collection, Howard-Tilton Memorial Library, Tulane University. A favorable evaluation of Stoddard is found in White, *Freedmen's Bureau in Louisiana*, p. 198. For additional information on Rogers, see Albert P. Subat, "The Superintendency of the Public Schools of Orleans Parish, 1862–1910" (M.A. thesis, Tulane University, 1947); Esther B. Klein, "The Contributions of William O. Rogers to Education in New Orleans" (M.A. thesis, Tulane University, 1942).

population (about 25 percent) dispersed throughout the city and not large enough to overwhelm local whites. In addition, New Orleans had only been part of the Confederacy for two years before its capture and had known some form of Reconstruction for over eight years before school integration. The vigorous, ambitious leadership of the New Orleans black population was also important.[19]

As with the rest of Louisiana, official reports of the New Orleans schools did not tabulate pupils according to race. The evidence available in records and newspapers indicates that about one-third of New Orleans's some seventy schools were integrated. At the height of Reconstruction between 500 and 1,000 blacks out of a total black school population of 5,000 to 6,000 attended schools with several thousand whites. Two of the city's three public high schools were probably integrated. The five mixed schools with seventy-five or more black pupils were all located in the second and third districts below Canal Street, an area where descendants of original French and Spanish settlers along with Irish, German, and Italian immigrants predominated. According to the Radical organ, the *Republican*, as of July 1873 New Orleans had between fifteen and twenty all-black schools, between thirty-five and forty all-white schools, and some fifteen mixed schools, the latter being "the best in the city," whereas the all-black schools were the poorest in every respect. Two specific examples of integrated elementary schools included the Fillmore School, which by June 1872 had 500 white and 100 black pupils and was described by a *Times* reporter as being in a thriving state. The Bienville School at this time had 320 pupils, one-third of whom were black. They were reputed to be in fine condition "morally, mentally, and physically, and the discipline is excellent."[20]

It was only during the first year of integration, 1870–1871, that enrollment in the New Orleans schools declined—from 24,892 to 19,091—and then it steadily increased each year to 26,251 in 1875.

19. Harlan, "Desegregation in New Orleans Schools," pp. 669–70, 672–74.
20. Eugene Lowrance, "Color in the New Orleans Schools," *Harper's Weekly* 19 (1875): 147; Fischer, "Segregation Struggle," p. 156; Harlan, "Desegregation in New Orleans Schools," pp. 666 n, 667; *Annual Report, Louisiana*, 1871, p. 375; ibid., 1872, p. 242; *New Orleans Republican*, April 12, 1873; ibid., July 18, 1873; *New Orleans Times*, June 7, 1873; ibid., December 13, 1873.

Of this figure about 21,000 pupils were white and 5,000 were black.[21] Certain contemporary observers, defying the Conservative party line, reported that integration was working well until activities of the White League threatened the existence of public schools in 1874. One congressman, Chester B. Darrall, a Pennsylvania-born Radical from Louisiana, declared that the ultimate effect of school integration in his adopted state had been the prospering of the school system rather than its destruction. Bright black pupils were eager to attend mixed schools, usually rated as "Grammar A," which had more and better-paid teachers than the all-black schools, most of which were classified as "Grammar B" institutions. Not only was the instruction at integrated schools far superior, but their facilities far exceeded those of black schools in comfort and convenience.[22]

One consequence of the integration of the New Orleans's public schools was a brief but sharp rise in the number of secular private schools for whites. There were only two such schools in 1868, but from 1871 to 1877 between forty-seven and sixty-three private (nonparochial) institutions provided a minimal education to children whose parents believed that racial composition of the classroom should be the primary factor in selecting a school. Most of these schools were small, being taught by needy white women and their families and were conducted in private homes. The great majority disappeared when the end of Reconstruction led to a resegregation of the public facilities. Nevertheless, according to one estimate, 16,000 white children in New Orleans were attending private schools (parochial and secular) by 1877, while 15,169 whites were attending public schools.[23]

Although New Orleans whites tolerated mixed schools from 1870 to 1874, the general reaction of most whites in rural Louisiana to integration was one of avoiding and ignoring public schools and either remaining uneducated or attending private institutions wherever possible. Conway's report for 1870 declared that there was probably no other state in the Union where popular education

21. *Annual Report, Louisiana,* 1871, p. 326; ibid., 1875, pp. 12–13.
22. Lowrance, "Color in the New Orleans Schools," p. 148; *Washington New National Era,* July 2, 1874; Harlan, "Desegregation in New Orleans Schools," p. 668; *New Orleans Times,* June 18, 1870.
23. Fischer, "Segregation Struggle," pp. 137–41.

faced so many disadvantages as in Louisiana. Not only did the system have to be rebuilt in the face of general apathy, which at times approached genuine antagonism, but the integration clause of the 1868 constitution had excited a "determined opposition on the part of many who would otherwise co-operate in the opening of schools, and in the raising of funds for their support." Conway admitted that a majority of older white citizens who had intelligence and time to promote popular education were "decidedly adverse to a system of instruction which made no distinction of race." In sections of Louisiana where the active, intelligent, and courageous leadership of native whites could not be enlisted, the superintendent granted by 1871 that the school system was a failure.[24]

Ephraim S. Stoddard, superintendent of the second division, reported a lack of sympathy by the oldest and most substantial part of the population toward public education, probably because of the race question. If not directly opposing the public school system, they did not encourage it unless motivated by "some selfish policy." He concluded that if this group had the power there would be no public schools. The treasurer of the Jefferson Parish (left bank) board of education reported in 1871 that five schools were under his jurisdiction, four attended exclusively by blacks, one exclusively by whites. "The whites will not mix with the blacks, and any attempt to mix them will prove disastrous to the public school system."[25]

Conway and his mixed school policy received severe criticism at the state education convention in 1872. After hearing several testimonials praising the great accomplishments of Louisiana in public education since 1869, Jasper Blackburn of Claiborne Parish declared that he believed the present school system was a failure, at least in rural parishes. The education laws of 1869, 1870, and 1871, based upon "an unfortunate article in the constitution," made the system a failure because they "alluded to and aroused the prejudices of white men." Blackburn said that he favored black education but opposed mixed schools. A black delegate denounced Blackburn's position, defending mixed schools and telling of their successful operation in his parish.[26]

24. *Report of the Commissioner of Education for the Year 1870–1871*, pp. 195–96.
25. *Annual Report, Louisiana*, 1870, p. 61; ibid., 1871, p. 132.

In January of 1875 David F. Boyd of Louisiana State University prepared his annual anniversary address to the institution on the subject of school integration. Although never delivered because of the "embattled condition" of the state at that time, it reflected the thinking of many serious-minded Louisiana whites. Boyd emphasized that it was the duty of the state to educate the black population but said that if one disregarded the race situation and mixed blacks and whites on the elementary and secondary levels, "the natural antipathy of the races will show itself *there* among the younger and less intelligent children," disorder and confusion would result, and "neither race can learn much." Boyd also believed that lack of good breeding and manners among black children would be a harmful influence on white children. He stated that Louisiana must retain separate elementary schools for a long time.[27]

Beginning in 1871 Conway faced a number of serious personal problems which may have influenced him not to run for reelection as superintendent in 1872. In October 1871 he suffered a severe case of yellow fever. The following year he lost his wife and son, Willie. Conway decided not to be a candidate for reelection in November 1872. In his last meeting on October 29, 1872, the state board praised him for his "vigilance and courage" in administering the public schools. Indulging in a bit of hyperbole, it declared that outside New Orleans where in 1868 there had been no schools, 700 now existed. Conway returned to the North in 1873 and after resuming his ministerial work in Vineland, New Jersey, he became pastor of the Centennial Baptist Church in Brooklyn, New York. Two years later he left the ministry to devote his full efforts to temperance work, organizing the New York Anti-Saloon League and a temperance insurance company. He died in Brooklyn on April 6, 1887, at age forty-eight.[28]

---

26. Ibid., 1872, pp. 49–50.

27. Reed, "David Boyd," pp. 210–12; David F. Boyd, "Some Ideas on Education: The True Solution to the Question of 'Color' in Our Schools, Colleges, and Universities, etc., etc.," in Walter L. Fleming Collection, Department of Archives and Manuscripts of Louisiana State University.

28. Letter Copy Book, 1871–1874, October 28, 1871, in Louisiana State Department of Education Archives; Beasley, "History of Education in Louisiana," p. 157; Louisiana State Board of Education, Proceedings and Minutes, October 29, 1872; *Appleton's Annual Cyclopedia for 1887*, new series, 12:578.

After Conway left Louisiana his successor, William G. Brown, revealed a financial scandal which involved Conway personally. The 1872 legislature had appropriated $6,000 for Franklin College in Opelousas for building repairs which had never been made. Brown conducted a heated correspondence with Conway, then in New York, in which the latter asked Brown not to mention the affair in his annual report. Exactly what Conway did with the money is not entirely clear. Eventually he returned $2,000 but never repaid the balance. For his exposure of Conway, Brown received considerable praise from the *Picayune*.[29]

A realignment of Louisiana Radical factions by August 1872 led to the nomination of William G. Brown for state superintendent of education. Brown belonged to the faction headed by Pinckney B.S. Pinchback. Little is known of Brown's background, except that he was a West Indian black, probably from Jamaica, and had served as enrolling clerk in the state legislature for two years before his election as state superintendent. According to an 1875 article in *Harper's Weekly*, Brown had been educated in an English school and then had emigrated to New Orleans where he became a teacher and editor before his duties with the legislature.[30] Brown achieved election as state superintendent in 1872 over Robert M. Lusher, thanks to a decision of the Radical-dominated returning board which allegedly turned Lusher's 11,000-vote margin into a majority for Brown.[31]

Although Brown has been described as an incompetent who allowed his white secretary, M. C. Cole, a Northern Baptist minister, to run the state Department of Education, contemporary evidence still available discounts this picture. David F. Boyd, who had no love for Radical politicians, declared in 1874 that Brown was one of the two best officers in the state and reflected credit on his race. Examination of some of Brown's letters in the Louisiana Depart-

29. *Legislative Documents, Louisiana*, 1877, Document no. 21, "Report of the Joint Committee of Investigation of the Department of Education," pp. 31–39; *New Orleans Picayune*, March 4, 1874.

30. John E. Gonzales, "William Pitt Kellogg, Reconstruction Governor of Louisiana, 1873–1877," *Louisiana Historical Quarterly* 29 (1946): 339–402; Thomas G. Thompson to William G. Brown, November 26, 1875, in Correspondence, East Carroll Parish, 1866–76, Louisiana State Department of Education Archives; *New Orleans Picayune*, October 17, 1872; Lowrance, "Color in the New Orleans Schools," p. 147.

31. Lusher, Autobiography Ms of May 31, 1889, p. 23, in Lusher Papers.

ment of Education Archives reveals the superintendent to have been capable of expressing himself in a clear and intelligent manner. Congressman Chester B. Darrall referred to Brown as a gentleman whose "energy, varied accomplishments and thorough education" qualified him for his office. Darrall believed that Brown performed his trying duties "in such a manner as to gain the respect and disarm the prejudice of all his political enemies." One reason for Brown's relative popularity may have been his reluctance and that of New Orleans superintendent Charles W. Boothby to push for more school integration, a situation that infuriated the pro-Radical *Republican*.[32]

Brown was serving as state superintendent when a series of incidents, later known as the New Orleans school riots, marred the prevailing calm. This followed failure of an 1872–1873 plan known as the unification movement, which proposed a fusion of native white and black voters in which blacks would promise to assist in removing the Radicals and cutting taxes, and whites would guarantee the blacks full civil rights and mixed schools. Proposed by idealistic businessmen, the unification movement failed because of rural voters' reluctance to make concessions and a belief among blacks that whites would not honor their commitments. Ex-Confederate General Pierre G. T. Beauregard was for a time one of the unification leaders as was the black lieutenant governor, Caesar C. Antoine. Many distinguished business and professional men participated, but this was a reform movement led by amateurs, and they barred professional politicians from their organizations. This fatal blunder caused both the Conservative and Radical parties to fight

32. Edwin A. David, *Louisiana, A Narrative History*, 2d ed. (Baton Rouge: Louisiana State University Press, 1965), p. 276; David F. Boyd Diary, 1874, vol. 1, August 8, 1874 (Ms in Boyd Collection, Department of Archives and Manuscripts of Louisiana State University); William G. Brown to Charles W. Keeting, June 2, 1873, Letter Copy Book, 1871–1874, in Louisiana State Department of Education Archives; *Washington New National Era*, July 2, 1874; *New Orleans Republican*, July 18, 1873. See also *New Orleans Picayune*, December 11, 1874, for reference to a slowdown of integration. Brown became the nemesis of the Conservative New Orleans press, when in June 1873 he rightfully dismissed a popular teacher and principal, Kate R. Shaw, for extreme discourtesy and refusal to acknowledge him as state superintendent. For an emotional account of this incident see Harris, *Public Education*, pp. 46–47. For Brown's careful description of the Shaw affair in his own words, see William G. Brown to Charles W. Boothby, June 20, 1873, in Letter Copy Book, 1871–1874, Louisiana State Department of Education Archives.

unification. With its failure whites in 1874 decided to keep blacks from the polls if they would not vote the white man's way. The anti-black White League developed in 1874, spreading from rural parishes to New Orleans where it promoted a three-day revolt in September which continued until federal troops arrived. After a Conservative city government assumed control in December 1874, the atmosphere was propitious for the school riots.[33]

The incident that the White League needed to start its campaign against mixed schools occurred on December 14 when eleven black girls, accompanied by a black teacher, attempted to apply for admission to Upper Girls High School. Mrs. M. E. McDonald, the principal, created a scene and asked her white pupils to leave, hoping to avoid further controversy. The girls went to a nearby house and drafted a petition declaring their refusal to go through graduation exercises unless authorities halted integration attempts. The black girls departed before arrival of superintendent Charles W. Boothby. Boothby calmed the white girls who returned to their classrooms. He disclaimed any prior knowledge of the affair although the *Picayune* declared that black members of the New Orleans school board had prearranged the whole affair. The following day Boothby returned to the high school to conduct an investigation of the previous day's events. When he got off the streetcar near the school, a group of fifteen white men attacked him, accusing him of using vile and insulting language to the girls the day before. They beat Boothby, threatened him with hanging, dragged him into Mrs. McDonald's classroom where they made him apologize, and compelled him to declare that he would prevent recurrence of similar events and that he opposed mixed schools.[34]

33. Harlan, "Desegregation in New Orleans Schools," pp. 670–71; T. Harry Williams, "The Louisiana Unification Movement of 1873," *Journal of Southern History* 11 (1945): 360; Fischer, "Segregation Struggle," pp. 145–47; Lowrance, "Color in the New Orleans Schools," p. 147. During this period the removal of the mixed school clause from Sumner's civil rights bill helped weaken the position of mixed schools in Louisiana.

34. *Annual Report, Louisiana, 1874*, pp. 60, 66; *New Orleans Picayune*, December 15, 17, 18, 1874; Harris, *Public Education*, pp. 45–46; "Notes on the Mixed School Imbroglio," Ephraim S. Stoddard Diary for 1874–75, in Stoddard Collection. The *New Orleans Bulletin* was convinced that the attempted integration of Upper Girls High School was a plot originated in Washington by advocates of Sumner's civil rights bill. *New Orleans Bulletin*,

The White League and its newspaper supporters, especially the *New Orleans Bulletin*, now assumed direction of mobs principally composed of men and boys not enrolled in high school. High school rowdies were used as fronts. According to one contemporary observer, "The city was for one week in the hands of a mob of school boys and no power existed competent to control them backed as they were by the White League."[35]

On December 15 twelve black youths arrived at Boys High School to take an entrance exam, but a group of white boys threatened violence and forced them to leave. The high school boys, directed by the league, then organized a committee and visited Lower Girls High School, ejecting students whom they believed to be black. Other groups, claiming to be high school boys, visited several elementary schools and removed suspected black students. Two of the girls forced to leave a school were the sister and daughter of Davidson B. Penn, a prospective Conservative candidate for lieutenant governor. A mob expelled a number of Jewish children from the Webster School because of their dark complexions. On December 17, after a mob ejected three or four pupils from Keller School, a riot ensued between white and black gangs resulting in the death of one black and injury to a black policeman.[36]

The mob was undaunted by the melee of the previous day and on December 18 proceeded to visit other white schools, searching for black or mulatto pupils. They encountered resistance at Beauregard School from a sizable group of black men. Shots were fired but no one was injured, and a group of adult whites forced the blacks to disperse. Responsible citizens then persuaded the White League to call off the mob. After the mob had insulted Judge Henry C. Dibble, the *Picayune*, thanking them for expelling the black pupils, remarked that the Dibble incident "affords sufficient evidence that the boys are no longer a useful or desirable element in the case."

December 16, 1874. For a favorable account of Boothby as New Orleans superintendent, see Subat, "The Superintendency of the Public Schools of Orleans Parish," pp. 35–39.

35. "Notes of the Mixed School Imbroglio," in Stoddard Collection: Harlan, "Desegregation in New Orleans Schools," p. 672; *New Orleans Weekly Louisianian*, December 26, 1874.

36. *New Orleans Picayune*, December 18, 20, 1874; "Notes on the Mixed School Imbroglio"; *New Orleans Weekly Louisianian*, December 26, 1874.

William G. Brown was furious when he learned that the *Picayune* had thanked the committee, and he blamed irresponsible journalism of the *Picayune* and *Bulletin* for motivating the "boys committee to commit outrages." He also accused certain New Orleans papers of manifesting "intense caste prejudice, bitter sectional hatred, and fierce political antagonism" in their editorials which motivated "gangs of idle and vicious men" to invade public schools and demand removal of black students.[37]

Word of the school crisis in New Orleans quickly spread throughout the nation. The *New York Tribune* incorrectly reported that the mixed school excitement in New Orleans had subsided and that nobody was hurt except H. E. Adams, a reporter for the Radical *Republican*, "who was cowhided for insulting some young ladies who called at his office." The *Atlanta Constitution* in a stern editorial warned that no power on earth would ever compel young white ladies to attend mixed schools in New Orleans or elsewhere, for "mixed schools are impossible, and we hope every honest man, and especially every honest legislator, will study the history of the New Orleans struggle, for it was an exact counterpart of what Sumner's civil rights bill would have produced in every Southern town, if it had become a law."[38]

The results of the New Orleans school riots are difficult to evaluate. The *Republican* declared it was unwise for blacks to force their legal rights "in face of the overwhelming popular prejudice arrayed against them." It suggested closing the schools temporarily and then reopening them on a separate-but-equal basis. The paper said that blacks would now prefer to attend separate schools rather than mixed schools where they would suffer abuse from white schoolmates. It believed that the recent outbreaks against mixed schools following two years of peaceful operation were a reaction against "the excessive prominence given to the colored population during the past few years,"—a backlash aided by recent Democratic and Conservative victories: "Let the colored people bear the reverse in patience and wait for better times."[39] Boothby reported unusually

37. Harlan, "Desegregation in New Orleans Schools," p. 672; *New Orleans Picayune*, December 19, 1874; *Annual Report, Louisiana*, 1874, pp. 49, 84–85.
38. *New York Tribune*, December 19, 1874; *Atlanta Constitution*, December 20, 1874.

heavy absenteeism during January and February after the schools reopened. He blamed some of it on the riots; however, in a few months he reported that all schools affected by the riots were calm and had returned to normal.[40]

Although most New Orleans whites were unaware of the situation, a small amount of school integration continued after December 1874. Boys High School retained some black students, although an incident in February 1875 led to the quiet withdrawal of twenty-two whites. This same school had a black mathematics teacher, the Paris-educated E. J. Edmunds, from 1875 until 1877, when he was placed in charge of the city's academic department for advanced black pupils. In September 1876 two black girls integrated the formerly all-white Paulding School, long considered to be a holdout against desegregation. As late as 1877 city superintendent William O. Rogers reported that although 5,500 black children were attending twenty-three separate schools, about 300 blacks attended schools where the large majority were whites.[41]

The school situation in New Orleans remained quiet for a few months until September 29, 1875, when citizens held a mass meeting in Lafayette Square to protest certain policies of the board of education, such as removing competent teachers to provide jobs for political favorites, appointment of Edmunds at Boys Central High School, and forced racial mixing in schools, which they termed "repugnant to the instinct of both races." The protesters drafted resolutions demanding that the board, which was 50 percent black, be reorganized in proportion to the population of the city, i.e. one-third black and two-thirds white. They requested the current board to resign and cease integration of schools, declaring that integration was detrimental to the cause of education and racial harmony.

39. New Orleans Republican, December 19, 20, 1874.

40. School Board Minutes, New Orleans, vol. 7, April 7, 1875; Annual Report, Louisiana, 1875, pp. 149–55.

41. New Orleans Picayune, February 19, 1875; Annual Report, Louisiana, 1875, p. 153; School Board Minutes, New Orleans, vol. 7, September 11, 1875, p. 60; ibid., vol. 9, November 7, 1877, p. 177; Annual Report, Louisiana, 1877, pp. 301–5. Fischer, "Segregation Struggle," pp. 154–56. According to one account, Edmunds was persecuted by the Conservative press, became ill, and lost his mind. See Rodolphe Desdunes, Nos hommes et nostre histoire (Montreal: Arbour and Dupont, 1911), pp. 101–2.

In a letter dated October 13, 1875, the New Orleans board denied charges of maladministration, incompetency, and corruption and stated that the meeting of September 29, attended by only 2,000–3,000 people, was hardly representative of the city's population or of public feeling, especially since less than fifty people had taken part in preparing charges against the board. The state board of education met on November 4 to hear accusations against the New Orleans board, but a committee of five who had presented the charges did not attend, and the state board dropped the matter.[42]

Racial integration in the public schools, although evidently not adopted on an extensive scale outside of New Orleans, had a number of consequences for the entire Louisiana school system. Among these was the reluctance of whites to attend public schools. In 1871 the population of school-age children amounted to over 246,000, but the number of children enrolled according to the state board of education's generous computations was only 91,500. This figure declined to 74,846 for 1874–1875, while the total school population increased to over 274,000. However, attendance in the most integrated system of all–New Orleans–showed a steady increase after 1871. William G. Brown in 1874 estimated the state's private school enrollment at about 60,000, which, when combined with the public school figure, did not bring total school enrollment in Louisiana to 50 percent of the school-age population.[43]

Hatred of many Louisiana whites for integrated public schools produced much violence against schools from 1870 to 1875. In 1874 fourth division superintendent Charles W. Keeting reported that in his area of northwestern Louisiana, he was able to visit only one-half the parishes because so many school officials, fearing personal violence, had been frightened from their homes. Assailants had murdered the president of the DeSoto Parish school board and the treasurer of the Red River board. By the end of 1875 schools of Lafayette Parish in south-central Louisiana were suspended indefinitely because of the opposition and interference of local whites who did not hesitate to threaten school directors with violence.[44]

42. *Annual Report, Louisiana*, 1875, pp. 40–46, 51–53. Former Confederate General James Longstreet was a member of the controversial New Orleans board.

43. Ibid., 1870, pp. 42–43; ibid., 1876, p. 149; ibid., 1874, p. 13.

44. Ibid., 1874, p. 29; ibid., 1875, p. 139.

In the state and national elections of 1876 both Louisiana Radicals and Conservatives claimed victory, although the returning board declared all Radical candidates, including William G. Brown, as elected. For a time Louisiana had two governors, two legislatures, and two sets of state officials. In April 1877 following removal of federal troops by President Rutherford B. Hayes, the Radical administration of Stephen B. Packard collapsed. Francis T. Nicholls became governor and Robert M. Lusher resumed his former office of state superintendent. Widespread criticism of inadequate black schools had been an important factor in the recent contest in encouraging many blacks to desert the Radicals and vote Conservative. In a later congressional investigation of the election, testimony revealed that in many rural areas blacks had no schools or schools that operated only for a term of one month a year. Blacks were also bitter about the hiring of incompetent, ignorant teachers of their own race to teach in what few black schools did exist and resented unequal distribution of school taxes.[45]

Upon assuming the office of state superintendent, Lusher requested an amendment to articles 135 and 136 of the 1868 constitution providing for mixed schools. He declared that school integration had either been ignored or avoided in rural parishes and that public schools had only gained favor where districts maintained separate schools. He believed that in New Orleans nine-tenths of the blacks preferred separate schools, erroneously stating that the only ones who desired integration were mulattoes whose parents had always been free. Lusher asserted that school integration was not a proper subject for constitutional enactment but "must be controlled and regulated by the enlightened conscience of the communities who are taxed for the support of free education."[46]

With the return of William O. Rogers as school superintendent

45. *New Orleans Picayune,* July 4, 1876; Gonzales, "William Pitt Kellogg," p. 485; Teddy B. Tunnell, Jr., "The Negro, the Republican Party and the Election of 1876 in Louisiana," *Louisiana History* 7 (1966); 109; *House Miscellaneous Documents,* 44th Cong., 2d sess., No. 34, pt. 3, pp. 96, 118, 128, 305; ibid., pt. 6, 59–60, 226.

46. *Annual Report, Louisiana,* 1877, pp. iv–v. Later, to accommodate mulattoes who had an aversion to attending school with dark-skinned blacks, authorities established a special school, Academy Number Four. For more information on the attitudes of freeborn blacks on sharing schools with freedmen, see White, *Freedmen's Bureau in Louisiana,* p. 179.

of New Orleans, mixed schools generally came to an end in the summer of 1877. Rogers clearly indicated his strong opposition to mixing either boys and girls or whites and blacks in public schools. On June 22, 1877, a new board of education recommended separate schools for New Orleans on the grounds that good discipline could not be maintained in mixed schools without undue severity. The board also declared that separate schools would best promote the education of both races. A group of approximately thirty prominent black citizens visited Governor Francis T. Nicholls on June 26 to protest the contemplated school segregation, pointing out that this would violate the 1868 constitution as well as recent pledges made by the governor. Nicholls stated that such matters were under the jurisdiction of parish or city school boards, and if a situation involved violation of the state constitution the courts could redress any wrongs. When members of the delegation protested the recent New Orleans board ruling against mixed schools, Nicholls expressed approval, explaining that the city would provide equal-but-separate facilities. He thought blacks now had every facility enjoyed by whites, and in some rural areas "they even had exclusive rights, as no white children attended the schools." The Conservative press lauded the governor for his stand while condemning the black delegation for its visit; the *New Orleans Democrat* viewed this as a threat by blacks to organize a "race party and begin a furious political warfare against the whites" if New Orleans resegregated its schools.[47]

The New Orleans board of education on July 3, 1877, voted 15–3 to establish separate schools for each race and authorized a committee of teachers to put this into effect during the vacation period. A black citizen sought an injunction to prevent this on the grounds that it violated his privileges and immunities. The Sixth District Court granted the injunction, but later dissolved it on the grounds that the plaintiff's petition declared no injury to himself and no cause of action. Blacks eventually lost three test cases despite

47. William O. Rogers to J. T. Leath, July 23, 1877, in William O. Rogers Correspondence; School Board Minutes, New Orleans, vol. 9, June 22, 1877, pp. 56–60; *Annual Report, Louisiana*, 1877, pp. 304–5; *New Orleans Times*, June 28, 1877; *New Orleans Democrat*, June 27, 28, 1877; *New Orleans Picayune*, June 28, 1877; *New Orleans Times*, June 28, 1877; Klein, "The Contributions of William O. Rogers to Education in New Orleans," pp. 12–16.

the mandatory provisions of the state constitution. Thus ended the only serious experiment with public school integration in the post-war South, especially significant because it occurred in a deep Southern state with a large black population.[48]

Louisiana, where controversy over mixed schools had raged most fiercely, was one of the last Southern states to enact a constitutional provision requiring separate schools. The constitution of 1879, in reality although not specifically, permitted separate facilities. The first legislative reference to segregated schools occurred in 1880 when the state established Southern University at New Orleans as an all-black institution, but there was no constitutional requirement until 1898, when a new constitution specified creation of separate schools for all black and white children between six and eighteen years of age.[49]

With the exception of a three-to-four-year period in New Orleans, Louisiana's experiment with integrated schools had proved a failure. There was virtually no desegregation in rural parishes, where mixed schools, as in the rest of the rural deep South, were doomed to failure by the weak economic position of black sharecroppers, a lack of demand for educated farm laborers, and the desire of white planters to maintain racial segregation as a method of social and economic control.[50] Whites in rural areas shunned public schools almost completely, attending private institutions or the semi-private Peabody Fund schools if they could afford to do so. Integration, whether in fact or theory, alienated most tax-paying whites from public schools. Some ninety years later, scenes of the New Orleans school riots of 1874 were revived when another battle erupted over school integration in the Crescent City in 1960–1961. Perhaps if the reasonably successful integration in New Orleans had been allowed to continue after 1877, it would have served as a pragmatic example to the rest of Louisiana and the South that school desegregation in

48. School Board Minutes, New Orleans, vol. 9, July 3, 1877, pp. 63–64; Garnie W. McGinty, *Louisiana Redeemed: The Overthrow of Carpetbag Rule, 1876–1880* (New Orleans: Pelican Publishing Co., 1941), pp. 228–30; Harlan, "Desegregation in New Orleans Schools," p. 672.

49. *Acts of Louisiana*, 1880, p. 54; Gilbert T. Stephenson, *Race Distinctions in American Law* (New York: D. Appleton, 1910), p. 172; *Constitution and Revised Laws of Louisiana*, 1904, p. 1981.

50. Harlan, "Desegregation in New Orleans School," p. 673.

certain situations could work to the advantage of both races. However, Louisiana's experience demonstrated the futility of attempting such a reform without sufficient support from the federal government, either in the form of troops or a federal police force to prevent a reoccurrence of the 1874 disaster and protect both children and teachers in integrated schools.

5. *Integration in Public Higher Education*

IN CONTRAST to public school systems, Southern public colleges and universities received little help from missionary teachers and Radical politicians during Reconstruction. The Freedmen's Bureau and benevolent associations did aid in the creation of numerous private institutions of higher learning for blacks such as Atlanta, Fisk, and Howard universities, but usually took little interest in state-supported colleges unless these schools could be included in their plan of Reconstruction.

Integration of state-supported colleges and universities was not usually a burning issue. In Arkansas the threat of racial mixing caused a brief flurry of controversy at the newly established (1872) Arkansas Industrial University—now the University of Arkansas—at Fayetteville. The board of trustees, meeting at Little Rock in mid-January 1872, declared that when necessity demanded it, the executive committee of the board would inform the president that he would admit white and black students into the same classes. The executive committee accepted the board's resolution at their April meeting. The following June, Albert Webb Bishop, a native of New York, member of the board of trustees, and later (1873–1875) president of the university, delivered a commencement oration in which he spoke of the University of Arkansas as a place where all were privileged to attend. Only one black applied for admission and was admitted by President Noah Putnam Gates. This unfortunate student, however, was forced to spend regular class hours in a nearby outhouse, and at noon and after school he met with Gates who heard his recitations in private. The black was forbidden to enter the classroom building used by white students. Evidently no other blacks applied for admission at this time—for obvious reasons. In 1875 the state established a normal school for blacks, now Arkansas Agricultural, Mechanical, and Normal College, at Pine Bluff.[1]

The Louisiana State Seminary and Military Academy at Alexandria reopened after the war in 1865; following a fire that destroyed the buildings, the college moved to Baton Rouge in 1869. After March 1870 the institution was known as Louisiana State University. President (or Superintendent) David F. Boyd maintained reasonably good relations with the Radical state governments at New Orleans until 1873, especially with the administration of Governor Henry C. Wormoth. On several occasions Wormoth promised to oppose all attempts to integrate Louisiana State University (LSU) and gave vital support to a legislative compromise which authorized cadet scholarships for blacks at Straight University in New Orleans. In 1871 an unpleasant incident occurred when Edward S. Cunningham, professor of natural philosophy and commandant of cadets, refused to shake hands with a black member of a visiting legislative committee, who took considerable offense at the affront. In that same year, relations became strained between Boyd and state superintendent Thomas W. Conway over the latter's desire to incorporate the university into the public school system with a strong implication that the institution would be open to all young men of Louisiana, regardless of race or color.[2]

The major problem of LSU, however, was one of dwindling finances. Most funds were appropriated in the form of depreciated state bonds which were exchanged for warrants. Frequently professors did not receive their salaries until cash could be obtained for

1. Thomas S. Staples, *Reconstruction in Arkansas, 1862–1874* (New York: Columbia University, 1923), p. 329; John H. Reynolds and David Y. Thomas, *History of the University of Arkansas* (Fayetteville: University of Arkansas, 1910), pp. 96–97.

2. Jean P. Bellier to Executive Committee of Louisiana State Seminary, June 24, 1868, in Walter L. Fleming Collection, Department of Archives and Manuscripts of Louisiana State University; Edward Cunningham to David F. Boyd, February 13, 1871, in ibid.; Germaine M. Reed, "David Boyd, Southern Educator" (Ph.D. diss., Louisiana State University, 1970), pp. 136–37, 142–45, 147, 224–25; Roger A. Fischer, "The Segregation Struggle in Louisiana, 1850–1890 (Ph.D. diss., Tulane University, 1967), p. 125; Leon O. Beasley, "A History of Education in Louisiana during the Reconstruction Period, 1862–1877" (Ph.D. diss., Louisiana State University, 1957), p. 193; E. Merton Coulter, *The South during Reconstruction 1865–77* (Baton Rouge: Louisiana State University Press, 1947), p. 329; *Annual Report of the State Superintendent of Education . . . to the General Assembly of Louisiana, 1871* (New Orleans: n.p., 1871), pp. 28–29.

the warrants, a difficult transaction to accomplish. Politics also complicated the university's existence. From March 1872 until January 1873 two rival governments, one led by William P. Kellogg, the other by John McEnery, contested for political control of Louisiana. The Kellogg administration, kept in power with federal troops, made no appropriations for the university, and the school received no further state support until 1877. Expenditures at LSU declined from $64,095 in 1870–1871 to $10,116 in 1873–1874, plummeting to a low of $3,428 for 1875–1876. In the state superintendent's annual report for 1874, LSU was listed under the heading of Private Institutions.[3]

Boyd and the university were caught between opposing ideologies on the mixed school controversy. Boyd angered the state board of education and legislature by his opposition to integration. An 1874 statute regulating university administration made no reference to racial equality in admission policies, and evidently this decision was to be left to the board of supervisors. The president voiced his despair when he declared, "Now the legislature won't support us, because we have no negroes here, and the whites are afraid to send us their sons, because the Negro may come here!" The university was deserted by the state "because we are not presumed to be in accord with the ignorance and villainy of the powers that be." Conversely, Louisiana whites boycotted the institution because of the law "which makes it obligatory on all schools, supported in whole or in part by the State, to receive Negroes as students." Whether by intent or circumstances, LSU remained a segregated and impoverished institution.[4]

3. David F. Boyd to W. L. Sanford, June 24, December 4, 1872, in Fleming Collection; New Orleans Picayune, May 21, 1872; Record of Expenditures, Louisiana State Department of Education Archives, Miscellaneous Records, Department of Archives and Manuscripts of Louisiana State University; Walter L. Fleming, Louisiana State University, 1860–1896 (Baton Rouge: Louisiana State University Press, 1936), pp. 195–97, 205, 264; Annual Report, Louisiana, 1874, p. 86; David F. Boyd to W. L. Sanford, March 4, 1875, in Fleming Collection.

4. Reed, "David Boyd," pp. 209–10; Louisiana State University . . . Enactments of the Legislature for its Organization . . . October 1, 1874, in Fleming Collection; David F. Boyd to W. L. Sanford, April 11, 1874, in ibid., David F. Boyd Diary, 1874, vol. 1, July 23, 1874, in David F. Boyd Collection, Department of Archives and Manuscripts of Louisiana State University.

The unification movement of 1873–1874 somewhat softened Boyd's stand against mixed schools, and in 1875 he drafted a proposal for limited desegregation of LSU, which he did not reveal to the public. Boyd still opposed integration on the primary and secondary levels but believed it foolish for a poor and weak state like Louisiana to support two state colleges simply to satisfy racial prejudice. Whites would gain nothing, morally or socially, and "at such a fearful sacrifice of educational facilities." Boyd suggested that Louisiana combine its resources into one good institution of higher learning for the whole state in which each student would "pursue his own chosen course of studies, . . . have his own select companions and . . . board or lodge, how or where he please without . . . hindrance, one of another." Somewhat illogically, the president did not believe that integrating LSU in its current status as a military school would succeed, therefore he suggested making the military school a separate department of the university with different units and barracks for each race. Other classes, however, were to be integrated.[5]

The unification movement had, of course, failed by December 1875 when Boyd presented his proposal and that, combined with the Conservatives' return to power two years later, precluded any racial mixing at LSU for many years to come. In 1877 LSU, remaining at Baton Rouge, was merged with the Agricultural and Mechanical College and returned to the status of a state-supported institution.[6]

In contrast to events of recent years, the University of Mississippi at Oxford did not face a genuine integration crisis during Reconstruction. The Radicals appointed a new board of trustees, but they never admitted blacks. In 1870 the faculty threatened to resign if integration were attempted and promised to eject any blacks who enrolled. However, none applied for admission and Alcorn University was soon established for blacks with former Senator Hiram R. Revels as president.[7]

5. David F. Boyd, "Some Ideas on Education: The True Solution to the Question of 'Color' in Our Schools, Colleges and Universities, etc., etc." in Fleming Collection; Reed, "David Boyd," pp. 210–12.

6. *Legislative Documents, Louisiana,* 1877, No. 7, pp. 25–26.

7. James W. Garner, *Reconstruction in Mississippi* (New York: Macmillan, 1901), p. 369.

North Carolina's state university at Chapel Hill faced many difficulties during Reconstruction, primarily a shortage of funds and students. Governor William W. Holden dominated the state board of education which in turn gained control of the university board of trustees in 1868. Virtually all trustees were replaced, and they in turn appointed a new president, Solomon Pool. Pool, an 1853 graduate of the university and former professor of mathematics (1861–1866), had been a severe critic of the university as overly dominated by certain aristocratic families. Pool was friendly with Holden, who also demanded a reorganization of the institution. The new faculty of five Radicals included Fisk P. Brewer, a former Yale tutor who had taught freedmen and had served as principal of a black high school.[8]

By May 1869 the university had ten students, two of whom were relatives of Pool. The threat of integration was remote—Conservative whites boycotted the institution simply because it was associated with the Holden regime. In 1868 two members of the board of trustees proposed that the state establish a branch of the university for blacks near Raleigh. The trustees agreed, but the plan was not implemented at this time. In the spring of 1869 rumors swept Chapel Hill that Pool had declared he would admit blacks if no whites attended the University of North Carolina. Such action was never seriously contemplated, and no integration took place during Reconstruction. Governor Holden, no friend of the university, was a self-made man from the poor white class who strongly opposed mixed schools. Speaking at the 1869 commencement, he declared that both races must be educated, but not together. Provisions would be made elsewhere for higher education of blacks, although Holden desired both the white and black universities to be part of the same system. Enrollment at the university continued to decline, reaching a nadir of two students by late January 1871. The

8. Phillips Russell, *The Woman Who Rang the Bell: The Story of Cornelia Phillips Spencer* (Chapel Hill: University of North Carolina Press, 1949), pp. 83, 111–15; Kemp P. Battle, *History of the University of North Carolina* (Raleigh: Edwards & Broughton Co., 1907), 1: 752, 774–75, 777; ibid. (1912), 2: 9–10, 35; Louis R. Wilson, ed., *Selected Papers of Cornelia P. Spencer* (Chapel Hill: University of North Carolina Press, 1953), pp. 612, 627–28; Hope S. Chamberlain, *Old Days in Chapel Hill* (Chapel Hill: University of North Carolina Press, 1926), p. 148. Fisk P. Brewer was a brother of David J. Brewer, associate justice of the United States Supreme Court, 1889–1910.

trustees suspended classes until further notice, and the venerable University of North Carolina, chartered in 1789 and opened in 1795, remained closed until September 1875.[9]

The University of South Carolina was the only institution of higher learning in the former Confederate states to integrate on an extensive scale. Originally South Carolina College, it survived Sherman's march and the burning of Columbia to enter a new decade of turmoil. Shortly after the Civil War the legislature changed its name to the University of South Carolina and expanded the curriculum to include modern languages, engineering, medicine, and law. Admitting blacks had caused no controversy by 1868 when Governor James L. Orr recommended a general policy of separate schools with the university reserved for whites and the Citadel at Charleston converted into a college for blacks.[10]

In the period 1868–1873 when the state was undergoing drastic changes through Reconstruction, the university remained generally unaffected. In a sense it prospered, for the Radical-dominated legislature increased its budget, appropriating $26,800 for the fiscal year beginning October 1, 1869, an amount double the last appropriation under the Orr regime. The situation remained uncertain, however, as Radicals threatened a transformation which could be accomplished under the 1868 constitution's mixed school clause, and students began transferring to other colleges. The pressure eased when the Methodist Episcopal Church established Claflin College for blacks at Orangeburg.[11]

A sign of impending trouble occurred in March 1869 when the General Assembly amended acts incorporating the university. Section 1 of this new act, proposed by William J. Whipper, black representative from Beaufort, stated that neither the board of trustees nor faculty "shall make any distinction in the admission of students or management of the university on account of race, color, or creed."

9. Wilson, ed., *Papers of Cornelia Spencer*, pp. 618, 620–22, 675–76; Battle, *University of North Carolina*, 2: 8, 35, 41.

10. Daniel W. Hollis, *College to University* (Columbia: University of South Carolina Press, 1956), pp. 3–17, 46; *Journal of the House of Representatives . . . of South Carolina*, special session of 1868, p. 30.

11. Hollis, *College to University*, pp. 46, 49; Oliver Otis Howard, *Autobiography of Oliver Otis Howard* (New York: Baker and Taylor Co., 1907), 2: 406.

On March 9, 1869, four days after Governor Robert K. Scott signed the new law, the General Assembly elected two blacks, Francis L. Cardozo and Benjamin A. Boseman, to the board of trustees. Among the white members were Franklin J. Moses, Jr., and state superintendent Justus K. Jillson. When the new board met in June, a white trustee, James L. Neagle, who was also comptroller general of the state, tried to have all university offices and faculty positions declared vacant in order to facilitate integration. Jillson and Governor Scott, an ex-officio member, opposed Neagle's plan, which was defeated. A similar proposal failed to pass at the board's July meeting, although a black replaced the incumbent bursar and registrar.[12]

For some whites in South Carolina, election of two black trustees was an indication that integration was imminent, and many undergraduates left the university in June 1869 with no intention of returning. A Columbia newspaper pointed out that although some citizens were treating the university's destruction as a foregone conclusion, the trustees had shown a "most discreet forebearance where action on their part might have compromised it."[13] Obviously the trustees were delaying integration, perhaps to test white support for the institution as a segregated school under Radical control.

South Carolina Radicals liked to point with pride to their support of the university, but enrollment was so low that it hardly appeared to justify the effort and expense of keeping the institution open. Enrollment declined from sixty-five in 1868–1869 to forty-two in 1869–1870, rose to eighty-eight in 1871–1872 and dropped to sixty-eight in 1872–1873. The highest appropriation for the pre-integration period was $37,850 in 1871–1872, $10,000 being designated for repairs. But the trustees' executive committee warned that unless the institution were better attended, it might not continue to

12. *Acts of South Carolina, 1868–69*, pp. 203–4; John S. Reynolds, *Reconstruction in South Carolina, 1865–1877* (Columbia, S.C.: State Co., 1905), p. 123; Hollis, *College to University*, pp. 50–51; Minutes of the Board of Trustees of the University of South Carolina, June 21, July 12, 1869, in South Caroliniana Collection, University of South Carolina, hereafter cited as Trustees Minutes. The Reynolds volume on South Carolina during Reconstruction presents a highly prejudiced and unreliable account of the university's integration, since Reynolds was one of those faculty members removed prior to integration. For an interesting account of this, see *Columbia* (S.C.) *State*, May 8, 1911.

13. *Columbia* (S.C.) *Weekly Gleaner*, August 18, 1869.

receive funds. In July 1871 the faculty promoted distribution of a circular stressing advantages of the university, its library, and scholarship program.[14]

This promotional effort slightly increased enrollment the next year from fifty-three to eighty-eight. Both old and new faculty members, Radicals and Conservatives, worked together in relative harmony to keep the university functioning. But fearing that blacks would soon be admitted and the faculty would then resign, prospective white students continued to boycott the faltering institution. This decline, combined with lack of a state-supported black college and a split in Radical ranks during the 1872 campaign, caused both factions to woo black voters with promises of admission to the university, and created a climate of opinion against the all-white institution, leading to its reorganization in 1873. It was absurd, of course, to expect a legislature with a black majority to continue supporting a university maintained exclusively for whites—especially if there were no satisfactory state college for blacks.[15]

The General Assembly elected a new board of trustees early in 1873 consisting of four blacks and three whites. Among the whites were Justus K. Jillson, future governor Daniel H. Chamberlain, and Governor Franklin J. Moses, Jr., ex-officio member and presiding officer of the board. Moses, a native South Carolinian, had attended the university briefly in 1855, leaving as a freshman. The black board members included some competent men. Two of them, Samuel J. Lee and James A. Browley, were members of the legislature. Another, W. R. Jervey, was a Methodist minister. Following election of the new trustees, the Euphradian Society, a literary and forensic club, proceeded to remove and hide its records to prevent blacks from becoming members should they enter the university. This followed an attempt to reinstate two scalawag members, Franklin J. Moses, Jr., and Thomas J. Robertson (elected United

14. *Reports and Resolutions of the General Assembly of South Carolina,* 1870–71, pp. 967–68; circular of July 1869, Minutes of the Faculty of the University of South Carolina in South Caroliniana Collection, University of South Carolina, hereafter cited as Faculty Minutes.

15. Hollis, *College to University,* pp. 57, 61–62. In 1872 the general assembly incorporated the Agricultural and Mechanical Institute for blacks at Orangeburg, but money for the school was diverted to other uses, and funds were not available until 1874.

States Senator in 1868), expelled in 1868 for being "a black stain on the society rolls."[16]

A gap in the trustees minutes for this period makes it difficult to ascertain exactly when the board decided to integrate the university, although this decision possibly was made by mid-summer of 1873. An unpleasant event of the previous April may have precipitated this action, for Associate Justice Jonathan J. Wright, a black member of the state supreme court, attended a lecture on campus and was incensed at the segregated facilities. Integration officially began on October 7, 1873, when Henry E. Hayne, a light-skinned black who was secretary of state for South Carolina, matriculated as a medical student. A Conservative local paper grudgingly admitted that Hayne possessed above-average intelligence and good character. Immediately after his admission, three professors, including the new faculty chairman, Maximilian LaBorde, resigned. On October 10 the trustees resolved to make public their conclusion that the resignations resulted from the admission of Hayne, "a gentleman of irreproachable character, against whom the said professors can suggest no objection except—in their opinion—his race." The board declared its satisfaction that a spirit "so hostile to the welfare of our state as well as to the dictates of justice and the claims of our common humanity" was no longer represented at the University, which was the property of all South Carolinians, regardless of race.[17]

The president pro tem of the board, Samuel J. Lee, later wrote that the professors' resignations, following the admission of a black student, "made necessary a change both in the corps of teachers and the university curriculum—a duty which we as a Board, had no hesitancy in assuming." Reviewing the past five years, Lee declared that white citizens of South Carolina should have been grateful to the legislature for supporting a university of a dozen bona fide stu-

16. Ibid., p. 63; *Columbia* (S.C.) *State*, May 8, 1911; Reynolds, *Reconstruction in South Carolina*, pp. 233, 261; Euphradian Society Minutes, April 11, 1868, May 24, 31, 1873, in South Caroliniana Collection, University of South Carolina.

17. Hollis, *College to University*, pp. 65–66; *Columbia* (S.C.) *Daily Phoenix*, April 6, 1873; *Columbia* (S.C.) *State*, May 8, 1911; University Ms, October 7, 1873, in South Caroliniana Collection, University of South Carolina; ibid., October 10, 1873; Faculty Minutes, October 3, 1873; Trustees Minutes, October 10, 1873.

dents from which his race had been excluded and retaining professors who "reviled them [Radicals] publicly and plotted against
them privately—men who used the leisure afforded by the university to stir up the opposition press and belittle every attempt at
progress."[18]

Hayne's admission occasioned considerable comment from the
South Carolina press. The Radical *Daily Union Herald* declared
that a new era had opened at the university, for all who enter would
now receive equal educational advantages. Another sympathetic
journal asserted that the university would be supported "at any
and every cost, and its campus filled with those who wish to learn."
The *Charleston News and Courier*, aghast at these events, predicted
that Hayne's admission marked the beginning of the end for the
University of South Carolina, for integration "must destroy any
institution of learning by forcing out the best classes of white
students and giving a practical monopoly of its advantages to the
colored people." The black-owned *New National Era* in Washington, D.C. countered the *Courier's* charges, saying it was hardly
possible that educating a few black students to "virtuous manhood,"
whether on an integrated basis or not, was capable of "destroying
an institution where great men have been instructed." Integration,
it continued, would not drive the level of white students down to
that of blacks; "the blacks will be raised to the level of whites."
Governor Moses also indicated his pleasure with integration of
the university and was certain that the "narrow spirit of bigotry
and prejudice" had been banished from its halls forever.[19]

By the end of December 1873 the university had about a dozen

18. *Reports and Resolutions of the General Assembly of South Carolina,*
1875, p. 756.

19. *Columbia* (S.C.) *Daily Union Herald,* October 8, 11, 1873; unidentified
clipping in Fisk P. Brewer Papers, South Caroliniana Collection; *Columbia*
(S.C.) *Daily Phoenix,* October 9, 1873; *Charleston News and Courier,* October
9, 1873; *Washington New National Era,* November 13, 1873; Reynolds, *Reconstruction in South Carolina,* p. 241. An ugly incident transpired the day Hayne
was enrolled. R. Gourdin Sloan, a white undergraduate, rushed into the library and inked out his name and that of his brother from the student register. The faculty proceeded to withdraw Sloan and his brother from school; the
trustees later changed the penalty to expulsion. *Washington New National
Era,* July 9, 1874; Faculty Minutes, October 7, 1873; Trustees Minutes, October
28, 1873.

students including a number of state officials, mainly blacks, who attended to prove the school was really integrated. Registered in the law school were Niles G. Parker, former state treasurer, C. M. Wilder, postmaster at Columbia, and state senators H. C. Corwin and George F. McIntyre—all whites. Also studying law were state representatives Lawrence Cain, Paris Simpkins, and the state treasurer, Francis L. Cardozo—all blacks. Few of these men attended regularly; only four of the students in the law school attended class and took examinations. The new faculty of seven men contained a number of carpetbaggers including Fisk P. Brewer, recently of the University of North Carolina. One of the more able professors was the Reverend Benjamin B. Babbitt, professor of physics and chairman of the faculty, who helped reorganize the university and demonstrated marked ability in dealing with difficulties. Probably the most capable of the group was Richard T. Greener, who taught mental and moral philosophy. Greener, the first black to receive a degree from Harvard (1870), later became dean of the law school at Howard University and served in several diplomatic posts abroad. Greener developed the reputation of a good, all-around scholar and polished speaker. While at the University of South Carolina he reorganized the library, restoring it to its former condition.[20]

The new faculty's attitude toward integration was, as might be expected, highly favorable. Babbitt declared that the university must be open to all. Greener, at a faculty conference with members of the legislature, stressed the necessity of abolishing the distinction of color, insisting that both races including poor whites should be educated together. Chairman Babbitt, predicting final success for the racially integrated institution, admitted this would be achieved only through trial and adversity.[21]

The university's enrollment problems increased with integration. Although the Conservative press insinuated that as of December 1873 the university had no students, minutes of the faculty indicate

20. Hollis, *College to University*, pp. 7, 80; Reynolds, *Reconstruction in South Carolina*, p. 234; *Charleston News and Courier*, December 19, 1873; *Columbia (S.C.) State*, May 8, 1911; *Dictionary of American Biography*, 7: 578–79.

21. Unidentified clipping dated December 12, 1873, in Brewer Papers; Report of the Chairman of the Faculty, November 26, 1873, University Ms.

that by June 1874 there were two juniors, six sophomores, and two freshmen. There was also a so-called subfreshman class (established to aid poorly prepared scholarship students) with sixteen students, a school of law with eighteen enrolled, and a school of medicine with three. The preparatory or high school department boasted sixty-seven pupils, most of them black, but it could not accurately be considered part of the university. According to these statistics, therefore, the University of South Carolina had fifty-seven college level students. Race classification was carefully avoided in all official records, but information still extant indicates that the student body was 50 percent or more black.[22]

To encourage attendance, in February 1874 the legislature established 124 state-financed scholarships of $200 each, to be divided among counties according to the number of representatives each county had in the legislature. Recipients had to pass two competitive examinations to obtain the grants which were paid either in a lump sum or at $20 a month for ten months. Extension of scholarships (they could be renewed for three additional years) required no stellar academic performance—a minimum general average of 60 percent sufficed.[23]

State superintendent of education and university trustee Justus K. Jillson attacked the scholarship program after it had been in operation for a year. He described it as a "miserable farce" and accused the faculty of assembling a motley crowd of youngsters, not qualified by virtue of "poverty, merit or scholarly attainment," to be recipients. The first twenty scholarships were awarded to four whites and sixteen blacks. Of twenty-four applicants, only four failed the competitive examinations. Faculty chairman Benjamin B. Babbitt insisted the scholarship students came from "all classes and conditions of men and fairly represent[ed] the population." But

22. *Columbia* (S.C.) *Daily Phoenix*, December 30, 1873; Board of Trustees to the Rev. Benjamin B. Babbitt, April 12, 1875, University Ms.; Faculty Minutes, June 20, 1874; Erastus W. Everson to E. M. Rollo, June 23, 1874, University Ms; unidentified clipping quoting letter from Judge Jonathan J. Wright, in Brewer Papers. For a fascinating account of the trials and tribulations of the reconstructed university, including an interesting comment on the subfreshman class, see Fisk P. Brewer's essay, "South Carolina University, 1876," in Brewer Papers.

23. *Acts of South Carolina*, 1873–74, pp. 555, 887; Faculty Minutes, February 20, 1874; ibid., February 19 and 26, 1875.

the anti-Radical *Columbia Phoenix* pictured the scholarships as a scheme to attract students and wondered when "this mockery of education, this outrageous imposition upon the people who pay taxes" would end. The Radical press countered, declaring the scholarship bill provided education for those who had no previous opportunity and that the real animus of Conservatives against the act was motivated by their hatred of black education.[24] This bill was clearly one of the most valuable constructive pieces of legislation ever enacted by any Reconstruction legislature, but since it provided education primarily for blacks to an integrated, formerly all-white state institution, it became anathema to Conservative taxpayers.

For several years the Radicals continued to give the University of South Carolina strong support, even though whites tended to boycott the institution. The legislative appropriation for 1873–1874 was $41,750, of which $6,400 was designated for scholarships. By June 1875 enrollment had increased to 166, including sixty-seven in the preparatory department. Excluding the subfreshman class, preparatory department, and normal school, enrollment in the college and professional departments was still approximately half-black. During these years the university proved to be a training ground for future black leaders including Thomas McCants Stewart, lawyer, journalist, and later associate justice of Liberia's supreme court; William D. Crum, a physician, later appointed collector of the port of Charleston by President Theodore Roosevelt; and Joseph W. Morris, later president of Allen University at Columbia, South Carolina.[25]

24. *Reports and Resolutions of the General Assembly of South Carolina,* 1875, p. 329; Hollis, *College to University,* p. 72; Erastus W. Everson to P. W. Phillips, April 4, 1874, University Ms; Report of Benjamin B. Babbitt to Trustees, December 1874, in ibid.; *Columbia* (S.C.) *Daily Phoenix,* December 30, 1873; *Columbia* (S.C.) *Daily Union Herald,* n.d., in Faculty Minutes, 1873–75.

25. *Columbia* (S.C.) *Daily Union Herald,* n.d., in Faculty Minutes, June 20, 1874; *South Carolina Statutes at Large,* vol. 15, p. 555; Hollis, *College to University,* 2: 72, 76; George B. Tindall, *South Carolina Negroes, 1877–1900* (Columbia: University of South Carolina Press, 1952), p. 204; *Washington New National Era,* April 16, July 9, 1874. For a long list of distinguished black graduates of the University of South Carolina from 1874 to 1877, see "When Negroes Attended the University," in the *Columbia* (S.C.) *State,* May 8, 1911. Written by Cornelius Chapman Scott, a black graduate of the university (1877), this presents a fascinating account of black graduates who went on to notable careers and reflected credit on their alma mater.

Another factor that did nothing to enhance the university in the esteem of white South Carolinians was the creation of a normal school on the campus in February 1873. Housed in university buildings, the normal school was open to boys of fifteen years of age and girls of fourteen of both races. University faculty occasionally lectured to normal school students who also used the university library. The school opened in September 1874 and after two years' operation had an enrollment of thirty-nine. Official reports do not give statistics on enrollment by race, but contemporary accounts indicate that the student body was heavily or completely black.[26]

According to Radical professor Fisk P. Brewer, integration at the University of South Carolina worked well. Most of the "advanced students of color" were gentlemen "and deserve to be treated as such." Brewer indicated that although both races attended class together, integration did not include sleeping or eating facilities. "It is an insult to . . . both colored and whites to stigmatize this institution as a 'miscegenation university.'" Evidently the interracial student body presented no greater disciplinary problems than their antebellum predecessors, although a former black student admitted years later that discipline was lax. Another contemporary observer believed that the University of South Carolina presented the finest argument in behalf of equality before the law: "The two races study together, visit each others rooms, play ball together, walk into the city together, without the blacks feeling themselves honored or the whites disgraced." One (presumably) black student, forced to leave school because of financial difficulties, referred to his experience at South Carolina "as among the most pleasing and beneficial of my college life."[27]

26. *Acts of South Carolina, 1872–73*, pp. 396–400; *Reports and Resolutions of the General Assembly of South Carolina, 1875–76*, pp. 496–502; Hollis, *College to University*, pp. 75–76. The normal school suspended operations on May 31, 1877, when eight young women received certificates representing completion of at least one year's work.

27. Brewer, "South Carolina University," passim, in Brewer Papers; *Columbia (S.C.) State*, May 8, 1911; *Columbia (S.C.) Daily Union Herald* (n.d.) in Brewer Papers; Hollis, *College to University*, p. 76; *Washington New National Era*, April 16, July 9, 1874; Paul S. Mishow to "President of the University," November 19, 1874, University Ms. See the *New York Times*, May 31, 1877, for commendation of the university's efforts to educate both races on an integrated basis, and how, under this "wise and liberal policy," the

The inauguration of President Rutherford B. Hayes and his withdrawal of federal troops from South Carolina in April brought about the downfall of Governor Daniel H. Chamberlain and the Radicals and signaled an end to the integrated university. On April 26, 1877, Conservative Governor Wade Hampton recommended a complete reorganization of the institution, stating that its benefits were not commensurate with the expense it entailed. Following this line of thought the local Conservative press attacked the university as a costly luxury. The *New York Times* correctly interpreted the situation by pointing out that the predominately Conservative legislature intended from the first to do away with the "nigger University." The legislature elected a new board of trustees and appointed Robert W. Barnwell as an all-purpose librarian, treasurer, and secretary. In June the General Assembly created a special commission to devise plans for two separate institutions of higher learning, one for whites, one for blacks. The following day it repealed the 1874 scholarship act and appropriated only a $1,500 university budget for the fiscal year that had begun on November 1, 1876, thus depriving the faculty of unpaid back salaries. Eventually, in 1878 the state did pay about one-third of the overdue faculty salaries for 1876–1877.[28]

The token appropriation of June 1877 forced the university to suspend operations, which were not resumed until 1880 when it became the segregated South Carolina College of Agriculture and Mechanics, offering a three-year course. The university was restored to its former academic status in 1888. The University of South Carolina, with its Radical staff, black students, and liberal support, by 1876 had become for Conservatives a symbol of all they wished to exterminate. The *Edgefield Advertiser* gloated that the "so-called professors" would not steal another cent from the state and that repeal of the scholarship act had forced "the miserable Negro boys *who were paid $20 a month to attend the institution*" to enjoy the

---

institution "has flourished, and scores of young colored men have graduated with the highest honors."

28. *Senate Journal, South Carolina*, extra session, 1877, p. 25; *Columbia (S.C.) Daily Register*, April 29, 1877; *New York Times*, May 31, 1877; *Acts of South Carolina*, 1877, pp. 256, 270, 314–15; Faculty Minutes, July 31, 1877; Trustees Minutes, July 31, 1877; *Acts of South Carolina*, 1877–78, p. 548.

pleasure "of footing it to their homes, and our beloved and honored university is freed forever from the Radical and the Negro." Many black students, forced to leave the university when it closed, completed their educations at all-black institutions in the South. J. J. Durham, later a physician and Baptist clergyman, was typical. He entered the University of South Carolina in 1874, staying until 1877. He then attended Atlanta University, Fisk University, and Meharry Medical College, graduating from the latter two schools.[29]

The closing of the University of South Carolina in June 1877 concluded the most successful phase of school integration in the entire South during Reconstruction. This integration is especially significant because it occurred in the state having the greatest proportion of blacks and, although deeply resented by most whites, it occasioned no riots or violence of any kind. In its brief existence as an integrated institution, the university did produce a surprisingly large number of black graduates who became a credit to their state, race, and alma mater. With its system of state-financed scholarships for needy but potentially able students, South Carolina was years ahead of its time. Proponents of the integrated university had no regrets. As one of the Radical faculty members later remarked, "We did what we thought to be our duty, and if we had our duty of '74 to do over again, we may not be able, with our then experience, to do any better."[30] Nevertheless, after the return of the state to Conservative control, it would have taken a sizable contingent of federal troops to have kept the university open on an integrated basis, a requirement that no national administration after 1877, whether Republican or Democratic, would have been willing to meet for many generations.

29. Hollis, *College to University*, p. 81; ibid., p. 83, citing *Edgefield* (S.C.) *Advertiser*, May 31, 1877; Tindall, *South Carolina Negroes*, p. 204.
30. *Columbia* (S.C.) *State*, May 8, 1911.

6. Congress & Integration

DURING the 1870s congressional Radicals led by Charles Sumner were interested in securing federal support for school integration throughout the nation and especially in the South. Although Southern Radicals had not been particularly successful in securing mixed school clauses in new state constitutions, certain Republicans in Washington attempted to do this when three former Confederate states applied for readmission to the Union. In 1870 the mixed school faction in Congress wished to incorporate guarantees for integrated schools in acts to readmit Virginia, Mississippi, and Texas. Much of their interest and concern resulted from the 1869 political campaign in Virginia where the mixed school question had emerged as a crucial issue. This campaign, which followed the constitutional convention, saw Conservative candidate Gilbert Walker assuring voters that if he and his party were victorious and the voters also approved the new constitution, its controversial provisions would never be enforced in a manner that was detrimental to whites. This was apparently understood as a pledge to block creation of mixed schools, for in July 1869 Walker was elected governor, the Conservatives won a large majority in the assembly, and voters ratified the constitution by a sizable margin.[1]

In January 1870 in Washington, D.C., a convention of loyal Republican citizens of Virginia petitioned Congress to intervene in the Old Dominion to secure establishment of mixed schools. The joint congressional committee on Reconstruction, then considering a bill to readmit Virginia, incorporated a provision that would in essence have required racial integration in public schools. According to Congressman E. Rockwood Hoar, this proposal raised a serious constitutional question because it imposed a "condition subsequent upon admission" on Virginia which implied a union of unequal states. Hoar declared that "it will clearly not be in the power of Congress to impose any requirements of additional qualifications upon them differing from those which . . . may be required in all the states." Even Radical stalwart John A. Bingham of Ohio attacked the constitutionality of the committee's proposal and moved an amendment to delete the controversial clause. This passed the House by a three-vote margin on January 14, 1870.[2]

The Senate, however, with Henry Wilson and Sumner, both of Massachusetts, leading the way, was determined to secure a mixed school requirement for Virginia. Ignoring Bingham's constitutional scruples, Wilson proposed an amendment declaring that the Virginia constitution should never be amended to deprive any class of citizens of their school rights and privileges. The Senate passed the bill with Wilson's amendment, 47–10, and on January 24 the House concurred by a large margin and the bill became law. Temperance leader Neal Dow of Portland, Maine, commended Sumner for his work in defeating the unconstitutional admission of Virginia, an action that Dow viewed as a "complement of the military defeat of the Rebellion." The condition-subsequent provision did not affect Virginia's schools, for in July 1870 the legislature passed an education law which contained a segregation clause. None of the Radicals in Congress including Sumner attempted to challenge the law.[3] A similar conditions-subsequent clause aimed at preventing racial segregation in public schools was added to the bill readmitting Mississippi in February 1870 and to the Texas bill the following month.[4]

Two years later in January 1872, Legrand W. Perce, a former New Yorker and Union Army colonel and now representing Missis-

1. *Congressional Globe*, 41st Cong., 2d sess., pp. 402, 543; Alfred H. Kelly, "The Congressional Controversy over School Segregation, 1867–1875," *American Historical Review* 64 (1959): 540–41; Hamilton J. Eckenrode, *The Political History of Virginia during Reconstruction* (Baltimore: Johns Hopkins Press, 1904), pp. 120–25; William T. Alderson, Jr., "The Freedmen's Bureau and Negro Education in Virginia," *North Carolina Historical Review* 29 (1952): 85.

2. *Congressional Globe*, 41st Cong., 2d sess., pp. 362, 390, 404, 440–41, 493–95, 502.

3. Ibid., pp. 643–44; Neal Dow to Charles Sumner, January 30, 1870; John W. Waltz to Charles Sumner, January 26, 1870; John M. Thayer to Charles Sumner, January 17, 1870, in Sumner Papers, Houghton Library, Harvard University; William T. Alderson, "The Influence of Military Rule and the Freedmen's Bureau on Reconstruction in Virginia, 1865–1870" (Ph.D. diss., Vanderbilt University, 1952), pp. 273–74.

4. *Congressional Globe*, 41st Cong., 2d sess., pp. 1173–84, 1253–61, 1365–66, 1969–71, 2271–72.

sippi, introduced a bill that would have created a national education fund out of proceeds from public land sales invested in 5 percent government bonds. The money was to be distributed annually among states and territories for educational purposes if they provided free education for all children between the ages of six and sixteen. Although the Perce bill contained no specific reference to mixed schools, certain congressional Democrats viewed it as the first step in compulsory school integration. Congressman John B. Storm of Pennsylvania called the bill a "Trojan Horse": "In its interior are concealed the lurking foe—mixed schools." Storm declared that if the Perce bill passed, within a year Congress would amend it to require that all states receiving money from the fund educate both races together. Democrat John T. Bird of New Jersey told the House that if Southern states complied with this hidden feature of the bill they would be accepting social equality, "the beginning of a degradation which awaits all who yield to miscegenation." Austin Blair, Republican of Michigan, pointed out that the bill did not provide for mixed schools but merely for free education of all children between six and sixteen years of age; the question of mixed or separate schools was left to the states.[5]

After John T. Harris, Conservative from Virginia, indicated his opposition to the Perce bill because of its mixed school implications and tendency to centralize the Government, William D. "Pig of Iron" Kelley of Pennsylvania facetiously retorted that if Congress forced mixed schools upon Virginia and other states the results would be temporary, "for all men know that the sun and atmosphere of the Southern States soon bleach the blackest African, both in hair and complexion, to the colors characteristic of purest Saxon lineage." On the following day, February 7, Southern congressmen decided to force settlement of the mixed school question before the Perce bill came to a final vote. Democrat Frank W. Hereford of West Virginia proposed an amendment providing that no money belonging to any state or territory under the act be withheld for reason of separate school laws or refusal to establish mixed schools. After a voice vote in which the Hereford amendment passed by two votes, George F. Hoar of Massachusetts, a strong supporter of mixed

5. Ibid., 42d Cong., 2d sess., pp. 535, 566, 569, 792, 854.

schools, called for yeas and nays. The tally now registered 115 yeas, 81 nays, with forty-three not voting.

Many leading House Radicals including John Bingham of Ohio, Ben Butler of Massachusetts, and William D. Kelley of Pennsylvania voted nay on the Hereford amendment. Virtually all those who refused to vote, thus assuring passage of the amendment, were Republicans. The House passed the Perce bill with the Hereford amendment on February 8 by a vote of 117–98. Nothing more was heard of it, for it later died in the Senate education and labor committee. The following March, Hereford asked for a suspension of House rules to vote on a proposal declaring it unconstitutional and tyrannical for Congress to force mixed schools on the states and "equally unconstitutional and tyrannical" for Congress to pass any law interfering with churches, public carriers, or similar subjects. Hereford's proposed gag rule failed, 61–85, with ninety-three not voting. The balance of power lay with a large group of Republicans, who, although unwilling to vote for mixed schools by defeating Hereford's amendment to the Perce bill, were also reluctant to go on record supporting segregation.[6]

Hereford's gag rule, although clearly aimed at preventing introduction of measures similar to the Perce bill, was also related to a growing controversy in the Senate where, in 1870, Charles Sumner of Massachusetts had introduced a civil rights bill with an explosive school desegregation clause. Sumner's struggle produced the first nationwide debate over federally enforced public school integration and created such a furor that Congress eventually deleted the mixed school clause.[7]

Sumner had been a champion of mixed schools for twenty years before introducing his civil rights bill. As early as 1849 in the celebrated Roberts case he condemned school segregation in Massa-

6. Ibid., pp. 855–56, 858, 902–3, 1582; Kelly, "Congressional Controversy," p. 544; Herbert C. Roberts, "The Sentiment of Congress toward the Education of Negroes from 1860–1890" (M.A. thesis, Fisk University, 1933), p. 133.

7. See also L. E. Murphy, "The Civil Rights Law of 1875," *Journal of Negro History* 12 (1927): 110–27; Kelly, "Congressional Controversy," pp. 537–63; James M. McPherson, "Abolitionists and the Civil Rights Act of 1875," *Journal of American History* 52 (1965): 493–510; William P. Vaughn, "Separate and Unequal: The Civil Rights Act of 1875 and Defeat of the School Integration Clause," *Southwestern Social Science Quarterly* 48 (1967): 146–54.

chusetts as contrary to the spirit of the Declaration of Independence and the Massachusetts constitution of 1780. In March 1867 he attempted to amend the second Reconstruction bill with a provision that would have required all states coming under the act to establish "public schools open to all without distinction of race or color." Although this was rejected by a 20–20 vote, Sumner tried a similar tactic five months later with an amendment to the third Reconstruction bill which would have forced legislatures of the former Confederate states to establish and maintain a system of public schools "open to all, without distinction of race and color." This proposal had little support and was defeated by a two-to-one margin.[8]

In his advocacy of mixed schools, Sumner could depend on a hard core of senatorial support which included Henry Wilson of Massachusetts, Theodore Frelinghuysen of New Jersey, Richard Yates of Illinois, Samuel Pomeroy of Kansas, George Edmunds of Vermont, John Sherman of Ohio, and Levi P. Morton of Indiana. In the House of Representatives, George Hoar, E. Rockwood Hoar and Benjamin Butler of Massachusetts were loyal to the cause. However, Sumner had great difficulty gaining substantial support for civil rights and school integration proposals from most Republicans in Congress. He received such support only "when it happened to coincide with the momentary, tactical or strategic interests of the Republican party." This situation occurred during the congressional fight over Southern amnesty in 1872 and during Republican maneuverings involved in passage of their post–1874 election program. Except for a few idealists, Republican Radicals used the mixed school question as a political stalking horse.[9]

Sumner's civil rights bill, introduced in May 1870, was the first major attempt on the national level to end public school segregation, an unpleasant and controversial subject which several states had ignored in their civil rights legislation and which Congress had avoided in the civil rights act of 1866. As late as 1874, when the debate over Sumner's bill was at its peak, only three Northern states —Massachusetts, New York, and Kansas—had passed civil rights

8. Charles Sumner, *Charles Sumner: His Complete Works* (Boston: Lee and Shepard, 1900), 3: 51–100; *Congressional Globe*, 40th Cong., 1st sess., pp. 165–70, 580–81; Kelly, "Congressional Controversy," p. 539.

9. Kelly, "Congressional Controversy," pp. 539–40.

laws. Both Kansas and New York had included public schools in the nondiscriminatory clauses of their acts. In the South the Reconstruction governments of Mississippi, South Carolina, Louisiana, Alabama, Arkansas, and Florida had enacted various forms of civil rights legislation which generally forbade discrimination in common carriers, inns, hotels, restaurants, and saloons. Arkansas's Act of 1873 alluded to discrimination in education by directing that similar and equal educational advantages be provided for both races, although it did not specifically prohibit segregation of facilities. Among Southern states, only Florida had a civil rights act (1873) which, on paper, attempted to deal with the school problem in a forthright manner. It declared that no citizen for reasons of race or previous condition of servitude should be excluded from full enjoyment of any facility or privilege by teachers, superintendents, trustees, or any other public school officials. By 1874 most of these acts were dead letters because of the failure of state courts to enforce them. As indicated, Louisiana and South Carolina both had forceful education laws which required integration of public schools and universities, a situation that created great controversy and bitterness in both states by 1874.[10]

One of the early pieces of federal Reconstruction legislation was the first civil rights act, passed on April 9, 1866. This measure, considered ineffective by the early 1870s, bestowed citizenship upon blacks and granted equal rights to all citizens except Indians, including "full and equal benefit of all laws and proceedings for the security of person and property." Although the 1866 statute never referred to mixed schools, some congressmen raised questions concerning this problem during debates over the measure and expressed fears that the bill would be used to integrate public schools. These solons were assured that the bill's sponsors had never contemplated mixed schools. Four years later Charles Sumner attempted to correct this omission when he introduced a new and comprehensive supplementary civil rights bill to the Senate on May 13, 1870, hoping it

10. Gilbert T. Stephenson, *Race Distinctions in American Law* (New York: D. Appleton, 1910), pp. 112–14, citing *New York Statutes*, vol. 50, sec. 9, pp. 583–84, and *Laws of Kansas*, 1874, chapt. 49, sec. 1; Francis E. Bonar, "The Civil Rights Act of 1875" (M.A. thesis, Ohio State University, 1940), pp. 5–11; *Acts of Arkansas*, 1873, pp. 17–18; *Laws of Florida*, 1873, No. 13, chapt. 1947, p. 25.

would be the "crowning work" of Reconstruction. It proposed equal rights on railroad cars, steamboats, public conveyances, hotels, licensed theaters, places of public entertainment, church institutions, cemetery associations incorporated by national and state authority, and "common schools and institutions authorized by law."[11]

Sumner's introduction and sponsorship of the civil rights bill produced hundreds of letters across the nation. Much of this correspondence dealt with the school integration clause. State superintendent Thomas W. Conway of Louisiana wrote Sumner two weeks after introduction of the bill and predicted that if it did not pass, "We shall be in agony here for years. Better strike out every relic of the old barbarism at once." A black from Philadelphia said that because of the civil rights bill, Sumner would be honored and revered "as long as this Republic lasts." The president of the board of trustees for black schools in Washington, Henry Johnson, promised to arouse the blacks of Georgetown and Washington to the importance of promoting Sumner's bill. Although most of the letters extant in the Sumner papers are praiseworthy, a handful condemned the senator for his course of action. A semi-illiterate Georgia pastor damned Sumner for introducing a social equality bill, which none but "the very worst of the Negroes" desired. Feminist leader Susan B. Anthony commended him for his civil rights efforts but wondered when he would add the word sex to color "in your every demand for justice and constitutional protection."[12]

Sumner, in replying to the school board president at Jefferson, Texas, wrote that there would be no lasting peace in the United States

11. U.S., *Statutes at Large*, vol. 14, p. 27; *Congressional Globe*, 39th Cong., 1st sess., pp. 1117, 1294–95; McPherson, "Abolitionists and the Civil Rights Act of 1875," p. 500; *Congressional Globe*, 41st Cong., 2d sess., p. 3434; David Donald, *Charles Sumner and the Rights of Man* (New York: Alfred A. Knopf, 1970), p. 531. Donald points out that under Sumner's bill, the only way a black deprived of his civil rights could secure redress was by bringing suit in the federal courts, a cumbersome and expensive process. Donald also indicates, however, that the lack of a national police force and general fears of an extensive federal bureaucracy really left Sumner no other option (when drawing up his bill) than to rely upon such a weak enforcement mechanism.

12. Thomas W. Conway to Charles Sumner, May 30, 1870, in Sumner Papers; "A Negro" to Charles Sumner, May 14, 1870, in ibid.; Henry M. Johnson to Charles Sumner, December 15, 1871, in ibid.; J. N. Glenn to Charles Sumner, June 11, 1870, in ibid.; Susan B. Anthony to Charles Sumner, February 19, 1872, in ibid.

until equality before the law was completely established—in the schoolhouse as well as in the courthouse. He declared, "You cannot give the colored child any equivalent for equality." In one of his most memorable Senate speeches defending the civil rights bill and school integration clause, Sumner asserted that separate-but-equal facilities were insufficient. To the black child, an integrated school was a necessity. The public school must be "a school for all"—black and white. "It is a theatre where children resort for enduring recreation. . . . it must be open to all."[13]

During 1870–1871 Sumner, unable to overcome apathy and overt hostility, failed to get the Senate to consider his civil rights bill. At the beginning of the second session of the Forty-second Congress, he attached his bill as a rider to an amnesty bill pardoning former Confederates disqualified from holding office under the Fourteenth Amendment. Sumner hoped that a general desire to pass the amnesty bill would carry his unpopular measure to victory. Former abolitionist William Lloyd Garrison warned Sumner that it would be a great disgrace if the civil rights bill should eventually be defeated and the amnesty bill passed. Sumner's proposal now became popular with Republican Radicals who despised amnesty as a nefarious means of reviving the Democratic or Conservative party in the South by removing the disabilities of the Fourteenth Amendment. They favored the civil rights amendment as a means of making amnesty distasteful to conservative Republicans and Democrats alike and thus preventing the two-thirds vote necessary for passage. At the same time the civil rights rider could be used as a sop to pacify black leaders demanding a federal mixed school law.[14]

After several weeks of heated debate in January and February 1872, Sumner's rider passed the Senate on February 9, with Vice President Schuyler Colfax casting the deciding vote. Virtually all Radicals voted for it, and their strategy proved successful, for adoption of the rider doomed the entire amnesty bill which was killed a few minutes later by failing to receive the necessary two-thirds

13. Charles Sumner to George W. Walker in Charles Sumner, *The Works of Charles Sumner* (Boston: Lee and Shepard, 1883), 14: 310, 393–96; *Congressional Globe*, 42d Cong., 2d sess., pp. 383–84.

14. William Lloyd Garrison to Charles Sumner, January 18, 1872, in Sumner Papers; Kelly, "Congressional Controversy," p. 547.

vote. A few days later the *Atlanta Constitution* predicted that Sumner would continue to bring up his civil rights amendment whenever an amnesty bill came before the Senate, since he wished to retain his position as champion of the black race and at the same time defeat amnesty as a means of injuring President Grant, with whom he had quarreled over the annexation of Santo Domingo.[15]

Although Sumner's dislike of amnesty proposals did not lessen, the attitude of the Republican power structure changed completely in the spring of 1872. Motivation for this shift was the adoption of a strong amnesty plank by the Liberal Republican convention in May. The regular or Grant Republicans were afraid this pro-amnesty stand might win many white Republicans to the liberal side, especially in the Southern states. They now decided to promote amnesty in order to heal the party schism and destroy Horace Greeley's candidacy in the South. Bellwethers of the Grant administration, such as the *New York Times*, began to denounce Sumner's killing of the previous amnesty bill with his civil rights amendment. The result of this strategy was a carefully negotiated bargain in the Senate between the Radical Republican clique, led by Roscoe Conkling of New York, and the Democrats, led by Allen G. Thurman of Ohio. The Democrats agreed to allow voting without further debate on an emasculated civil rights bill that would not contain the jury and school provisions. In return Republicans promised that immediately after the civil rights vote they would call up one of the pending amnesty bills enacted by the House and pass it at once. The black-owned *Washington New National Era*, anticipating the outcome, declared that national opposition to Sumner's civil rights bill indicated that the country was not yet ready for universal amnesty. "Let the two measures be united and fall or flourish together. When the people are ready for equal rights to all men, then it may be ready to restore the late slaveholding rebels, the deadly enemies of equal rights, to their old *status* as American citizens."[16]

The prearranged plot was followed without deviation during a late evening session which Sumner had left briefly, feeling ill. The

15. *Congressional Globe*, 42d Cong., 2d sess., p. 919; *Atlanta Constitution*, February 13, 1872; Donald, *Charles Sumner and the Rights of Man*, pp. 495–97.

16. *New York Times*, May 9–11, 1872; *Congressional Globe*, 42d Cong., 2d sess., pp. 3730–36; *Washington New National Era*, May 16, 1872.

clause relating to schools, churches, cemeteries, and juries was deleted by an amendment of Matthew Carpenter of Wisconsin, and the civil rights bill, as amended, was approved, 28–14, with thirty-two senators absent. This was the last ever heard of this particular measure, for it was never considered by the House. The amnesty bill then passed as previously arranged, 32–2, one of the negative votes being cast by a furious Sumner, who had hastily returned.[17]

A black citizen of Washington, D.C., named Piper declared that removal of the mixed school clause from the civil rights bill made the bill of little use to those whom it was intended to benefit, for the school clause was the most vital principle of the entire measure. Piper said that the Senate's action humiliated him both as a father and as a Republican, for although his children lived practically next-door to a public school, they could not attend it because it was a white school and they had to walk more than a mile to a black school. William Lloyd Garrison regretted that the Senate had modified Sumner's bill and sensed that it was doomed. He concluded rather bitterly, "What a marked difference in the unanimity of the Senate for amnesty and the division that was shown in the matter of Civil Rights."[18]

Sumner waited seventeen months until December 1873 before reintroducing his bill, which was identical to one the House judiciary committee reported about three weeks later. Both bills contained the school integration clause. The subject of civil rights and especially federally enforced integrated schools caused acrimonious debate in Congress in January 1874. Southern representatives immediately denounced the House bill (H.R. 796) containing the school provision. Alexander H. Stephens asserted that the bill was unconstitutional and that Georgia blacks did not want mixed schools: "All they want is their right and just participation in schools of their own. This they now have in Georgia." Stephens's remarks prompted black citizens of Atlanta to send petitions and telegrams to the House and Senate judiciary committees denying Stephens's assertion that Georgia blacks opposed integrated schools. One group of petitioners declared that integration would not destroy public

17. *Congressional Globe*, 42d Cong., 2d sess., pp. 3735–36, 3738.
18. H. Piper to Charles Sumner, May 23, 1872, in Sumner Papers; William Lloyd Garrison to Charles Sumner, May 27, 1872, in ibid.

schools in the South but would create new schools which would include any children currently excluded.[19]

The Southern press, which hitherto had tended to ignore the far-reaching implications of Sumner's proposal, now devoted much attention to the whole civil rights issue. This press, including some Radical papers, together with Southern public school officials and sympathetic congressmen from all parts of the nation, cried that integration would destroy struggling school systems in the South as white taxpayers refused to support schools and white parents withdrew their children from mixed schools. William H. Ruffner, state superintendent of education in Virginia, noted in his annual report for 1874 that public sentiment in many counties was affected by fear of the bill. Fifteen Virginia counties reported increased opposition to public schools and the superintendent of Hanover County stated that threatened passage of the measure had done more to retard his work and weaken the cause of public education among the taxpayers than any other factor. The superintendent of Franklin County schools warned that should integration be required by federal law, "the white people of this county will, with one voice, say 'away, away with the public school system.' "[20]

The Virginia legislature reflected overwhelming sentiment of white citizens in the state, when in January 1874 it passed five resolutions denouncing the bill. It declared that the measure was a violation of the Fourteenth Amendment; that it was an infringement on the constitutional and legislative powers of the states; that it was sectional in its operation and injurious alike to whites and blacks of the Southern states; that its enforced application in these states would prove destructive of their educational systems and "produce continual irritation between the races, counteract the pacification and development now happily progressing . . . and reopen wounds now almost healed."[21]

The *Richmond Enquirer* bitterly criticized Southerners for accepting without opposition anything Congress wished to do to

19. *Congressional Globe*, 43d Cong., 1st sess., pp. 318, 381; Records of the House and Senate Committees on the Judiciary (unpublished), 43d Cong., 1st sess., January 1874.

20. *Fourth Annual Report of the Superintendent of Public Instruction* [Virginia] *for the Year Ending August 31, 1874*, p. 52.

21. *House Miscellaneous Documents*, 43d Cong., 1st sess., No. 60, pp. 1–2.

them. It found Sumner's bill revolting because it intended to put blacks and whites on the same social level and alarming because it abrogated every right left to the states since adoption of the Fourteenth and Fifteenth amendments. A leading Radical paper in Virginia, the *State Journal,* surprisingly opposed the bill, saying its passage would destroy public schools and it urged blacks to petition Congress at once to desist from any legislation enforcing mixed schools. In so doing, the freedmen would establish a new claim to the respect of whites. The *Atlanta Constitution* feared passage of Sumner's bill would prove destructive to Southern progress and civilization and that the "madmen and fanatics" who were trying to force it on the country knew little of the detriment the bill would work. The *Memphis Appeal* insisted that consideration of Sumner's bill by Congress was simply another instance of renewing the black question in "some of its most detestable aspects" in order to avoid such pressing economic problems as tariff and currency reform. Even an educational journal published at Columbus, Ohio, came out against the school clause, saying that race prejudices were too strong to support such a measure. It advocated separate-but-equal accommodations, instruction, and length of sessions for black children.[22]

Interest in the progress of the civil rights bill was momentarily transferred to its author in the spring of 1874, when Charles Sumner suddenly died of heart disease on March 12. Before he died Sumner extracted a death-bed promise from his close friend, E. Rockwood Hoar, that he would not let the civil rights bill fail. Hoar complied in the House, and Theodore Frelinghuysen of New Jersey continued to promote it in the Senate. Frelinghuysen insisted the school clause be retained since the object of the bill was to destroy racial distinctions rather than to recognize them. However, he tried to calm the opposition by pointing out that adoption of the bill would not preclude existence of two schools in a single district, each attended by a different race, and that blacks and whites in the South would, in most cases, voluntarily arrange for separate schools after the bill became law.[23]

22. *Richmond Enquirer,* January 4, 7, 1874; *Atlanta Constitution,* January 6, 1874; *Memphis Appeal,* January 6, 1874; *National Teacher* 4 (1874): 67–68.
23. *New York Tribune,* March 12, 1874; *Congressional Record,* 43d Cong., 1st sess., p. 3452.

Not all congressional opposition to the school clause came from Southerners. In May 1874 Senator Aaron A. Sargent of California proposed that nothing in the bill should be construed to prohibit any state or school district from establishing separate schools. The Senate defeated Sargent's amendment by five votes. Another western senator, William N. Stewart of Nevada, believed that amnesty for ex-Confederates and black suffrage were more important than civil rights bills. He feared the mixed school provision of Sumner's bill would endanger many public school systems and deprive thousands of children of an education. Stewart declared that if it were not for the 800,000 potential black votes in the nation, not more than five or ten congressmen would have voted for the school clause. One of the bill's most ardent defenders in the Senate was George F. Edmunds of Vermont, often described as the best constitutional lawyer in Congress. Edmunds insisted that the bill merely intended to enforce inherent rights secured to every citizen by the Constitution. He produced statistics illustrating the low percentage of blacks enrolled in Southern schools and declared that if Congress did not act to prevent discrimination in schools, blacks would be denied educational opportunities and racial aristocracy would be restored.[24]

The civil rights bill containing the school clause finally passed the Senate on May 22, 1874, 29–16, with twenty-eight not present. Many voting for the bill did so out of respect for Sumner, viewing it as a memorial to him. The Southern press generally condemned its passage; and the New York Times, still a pro-Grant paper, described the school clause as the most vital part of Sumner's bill but, fearing destruction of Southern schools, opposed its inclusion. The Times insisted that blacks would benefit more if Congress merely recommended school integration to Southerners "instead of legislating on the education question and creating turmoil and chaos where something like steady progress has been, after many years of striving with prejudices, at last secured."[25]

In some Southern states a fear that Sumner's bill might become

24. Congressional Record, 43d Cong., 1st sess., pp. 4167–69, 4173; Robert J. Harris, The Quest for Equality (Baton Rouge: Louisiana State University Press, 1960), pp. 39, 49.
25. Congressional Record, 43d Cong., 1st sess., pp. 4173–76; New York Times, May 23, May 29, 1874.

law and create havoc in public schools led to long delays in signing contracts for construction of new schoolhouses; superintendents declined to hire new teachers and school officials resigned in anticipation of impending trouble. Georgia's state superintendent of education, Gustavus J. Orr, believed that congressional debates over the civil rights bill had hurt schools in his state, especially regarding forthcoming legislative appropriations. Orr declared that if the bill became law and were enforced, it would kill Georgia's public schools. David F. Boyd of Louisiana State University wrote that the mere reference of civil rights had almost destroyed public schools and colleges in some states, "or they starved 8 years, as we have done, with the Civil Rights Law actually in existence. In Louisiana, the *Negro* has been 'on top' since 1868–or earlier." John M. Fleming, state superintendent of schools in Tennessee, voiced similar sentiments, while state superintendent Alexander McIver of North Carolina asserted that federally enforced school integration was unconstitutional and exclusively within the jurisdiction of state legislation.[26]

Not everyone living in the South during the spring of 1874 believed that the mixed school clause of Sumner's bill would kill public schools. Methodist Bishop Gilbert Haven of Georgia, a former Massachusetts abolitionist preacher, declared it was fallacious that Southern schools would be ruined "if this law should prevail. . . . But perhaps they had better be ruined than perpetually to train little children and youth to abhor each other who had no natural antipathies." One notable exception to the opposition emanating from the South was a resolution prepared by the predominantly black General Assembly of South Carolina and sent to the House of Representatives. It called for passage of the bill with the mixed school clause, stating that attendance in public schools came under the principle that every right or occupation dependent upon our public laws should be for the benefit of all.[27]

26. Edgar W. Knight, *Public School Education in North Carolina* (Boston: Houghton Mifflin, 1916), p. 255; *Proceedings of the Board of Trustees of the Peabody Education Fund* (Cambridge: by the Trustees, 1875), 1: 420, hereafter cited as *Proceedings, Board of Trustees*; David F. Boyd Diary, 1874, vol. 1, October 3, 1874, in Boyd Collection, Department of Archives and Manuscripts of Louisiana State University.

27. McPherson, "Abolitionists and the Civil Rights Act," p. 505; *House*

Politics once again intervened in the civil rights imbroglio following the congressional elections of November 1874. Economic depression, charges of political corruption, and reconstruction problems in the South helped bring about a disaster for the Republicans, who lost their majority in the House of Representatives. Over half of the Republican incumbents failed to achieve reelection and were lame ducks for the second session of the Forty-third Congress. President Grant indicated his belief that popular opposition to the social equality features of the civil rights bill, especially in the Southern and border states, was partially responsible for the Republican debacle. Journalist Charles Nordhoff declared that the small white farmers of Alabama's northern counties who had voted Republican in previous years went over en masse to the Democrats in November 1874, being "alarmed at the prospect of Negro equality" in Sumner's bill. Benjamin Butler, chairman of the House judiciary committee, was one of the lame ducks, having been defeated for reelection by less than 1,000 votes. Butler was in an unforgiving mood and had no intention of remaining silent during the forthcoming short session of Congress. He would leave in a blaze of glory, and one way of achieving this might be through promotion of Sumner's civil rights bill.[28]

In the brief time that remained for both houses of Congress to be under Republican control, the Radical wing, led by Butler and Levi P. Morton, developed a new program which they hoped could be enacted before the new Congress convened. This included a variety of subsidy bills for various railroad interests and several bills to strengthen the Radical party in the South. Among the latter was a new enforcement bill giving the president power to suspend the writ of habeas corpus in several Southern states, an army appropriations bill to insure maintenance of troops in the South for two years without securing congressional approval, and passage of

Miscellaneous Documents, 43d Cong., 1st sess., No. 111, pp. 1–2. This assembly, elected in November 1872, was composed of 106 blacks and 51 whites. Radicals held 130 of 157 seats. John S. Reynolds, *Reconstruction in South Carolina, 1865–1877* (Columbia, S.C.: State Co., 1905), p. 226.

28. *New York Tribune,* November 7, 1874; Charles Nordhoff, *Cotton States in the Spring and Summer of 1875* (New York: D. Appleton, 1876), p. 91; Hans Louis Trefousse, *Ben Butler: The South Called Him Beast!* (New York: Twayne Publishers, 1957), pp. 230–31.

Sumner's civil rights bill, now under the guidance of Butler as chairman of the House judiciary committee. Although Radicals argued that Republican success in 1876 depended upon enactment of these bills, many party moderates including James A. Garfield and Speaker of the House James G. Blaine opposed all or part of this program.[29]

The Radical program had little chance of passage without a change in House rules to prevent a Democratic filibuster. Suspension of the rules required a two-thirds vote. For reasons that are clouded in mystery, Butler decided to make the civil rights bill the forerunner of a House battle to change the rules. Thus, the bill suddenly assumed a political significance out of all proportion to its initial place in the Radical spectrum.[30]

On December 16, 1874, Butler reported the bill H.R. 796, with amendments, from the judiciary committee where it had been under consideration since January. It was read and referred back to committee. The fight over the House rules occurred in late January 1875. Out of a most intricate series of maneuvers and manipulations emerged the basic plot. On January 25 one of Butler's lieutenants, John Cessna of Pennsylvania, introduced a motion to forbid all dilatory motions during the remainder of the current session. This proposal failed to muster the necessary two-thirds vote, everyone realizing that Butler's true object was passage of the enforcement and army appropriations bills. Two days later Butler moved to call up the civil rights bill and place it on the House calendar. Technically this was a motion to reconsider the vote whereby the bill had been recommitted to the judiciary committee in January 1874. Passage of this motion required a two-thirds vote, which Democrats tried to prevent by a forty-eight-hour filibuster that included seventy-five votes on dilatory motions. Finally, Butler permitted an adjournment.[31]

Over the weekend, Speaker Blaine called the House rules committee together, and that body proposed a permanent rules change whereby dilatory motions during debate would be virtually pro-

29. Kelly, "Congressional Controversy," pp. 556–57.
30. Ibid., p. 557. The Benjamin F. Butler Papers at the Library of Congress are virtually silent on anything pertaining to the civil rights act of 1875.
31. *Congressional Record*, 43d Cong., 2d sess., pp. 116, 700, 785.

hibited. In return there could be no cloture on the first day of debate without a three-fourths majority vote. Garfield proposed this on the floor of the House, but the House adopted it only after a bitter forty-six hour continuous session. Garfield's proposal was amended to permit cloture on the first day of debate by a two-thirds vote.[32] This made passage of the civil rights bill possible, but precluded enactment of the remainder of the Radical program because there was insufficient time for consideration of other measures.

Removal of most major obstacles to passage of Sumner's bill permitted Butler to call it up for debate. On February 3, 1875, he declared that as instructed by the judiciary committee he would 1) agree to substitute the provision of the Senate bill for H.R. 796; 2) allow Congressman Alexander White to make an amendment; and 3) "then yield to a motion to amend the bill by striking out all relating to schools. I do this in order that all shades of republican [sic] opinion may be voted upon." White, a Radical from Alabama and the only Southerner on the House judiciary committee, then introduced his amendment to the Senate version of the bill. This differed from Sumner's original bill in that the cemetery provision was missing and it contained a new provision for separate-but-equal public accommodations and school facilities.[33]

More important in terms of the final outcome was Stephen W. Kellogg's brief amendment which proposed to delete the following clause from H.R. 796: "and also all common schools and public institutions of learning or benevolence supported in whole or in part by general taxation."[34] If passed, this amendment would com-

32. Ibid., pp. 901–2. Two members of the rules committee, Samuel Cox, Republican of New York, and Samuel J. Randall, Democrat of Pennsylvania, were so angry at the change in House rules they resigned from the committee. See also Richard S. West, *Lincoln's Scapegoat General: A Life of Benjamin Butler, 1818–1893* (Boston: Houghton Mifflin, 1965), p. 358; Kelly, "Congressional Controversy," pp. 559–60.

33. *Congressional Record*, 43d Cong., 2d sess., pp. 938–39.

34. Ibid. Kellogg was a Republican from Connecticut who had served in the House since the 41st Congress (1869) but was defeated for reelection in 1874 and thus had less than a month in office at the time he introduced this amendment. Although not a member of the Committee on the Judiciary, he was obviously on good terms with Chairman Butler who introduced him for the purpose of offering the crucial amendment. "Biographical Directory of the American Congress, 1774–1961," *House Documents*, 85th Cong., 2d sess., No. 442, pp. 1150–51.

pletely eliminate any reference to schools in the civil rights bill. The heated discussion that occurred over this did not take place immediately, for various other proposals were placed before the House ranging from the Senate's bill including schools and cemeteries to the White amendment which allowed separate facilities, providing they were equal in all respects. However, it was now obvious that Butler had decided to omit the school clause.

Advocates of mixed schools including William Lloyd Garrison comprehended the significance of the White and Kellogg amendments. Sensing that elimination of the school clause was imminent, Garrison wrote to C. T. Garland of the *Chicago Inter-Ocean*, on February 1, 1875, two days before the proposals were presented, that he would rather see the bill defeated than adopted without the mixed school clause. Garrison denied the constitutional right of that body or any state legislature to recognize racial distinctions.[35]

Introduction of the Kellogg amendment rekindled the flames of controversy in the House of Representatives over the school clause in the bill and the problem of integrated schools in general. John Lynch, black Radical and former slave from Mississippi, declared that passage of the bill with the school provision would not break up public school systems in the South; in fact, he believed that this was the most harmless portion of the bill. Lynch thought that if Congress passed and enforced the school clause, mixed schools would result only in those areas of the South where one race was in a small minority. In his opinion such a provision was necessary to nullify the separate school requirements of some Southern laws and constitutions. Richard Cain, a black representative from South Carolina, thought that blacks would lose nothing if the school proviso were cut out but stated that the party "could afford, for the sake of peace in the Republican ranks, if for nothing else—not as a matter of principle—to accept the school clause." Milton Southard of Ohio did not believe school integration was within the scope of federal authority, for he considered schools to be a state and local prerogative.[36]

Kellogg defended his amendment by saying that it was made in the interest of education, especially the education of black chil-

35. As quoted in the *Washington Chronicle*, February 5, 1875.
36. *Congressional Record*, 43d Cong., 2d sess., pp. 945, 951, 996.

dren in the Southern states. He believed that the civil rights bill proposed to make a distinction of race in the area of education, and he did not wish to see this happen. He emphasized that if Congress passed the bill with the school clause, "You will destroy the work of the last ten years and leave them [the schools] to the mercy of the unfriendly legislation of the states where the party opposed to this bill is in power." Barbour Lewis of Tennessee favored Kellogg's amendment because laws cannot always control public opinion. He referred to Mississippi, which possessed a mixed school law but had virtually no mixed schools because the people had, of their own choice and without legislation, maintained separate schools simply as a matter of taste. A political independent from New Jersey, William W. Phelps, told his colleagues that if they enacted the school clause they would shut the door of every public school in the South: "Let one more autumn come, and there will not be a state in the South whose legislature shall vote one single dollar for their creation and support."[37]

Speeches against Kellogg's proposal were in the minority. Charles Williams of Wisconsin argued that mixed schools would help develop a tolerant spirit between races whereas segregated facilities would encourage hatred and prejudice among children. Kansas Republican William A. Phillips believed that if Congress adopted the Kellogg amendment, no provisions for black education would be made in districts containing a small black population. Benjamin Butler said that he favored equal privileges for both races in schools, but that he also believed the prejudice against mixed schools was so great in the South that their weak public school systems would be broken up if the school clause were incorporated into the bill. He concluded that he would rather have the entire section relating to schools struck out than see Congress approve his judiciary committee's provision for mixed schools.[38]

Butler's pronouncement was an indication of how the power structure in the Republican party, including President Grant, regarded this controversial matter. House Republicans reflected this attitude in their voting on the Kellogg amendment, February 4, 1875. The House accepted the amendment, 128–48. The civil rights

37. Ibid., pp. 997–1002.
38. Ibid., pp. 999–1006.

bill, as amended and therefore without the school clause, passed on the same day by a vote of 162–99. All affirmative votes were Republican; not a Democrat voted for it. Fourteen Republicans voted against the bill, twelve of them from the South.[39]

Most leading Southern newspapers seemed relieved that the school proviso was omitted from the bill but did not comment extensively. The *Charleston News and Courier* said that since mixing in the schools was not to be compulsory, it saw no reason why whites and blacks with a little tact and forbearance on each side could not live harmoniously and prosperously under the protection of a just system of laws which gave the same public rights and privileges to all citizens. The *Atlanta Constitution* was pleased at deletion of the school provision from the bill but described other sections as "all that the most revolutionary white villain or the densest negro brain could desire." It believed the bill meant malicious persecutions, unnumbered troubles, and even civil war in the South. The *Times* in New Orleans pointed out that the bill, "shorn of its obnoxious features with reference to the public schools," was less radical than the Louisiana law which contained a strong mixed school provision.[40]

In North Carolina two Radical members of the lower house of the state legislature were so upset over House passage of the bill, even without the school clause, that they resigned from their party, one declaring that he was aligning himself with "the great party that is now building up in the South and North for the preservation of constitutional government and the purity and salvation of the Anglo-Saxon race of our great land."[41]

The Senate soon approved the House bill without a struggle. Republicans generally felt that to amend the measure was to lose it, and senators who had previously favored mixed schools and declared them to be the foundation of racial equality now remained silent when the bill came up for a vote on February 27. Among the most prominent of these was George Boutwell of Massachusetts,

39. Ibid., pp. 1010–11. There were 194 Republicans and 92 Democrats in the House in the 43d Congress.

40. *Charleston News and Courier*, February 8, 1875; *Atlanta Constitution*, February 6, 1875; *New Orleans Times*, February 6, 1875.

41. *Wilmington* (N.C.) *Journal*, February 9, 1875.

who a week earlier had argued against removal of the vital school clause. The bill passed the Senate, 38–26. President Grant quickly signed the measure and it became law on March 1, 1875. The *Chicago Inter-Ocean* viewed this event as a great advance but considered absurd the situation whereby "the child of the black man, who in the halls of Congress, perchance, vanquished his white brother in the tilt of argument and eloquence, may not attend the same school with the child of the conquered white Congressman."[42]

Many Southern newspapers looked upon the new law as a conglomeration of empty legal phrases which would never be enforced. The *Charleston News and Courier* was pleased that the law did not contain the school and cemetery provisions and stated that it was innocuous. The *Atlanta Constitution* echoed these sentiments, referring to the law as "a bill as full of false promises to the negro as it is of imaginary terrors to the white." Another Georgia paper reminded its readers that the law in final form was not the measure desired by Sumner; Congress had wiped out the most objectionable features, the school and cemetery clauses.[43]

The Northern press generally concurred with its Southern counterpart, the *New York Tribune* declaring that it attached far less importance to the law than the amount of noise made over it would seem to warrant, for Congress had omitted the most objectionable feature—that of enforcing mixed schools. It believed that the section prohibiting discrimination in theaters or restaurants was poor statesmanship and would not amount to much; the clause securing equal rights to blacks on railroad cars and steamboats was more practical. The act, however, was likely to prove more irritating to both races than either beneficial to one or injurious to the other. The *Nation* declared the law to be harmless, noticing that its passage seemed to have little effect on Southern public opinion. It believed that the chief objection to the new statute was its unconstitutionality. Benjamin Butler, in temporary political retirement, perhaps revealed his true feelings about the civil rights act when he wrote that it gave "the colored man every right I have, no more no

42. *New York Tribune*, March 1, 1875; *Congressional Record*, 43d Cong., 2d sess., 1870; *Chicago Inter-Ocean*, March 1, 1875.

43. *Charleston News and Courier*, March 2, 1875; *Atlanta Constitution*, March 2, 1875; *Augusta* (Ga.) *Constitutionalist*, March 3, 1875.

less, but it gives to the colored man one privilege which I have not, and that is to bring suit in the United States court when his rights are infringed in this regard. . . . I don't see what cause any colored man has to complain of it."[44]

What many whites feared to be the greatest threat to Southern public schools since their reorganization had failed to materialize. Under the highly political motivation of forcing a rules change to prevent a Democratic filibuster and thus ensure passage of their new program, Republicans of the Forty-third Congress agreed to delete the school provision from the civil rights law, and federal prohibition of segregated schools was postponed for seventy-nine years until the Supreme Court decision of 1954. Perhaps if Congress had included the school clause in the law, it would have affected, at least for a time, the meager appropriations provided by Southern state and local governments for maintaining schools. The course of time and the Supreme Court's decision of 1883 made the law a dead letter,[45] but this could not be foreseen by Reconstruction-weary superintendents, teachers, and advocates of public education. Nevertheless, failure to provide federally enforced school integration in the 1870s made acceptance of this social, cultural, and legal necessity a far more difficult task ninety years later.

But Congress was not the only force outside the South to perpetuate school segregation. Unknown to many Americans, a highly respected philanthropic agency was actually fighting integration and promoting separate schools for blacks throughout the Reconstruction period.

44. *New York Tribune*, March 2, 1875; *Nation* 20 (March 4, 1875): 141; Benjamin F. Butler to C. H. Mercier, May 12, 1875, in Benjamin F. Butler Papers, Library of Congress.

45. The unconstitutionality of the 1875 civil rights law was affirmed by the United States Supreme Court in 1883 when the court rendered a decision in five cases involving the civil rights of blacks in hotels, railroad cars, and theaters. Justice Joseph P. Bradley, delivering the opinion of the court, stated that the first and second sections (the second section made it a penal offense to deny any citizen any of the accommodations or privileges mentioned in the first section) of the law were unconstitutional because they were not authorized by the Thirteenth Amendment, for separation of races in public places was not a symbol of servitude. Nor was the civil rights law authorized by the Fourteenth Amendment, which referred to action by states, whereas the law applied to individual discrimination. *Civil Rights Cases*, 109 U.S. (1883), pp. 3–25.

7. The Peabody Fund & Integration

IN THE DECADE following the Civil War, Southern school systems received vital financial assistance from a fund established in 1867 by the Northern philanthropist George Peabody.[1] The fund, as administered by the well-known educator and former college president Barnas Sears, was eventually distributed on a segregated basis, with no monies going to integrated schools. Although bitterly criticized by some Southern Radicals for promoting segregation and blocking integration, Sears and the Peabody Fund trustees insisted that they had to work within the realities of the Southern social system in order to secure the improvement and educational advancement of as many children as possible, albeit with segregation.

Peabody was a banker and financier who had been born in Danvers, Massachusetts, in 1795 but made his fortune in England as a merchant and money broker. His philanthropic endeavors began in 1852 when he gave $10,000 to the United States exhibit at the world's fair in London and a similar amount to the Grinnell Arctic expedition. By 1867 he had donated $4,480,000 to projects as varied as housing for the poor in London and the museum of Archaeology and Ethnology at Harvard. Washington College at Lexington, Virginia, was the recipient of a $60,000 gift in 1867. In that year Peabody bequeathed $1 million for public school education in the South, the investment income to be used and applied "for the promotion and encouragement of intellectual, moral or industrial education among the young of the more destitute portions of the South and South Western States of our Union." He declared that this fund should benefit the entire population, "without other distinction than their needs and the opportunities of usefulness to them."[2]

A short time later Peabody increased his original donation with $1.5 million worth of Mississippi bonds, which were soon, however, repudiated by the state. In July 1869 he donated an additional

$1 million for the promotion of Southern education and also gave $384,000 worth of Florida state bonds, which later proved to be valueless. If one subtracts the worthless bonds from the total contributions, the fund equaled $2 million and not the oft-quoted $3 million. Since only the investment income from the fund could be used for educational purposes, donations by Peabody trustees to public schools from 1868 to 1880 never exceeded $143,125 for a given year, and that figure was reached in 1874. In February 1867 Peabody selected fifteen prominent Americans to serve as a board to administer the fund. They included politicians and statesmen such as Robert C. Winthrop of Massachusetts and Hamilton Fish of New York, as well as General Ulysses S. Grant and Admiral David G. Farragut. Also appointed were five Southerners: William C. Rives of Virginia, William Aiken of South Carolina, George W. Riggs of Washington, D.C., Edward A. Bradford of Louisiana, and George N. Eaton of Maryland. Peabody picked Winthrop, a former Whig congressman and senator, as chairman.[3]

At their first meeting the trustees learned that as the immediate goal of the fund, Peabody favored promotion of elementary education for the greatest possible number of Southern children. The philanthropist was quite adamant on this point and until his death in 1869 continued to insist on encouragement of primary education rather than providing college educations for gentlemen's sons. The board resolved to promote "Primary or Common School Education by such means or agencies as now exist or may need to be created." It agreed to appoint a general agent to supervise administration of

1. Hoy Taylor, *An Interpretation of the Early Administration of the Peabody Education Fund* (Nashville: George Peabody College for Teachers, 1933), p. 4; Jessie P. Rice, *J. L. M. Curry, Southerner, Statesman and Educator* (New York: King's Crown Press, 1949), p. 94; William P. Vaughn, "Partners in Segregation: Barnas Sears and the Peabody Fund," *Civil War History* 10 (1964): 260–74. For an interpretation that attempts to absolve Sears of being a racist on the grounds that he permitted temporary discrimination in order to achieve long-range justice, see Earle H. West, "The Peabody Fund and Negro Education, 1867–1880," *History of Education Quarterly* 6 (Summer 1966): 3–21.

2. Taylor, *Peabody Fund*, p. 6; *Proceedings of the Board of Trustees of the Peabody Education Fund* (Cambridge, Mass.: printed by order of the trustees, 1875), 1: 3.

3. Taylor, *Peabody Fund*, pp. 6, 88, 12; Charles W. Dabney, *Universal Education in the South* (Chapel Hill: University of North Carolina Press, 1936), 1: 104.

the fund. Peabody later informed the trustees that they had absolute discretion where the money was to be spent. He hoped that sooner or later all states suffering from the war might receive some aid.[4]

The trustees selected as their general agent Barnas Sears, a man who probably did more to make the Peabody Fund an influential factor in Southern education than any other person connected with its administration. Sears had been active in the field of education for many years. Born and raised in rural Massachusetts, he was educated at Brown University, Newton Theological Seminary, and in Germany. He served as a Baptist minister in Hartford, Connecticut, taught at Madison University, and then became professor of theology at Newton Seminary, of which he later became president. From 1848 to 1855 Sears acted as secretary and executive agent of the Massachusetts Board of Education, succeeding Horace Mann. In 1855 he was called to the presidency of Brown University. He was serving in this capacity when Winthrop asked him to draw up a policy statement for administration of the fund. His suggestions so impressed the trustees that they invited him to become general agent.[5]

Sears's outline to the board of trustees contained two possible courses of action: establishment and operation of a system of Peabody Schools not connected with any existing system, or disbursement of funds to struggling but established schools. He asserted that the first plan was far too complicated because it would require a great amount of supervision and direction from the trustees. There would also be the problem of collecting official reports as well as complications arising from trustee ownership of buildings and lots, a situation that might cause local communities to become jealous or indifferent. Sears believed that it would be much simpler and wiser to strengthen and revive existing facilities. "Let good schools," he implored, "springing up on the soil, growing out of the wants of the people, and meeting those wants, be sprinkled all over

4. Barnas Sears to Robert Winthrop, July 21, 1869, in Jabez L. M. Curry Papers, microfilm, Library of Congress; *Proceedings, Board of Trustees*, 1: 16, 21–22.

5. *Dictionary of American Biography* 16: 537–38; Jabez L. M. Curry, *A Brief Sketch of the Peabody Fund through Thirty Years* (Cambridge: [Harvard] University Press, 1898), p. 68.

the South, as examples and be made the *nuclei* for others, and let them be established and controlled, as far as possible, by the people themselves, and they will in time grow into state systems." The general agent also recommended creation of normal schools, scholarships to potential teachers who would be required to teach for designated periods of time, encouragement of teachers' associations by financing speakers, and financial assistance to education periodicals.[6]

In his work, much of which consisted of touring the South, Sears claimed to exercise great caution and avoid controversy. He later wrote to Winthrop in 1872 that "politics I eschew altogether. I neither vote, nor discuss political questions, even privately." During the autumn of 1867 he made his first long trip into the South, visiting parts of Virginia, Tennessee, Georgia, and North Carolina, where he inspected conditions and talked with teachers, school officials, and ordinary citizens. After returning to his headquarters at Staunton, Virginia, he recommended to the trustees at their January 1868 meeting certain limitations on fund expenditures. He wanted to confine financial aid, as much as possible, to a relatively small number of urban public schools which might serve as models of progress for their rural counterparts. Sears also urged the use, whenever feasible, of state education systems as agencies to handle the Peabody appropriations. The board of trustees adopted these suggestions as general policy.[7]

During the first three years of the board's operation, Sears had

6. Barnas Sears to Robert Winthrop, March 14, 1867, in Curry Papers. Most of these suggestions were eventually adopted. The fund aided a number of normal schools and eventually established one of its own in Nashville, Tennessee, in September 1875. Taylor, *Peabody Fund*, p. 137. The cause of popular education in Georgia was furthered in 1875–1876 by a lecture trip throughout the state made by state superintendent Gustavus J. Orr. He gave forty-four addresses, and his expenses were paid by the Peabody Fund except for transportation, which was furnished by the railroads of Georgia. *Report of the Commissioner of Education . . . for the Year 1875–1876* (Washington: Government Printing Office, 1876), p. xxxiv. The *Arkansas Journal of Education*, established in 1871, was subsidized by the Peabody Fund, and in 1873 it became the official publication of the state board of education. Thomas S. Staples, *Reconstruction in Arkansas, 1862–1874* (New York: Columbia University, 1923), p. 326.

7. Barnas Sears to Robert Winthrop, September 6, 1872, in Curry Papers; *Proceedings, Board of Trustees*, 1: 56–57.

trouble finding enough schools to qualify for assistance. Then, from 1871 to 1874, supply and demand tended to balance each other. After 1874, however, the general agent was able to approve only 50 percent or less of the applications. As the number of schools pleading for assistance increased, Sears tried to follow a policy, except in Louisiana, of aiding those which he considered had a good chance of winning public support.[8] To qualify for aid a school had to meet certain requirements: it must be a public institution; it must have a term of approximately ten months; and it should have an average minimum attendance of 85 percent. Local citizens were to pay toward current expenses at least twice as much as they received from the fund, and they were to bear all the expense of erecting, repairing, and furnishing schoolhouses. The community had to supply one teacher for each fifty pupils and assign the pupils to grades.

Sears decided that enrollment would determine the annual subsidies. If the applying institution met the qualifications and had no fewer than 100 pupils, it received $300; 100–150 pupils, $450; 150–200 pupils, $600; 200–250 pupils, $800; and 300 pupils or more, $1,000. From the beginning there was discrimination in payments to black schools, a policy that Sears believed was justified by the lower fiscal needs of black schools. In September 1869 Sears wrote to Winthrop that he was inclined to adopt a scale for blacks that was one-third less than the scale for whites because it costs less to maintain schools for black children. He admitted that "some will find fault with our making any *distinction* between the two races." Evidently Winthrop and the other trustees approved of this scheme, for the official proceedings of 1870–1871 presented the scale of payments to white schools with the notation: "At present, we pay for colored schools two-thirds of the rates above named."[9]

Sears's plan of appropriations based upon enrollments of schools, with the local community contributing at least one-half of the expenses, enabled the trustees to help educate a large number of children at a low per capita rate, less than $1.50 per pupil on the basis of a $1,000 contribution to a school with 700 students.[10] The

8. Rice, *J. L. M. Curry*, p. 94.
9. *Proceedings, Board of Trustees*, 1: 236; Barnas Sears to Robert Winthrop, September 21, 1869, in Curry Papers.
10. Barnas Sears to Robert Winthrop, February 8, 1868, in Curry Papers.

general agent was always willing to grant aid to communities that needed it and were disposed to abide by regulations; he never withdrew money from towns that had qualified for aid until they could sustain their own schools. His entire theory of assistance, however, was a trickle-down approach. The Peabody Fund assisted only larger towns and cities that were able to meet the requirements; however, country schools were often the ones that most desperately needed direct aid but could not afford to meet Sears's standards. In the realm of Southern rural education, therefore, the effectiveness of the Peabody Fund is questionable.

Sears's activities at Yorkville, South Carolina, offer an example of how he introduced the fund to a specific community. He arrived there in March 1868 and immediately called a meeting of city officials and other leading citizens interested in education. Sears then submitted a proposal by which the fund would give Yorkville two-fifths of the money necessary to open free schools for all children of the town, the remainder to be raised by local citizens. The town council would supervise expenditure of the money and maintenance of the schools. The schools for black children were to be separate, and "everything controlled as the council deem best."[11]

During this early period of his work Barnas Sears had notices printed in numerous Southern newspapers stating the purpose of the Peabody Fund and the requirements a community must meet in order to receive assistance. These notices declared it to be the aim of the fund to encourage and aid public schools in the South, but these facilities must be established, supported, and supervised by the local people. Schools languishing because of inadequate support would receive financial assistance in moderate amounts. Places where there were no schools would also receive aid, provided citizens would inaugurate schools and undertake their support. Sears warned, however, that such aid was to be regarded as temporary. The fund would select schools on a basis of need and number of pupils to be benefited. Normal schools were to receive particular attention, especially a small number that would furnish the "most perfect models of instruction," but there would be no assistance for literary or professional schools. Sears emphasized that only

11. *Charleston Courier*, March 14, 1868, citing the *Yorkville (S.C.) Enquirer*, March 10, 1868.

in rare instances would he himself hire teachers and would "aid such in obtaining places only by giving their names to school committees."[12]

The Southern press tended to ignore the work of the Peabody trustees and Barnas Sears.[13] Available materials do not indicate whether this situation resulted from a lack of interest in the Peabody Fund, a paucity of information about it, or hostility toward Northern charity.[14] Most Southern papers of any consequence paid great attention to the death of Peabody in November 1869, and in listing his many accomplishments and philanthropies they noted he had donated large sums of money to Southern education. But they ignored or were unaware of the fund's operations and Sears's work. In contrast, the *New York Times* in a long eulogy about Peabody made direct reference to monies "placed in the hands of trustees of the highest character . . . to be applied to assist schools and to promote the education of the people, without distinction of race or color, in the Southern States."[15] As events proved, this last statement concerning racial non-discrimination was false.

Sears did not intend that the Peabody Fund should become involved in the crosscurrents of political and social strife that swept through the South during Reconstruction. However, the general agent unconditionally opposed mixed schools. Whenever he offered aid to a town it was understood that blacks would have separate facilities. He created a scale of payments to black schools that was one-third less than that for white schools. Many of his critics did not hesitate to declare that Sears had acquired a Southern prejudice against blacks, and one unnamed gentleman referred to him as one of the most prominent "doughfaces in the whole Southern region." The Peabody Fund did assist numerous black schools, but only according to Sears's reduced scale of payments. Many of these schools

12. *Charleston Courier*, June 7, 1867.
13. For a discussion of this, see the *Baltimore Gazette*, July 7, 1869; Barnas Sears to Robert Winthrop, July 15, 1869, in Curry Papers.
14. *Atlanta Constitution*, November 20, 1869; *Charleston Courier*, May 17, 1870.
15. *New Orleans Picayune*, November 5, 1869; *Galveston Daily News*, November 6, 1869; *Memphis Appeal*, November 6, 1869; *Wilmington* (N.C.) *Journal*, November 14, 1869; *Atlanta Constitution*, November 10, 1869; *Augusta Constitutionalist*, November 9, 1869; *New York Times*, November 5, 1869.

were still under supervision of the Freedmen's Bureau with teachers supplied by various benevolent societies. Ralza M. Manly, bureau superintendent of education in Virginia, reported that in July 1869 Sears had sent him $4,000 to aid needy black schools and supplement what the freedmen were doing for themselves. But six months later Sears refused school aid to the bureau superintendent in Texas because his schools were not state-supported.[16]

Sears made his official position and that of the trustees quite clear when he declared in 1869 that the board assumed no control over admission policies of schools assisted by the fund. The situation that forced the trustees and Sears to adopt a policy regarding racially integrated schools was the attempt to establish mixed schools in South Carolina and Louisiana after 1868. In a letter to the *New Orleans Republican,* Sears explained his policy and that of the board concerning mixed schools. He believed it was not the place of the board to pronounce judgment on integration. "Let the people themselves settle that question." If the government ventured upon an experiment which worked badly, "we cannot help it. We leave the responsibility where it belongs. We must go our own way, and do our duty." The general agent asserted that the trustees should only encourage education and not meddle in politics. If separate schools were provided for both races and both were pleased with the arrangement, the trustees would have no compunctions in cooperating with the state authorities. If the law required mixed schools and both races attended them, "we shall have no difficulty in our work. But if the State supports only mixed schools, and the white children do not attend them, we should naturally aid, not the colored children who enjoy exclusively, the benefit of public school money, but *the white children* who are left to grow up in ignorance."[17]

Privately, Sears referred to mixed schools as a curse because Southern whites would neither support nor attend integrated facilities. On several occasions he wrote to Winthrop about the difficulty mixed schools were causing in South Carolina and Louisiana. In 1868 the board officially took a position that, because of the furor over integration and desertion of the school by white pupils, the public schools of Louisiana no longer served white citizens. Sears

16. Curry, *Peabody Fund,* p. 60; "Synopsis of School Reports," 2: 35, 205.
17. Curry, *Peabody Fund,* p. 61.

directed Robert M. Lusher, former state superintendent of education, to make arrangements for the distribution of $17,000 for the sole benefit of white children. The board gave money to larger towns, excluding New Orleans, on a basis of $5.00 per pupil, and Lusher voluntarily acted as the fund's special agent in Louisiana until 1877. By 1871 the fund was aiding twenty-eight Louisiana communities, selected according to "importance, influence, and ability to share expenses." With the aid of Peabody money seven institutions in rural Louisiana established free teacher-training departments, and the fund supported them entirely from 1868 to 1884. Donations from the fund to selected schools enabled them to extend their terms from six to nine months.[18]

Lusher, as Peabody agent for Louisiana, proved to be a staunch segregationist. Attempting to spite Conway and the state board of education, he removed a portrait of Peabody and some books from a New Orleans normal school after Conway had integrated the public schools. This school eventually closed, and in 1870 Lusher helped organize a new normal school supported entirely by Peabody money. In his autobiography Lusher later recalled his work as Peabody agent, helping to provide ten months a year of thorough education for "9000 white children, who were at the same time protected from moral contamination, and redeemed from the sway of ignorance."[19]

Louisiana's superintendent of education, Thomas W. Conway, was naturally incensed that Sears refused to appropriate any money to schools under his jurisdiction and instead rendered assistance to all-white schools that were in reality private institutions. In 1869 Conway remarked that as disbursement of Peabody monies had not yet been entrusted to the state officers of Louisiana, he was unable to determine what benefits had been received, or by whom. He concluded that it would contribute to the efficiency of his educational work if the Louisiana board of education distributed the fund. By

18. Barnas Sears to Robert Winthrop, June 14, September 18, 1870, in Curry Papers; *Proceedings, Board of Trustees*, 1: 91, 262; Howard Turner, "Robert M. Lusher, Louisiana Educator" (Ph.D. diss., Louisiana State University, 1944), p. 171.

19. Robert M. Lusher, Autobiography Ms of May 31, 1889, pp. 17, 19–31, in Robert M. Lusher Papers, Department of Archives and Manuscripts of Louisiana State University.

1870 Conway was less moderate when describing the work of the Peabody trustees. He complained of occasionally encountering an exclusively white school of "complex character" sustained by the Peabody Fund, tuition fees, and organized local groups. In Conway's opinion local authorities embarrassed state officials by granting use of public buildings to the Peabody schools, as had happened at Baton Rouge.[20]

De Bow's Review, arch-champion of the antebellum way of life, commended the efforts of Peabody and his "excellent selection of agents to carry out his trusts." The editor, William M. Burwell, remarked that he had read with much interest a letter from Sears to Lusher in which Sears revealed that the trustees had decided to cooperate as much as possible with the state public school systems, and there would be no difficulty in doing this if the two races were taught in separate facilities. Sears had pointed out that there were no mixed schools in Florida, South Carolina, or any other state and that he could not "suppose that Louisiana would venture on so bold an experiment."[21] Obviously the general agent was extending a gentle hint to Louisiana officials to segregate their schools or expect no Peabody largesse.

In October 1870 Conway presented Sears with a resolution which declared that the Louisiana board of education "would seem to be the proper medium for the care and disbursement of the portion of the said endowment to which the State is entitled." The superintendent insisted that Sears should remove the uncooperative Lusher and change his agency to the state board. Conway accused the Peabody trustees of trying to create a school system in opposition to that of the state and declared that certain teachers, aided by Lusher, were doing their utmost to destroy public schools, in some cases even issuing circulars urging citizens to oppose mixed schools. Conway declared that Lusher had placed the Peabody trustees in the false position of establishing a "caste system of education." Conway further accused Sears and Lusher of exciting widespread

20. Louisiana State Board of Education, Proceedings and Minutes, April 30, 1869; *Annual Report of the State Superintendent of Education . . . to the General Assembly of Louisiana, 1869* (New Orleans: n.p., 1870), pp. 20–21; *Report of the Commissioner of Education for the Year 1870–71*, pp. 193–94.

21. Cited in *De Bow's Review* 40 (October 1869): 909.

opposition to public schools, of unharmonious conduct toward school officers and of neglecting the educational interests of Louisiana blacks. "We think," he said, "the fund for this State can be used by the State board of education to far better advantage than if it remains in the hands of Mr. Lusher." Conway promised that if state authorities took over the fund it would be distributed to both races without exciting the jealousy or opposition of either one.[22]

Sears tersely replied that under ordinary circumstances he would be most happy to cooperate with the state authorities, but because Louisiana's schools were integrated, most whites were unwilling to patronize them and consequently public money went chiefly to black schools. If this situation could be remedied, the Peabody trustees would no longer need to maintain a representative in Louisiana. "We ourselves," Sears said, "raise no questions about mixed schools. We simply take the fact that the white children do not generally attend them, without passing any judgment on the propriety or impropriety of their course. We wish to promote universal education to aid whole communities, if possible. If that cannot be, on account of peculiar circumstances, we must give preference to those whose education is neglected. It is well known that we are helping the white children in Louisiana, as being the more destitute, from the fact of their unwillingness to attend mixed schools. We should give the preference to colored children, were they in like circumstances."[23]

This exchange only succeeded in angering Conway even more. The irate superintendent commented upon Sears's letter in his annual report for 1870. He doubted that the unwillingness of white children to avail themselves of public schools constituted any destitution in the true sense and insisted that the number of whites enrolled in public schools was three times that of black children. He accused the Peabody Fund of pandering to those who refused their offspring an education unless it was "in harmony with the spirit of caste." The creation of the Peabody schools for white children, according to Conway, enabled opponents of public schools to deny educational facilities to blacks without injury to white pupils.[24]

22. *Report of the Commissioner of Education for the Year 1870–71*, p. 198.
23. Barnas Sears to Thomas W. Conway, November 8, 1869, in ibid., pp. 198–99.
24. *Annual Report, Louisiana*, 1870, pp. 42–43.

Conway's complaints against the work of Lusher and the Peabody Fund continued until the end of his term in 1872. His 1871 report declared that the board had used the fund to oppress the poor and strengthen the "heel of caste, that it [may] more effectually crush those it would make its victims." The direct effect of Sears's misguided policy was to keep alive segregationist prejudices which otherwise would be entirely removed. One of Conway's subordinates, R. K. Diossy, claimed that in one Peabody school the principal was a notorious drunkard, while in others "favourites are pensioned upon the fund."[25] The editor of the *New Orleans Picayune* severely criticized Peabody money placed under his control. He accused the state superintendent of possessing a "lust of power and private avarice," of being dissatisfied with his almost "unprecedented powers" and salary of $7,000 a year, and of being unable to "view without coveting the paltry patronage confided to another."[26]

Although Conway retired from office in 1872, the victory of William G. Brown over Robert M. Lusher in the hotly disputed election of that year continued and increased the enmity between the state board of education and the Peabody agent for Louisiana. In October 1873 Brown wrote to Lusher demanding from the Peabody fund in Louisiana a report giving such information as the number of teachers employed, their salaries, and the number of scholars enrolled. Lusher angrily replied that if it could be proved that Brown were the legally elected head of the schools, he would consider giving him the desired information. "As long, however," he added, "as you remain a beneficiary of the *prima facie* fraud and actual usurpation by which the liberties of the people of Louisiana have been sacrificed. . . , no self-respecting citizen of the State can deem it an honor to appear in your 'annual report' as an auxiliary in the compilation of educational statistics."[27]

The Peabody Fund continued to aid white schools in Louisiana until the Conservatives returned to power and Lusher once again became state superintendent. Until 1877 Radicals kept up their demands for transfer of Peabody monies from Lusher to the state board of education. The *New Orleans Republican* declared that,

25. Ibid., pp. 37–38, 188.
26. *New Orleans Picayune*, May 21, 1872.
27. *Annual Report, Louisiana*, 1873, pp. 31–32.

if still alive, George Peabody would be distressed to see how Sears had misused the fund by failing to aid black pupils. It accused Sears of subletting his authority "to those who are notoriously hostile to universal education." The following day the Conservative *Bulletin* printed a stirring defense of Sears, the Peabody trustees, and Lusher, describing the *Republican*'s editorial as a thoughtless, senseless attack on those who are "beyond the reach of Radical malice"—an attack based upon "ignorance, most certainly dictated by jealousy and malice" that was unworthy of Lusher's notice.[28]

Barnas Sears proved implacable in his refusal to aid integrated school systems, steadfastly maintaining that mixed schools failed to receive support from a majority of white Southerners and therefore was detrimental to the entire future of public education in the section. When South Carolina integrated its state university in 1873–1874, he cut assistance to that state from $1,000 to $2,000.[29]

In 1874 Sears actively involved himself in the controversy over Sumner's civil rights bill, then pending in Congress, which contained the school integration clause. Sears declared that he could not remain a passive spectator while men in power were unwittingly urging a measure which would undo all the good accomplished by the Peabody Fund. As he later explained to the trustees: "I felt constrained to go twice before the committee and leading members of Congress and utter a voice of earnest warning against a futile attempt to enforce mixed schools, and to show, as best I might, what would be the necessary operation of such a law—a law that would prove a nullity if not followed by another requiring each state to maintain public schools of a given character, and still another requiring the attendance of white children."[30]

Available records and manuscripts reveal only one such trip made by Sears to Washington. This occurred in January 1874 during the House's early debate on its version of Sumner's bill, presented by Benjamin Butler of Massachusetts. Sears first visited friends of

28. Robert M. Lusher Diary, September 14–15, 1875, in Lusher Papers; *New Orleans Republican*, September 14, 1875; *New Orleans Bulletin*, September 15, 1875.

29. Taylor, *Peabody Fund*, p. 88.

30. *Proceedings, Board of Trustees*, 1: 405. The records of neither the House nor the Senate judiciary committees, 43d Cong., 1st sess., indicate Sears's presence before those bodies.

the measure—Butler, Hoar, Dawes, and others—and convinced them that, if the school proviso were left intact, it would lead to destruction of Southern public schools and leave blacks and poor whites bereft of education. Congress would then be responsible for forcing popular ignorance upon the South in order to uphold a vague abstraction. According to Sears's own statement to Winthrop, everyone admitted the weight of his argument. Butler himself said the bill should be recommitted and that he was willing to make a reasonable compromise. In the next phase of his campaign, Sears called upon several leading senators—"not Sumner nor his trained Negroes," but Oliver P. Morton of Indiana, William A. Buckingham of Connecticut, and others who would work against the objectionable clause or aid in defeating the entire bill. Finally, he visited President Grant at the White House, where he also talked with Butler and learned that Grant shared his negative views on integrated schools. Sears told the president and Butler that blacks themselves thought it best to have separate schools and that a delegation of black preachers and a black lawyer had strongly expressed these opinions to him while on a visit to Memphis. He also declared that the bill ignored Southern white sensitivities, for Southerners cared much more about preserving separate schools than segregated public accommodations. According to Sears, if Congress passed the bill with the mixed school clause it would destroy the entire work of the Peabody Fund during the past six years "and leave us without a promising field of action by taking away public schools and leaving nothing in their places."[31]

The House voted on January 7, 1874, to recommit the bill to the judiciary committee, from which it did not emerge until December, following Sumner's death. In the interim Sears took his fight against the school clause to the people. One of a number of speeches he made that year was to a Baptist meeting in New Orleans. Passage of the civil rights bill in its present form, he argued, would destroy the free school system in the South where many of the best workers in the cause of education would resign their positions in despair. Sears's old enemy, Thomas W. Conway, answered these charges in a letter to the *New Orleans Republican*. The former superintendent declared that although he had the highest regard for Sears, he

31. Barnas Sears to Robert Winthrop, January 8, 1874, in Curry Papers.

thought him greatly mistaken regarding the consequences of the civil rights bill. He believed that Sears had arrived at false conclusions about mixed schools because his acquaintance in the South "is known to be confined chiefly to those who in war times were known as rebels." Sears had made several visits to Louisiana while Conway was state superintendent, and the latter knew that "his [Sears] advisers there were chiefly of the class who hate the equality of the Negro in any shape."[32]

In a short essay printed anonymously in the education column of the *Atlantic Monthly*, Sears sought to arouse citizens of all sections against the mixed school clause. "Southern charity will be dried up if the negro is made the instrument of breaking up the existing systems of public instruction," he asserted, while Northern contributions to black education had been dwindling for some time. The black, said Sears, possessed neither sufficient funds nor intelligence to carry on the work of education, and nothing but public schools maintained by the Southern states could meet their needs. If there were a difference between educational advantages offered to blacks and those given to whites, it was only in certain localities and was both accidental and temporary. Sears believed that if Congress preserved the present plan of separate schools, the education of the "whole colored population at the expense of others" was secure. "But let them [the schools] be disturbed by any unhappy excitement, and the disaffected will seize upon the opportunity to *abolish* the public schools and to return to their favorite plan of private schools."[33]

Sears reiterated much of what he had written for the *Atlantic Monthly* in his report to the Peabody trustees in October 1874. He stated that seven years' personal contact with all classes of men in the South and "an opportunity which few have enjoyed of knowing the opinions and feelings of the people in regard to schools," had led him to the unalterable conviction that any authoritative interference in that region would be disastrous "for that class of citizens in whose behalf such measures have been proposed." In his opinion the mixed school clause of Sumner's bill would prove a calamity to Southern blacks, who in most cases would be left completely without schools.

32. As cited in *Washington New National Era*, June 4, 1874.
33. [Barnas Sears], "Education," *Atlantic Monthly* 34 (1874): 381–82.

Like many twentieth-century segregationists, the general agent declared that legal statutes proved that blacks had the same educational advantages as whites. Sears warned that no distinction would be made in administering these laws. The state governments must in the end apply the laws equally. Sarcastically referring to the mixed school clause of the civil rights bill as a "grand provision for the education of the whole colored population, chiefly at the expense of others," Sears warned again that if any strife disturbed the school systems certain whites who opposed public schools in principle would take the opportunity to abolish them all and return to a system of private academies, with black children being "left to grow up as brutes."[34]

The Peabody trustees gave overwhelming approval to Sears's actions in opposing mixed schools in Louisiana and fighting for removal of the school clause from the civil rights bill. A report adopted unanimously by the board sustained Sears and declared that compulsory legislation by Congress in favor of mixed schools would be pernicious to many communities and that blacks would suffer the greater share of this "disastrous influence."[35]

Southerners, aware of Sears's actions to remove the school clause, clearly appreciated his efforts. Virginia's superintendent of public instruction, William H. Ruffner, publicly thanked Sears for his effective aid during the past year, "in spreading before the members of Congress and the country generally the ruinous consequences which would follow the passage of the Civil Rights Bill."[36]

By the end of Reconstruction the Peabody trustees believed that they had won the battle in behalf of popular acceptance of public education in the South and began to devote more attention to training teachers. Private schools first received aid for developing teacher education programs; then the fund assisted states in establishing normal schools. The states were slow to act, and Sears conceived the idea of a central normal college to serve the entire South. The outgrowth of this idea was George Peabody College for Teachers, established in Nashville in 1875.[37] Until its dissolution in 1914 the

34. *Proceedings, Board of Trustees,* 1: 405.
35. Ibid., pp. 437–39.
36. *Fourth Annual Report of the Superintendent of Public Instruction, for the Year ending August 31, 1874* [Virginia] (Richmond: n.p., 1874), p. 130.

fund worked toward general development of Southern education, with particular emphasis on improving the training of elementary and secondary teachers.

Barnas Sears continued to serve as general agent of the Peabody Fund until his death in 1880. Overshadowed by his successor, Jabez L. M. Curry, he is today a relatively forgotten figure. Yet his significance would be hard to exaggerate. A Northern educator of experience and prestige, he lent his own considerable energies and the resources of the Peabody Fund to supporting a policy of racial segregation in Southern schools. Had the Peabody Fund financed integrated schools exclusively, however, its efforts would have aided only a few schools in Louisiana, mainly in New Orleans, and would have left the great majority of Southern school children, white and black, totally without the benefits of Peabody support. It is unrealistic to have expected Sears and the Peabody trustees to have worked actively for integration, a situation evidently contemplated by Conway in Louisiana. By the time that appropriations from the fund had reached their peak in 1874, all but three Southern states (Louisiana, South Carolina, and Florida) had returned to Conservative control, and any attempts by Sears to have fostered integration in the states under Conservative domination would have been blocked immediately. Sears quite clearly believed that in order to benefit as many children as possible, he must work within the *modus operandi*.

Nevertheless, Sears's refusal to give any money to the integrated public schools of Louisiana and his drastic curtailment of South Carolina's funds after integration of the university is less defensible. Sears could have distributed some funds to the integrated public schools of Louisiana as well as to the all-white Peabody schools. His policy in Louisiana meant that black children in that state received no Peabody benefits whatsoever. Sears's successful stand against the school clause of Sumner's civil rights bill, although undoubtedly motivated by a sincere belief that federally enforced school integration in the South would mean an exodus of virtually all white children from the public schools, indicates his lack of interest in working for the genuine betterment of blacks.

------

37. Taylor, *Peabody Fund*, pp. 159–61.

His actions of 1874 give credence to the Radical charge that Southern Conservatives had brainwashed Sears into believing that segregated schools must be preserved at all costs.

The struggle for black education in the South during Reconstruction produced many achievements. Black schools, either illegal or severely circumscribed before 1860, became viable institutions. Whereas less than 10 percent of the black population was literate by 1860, within a decade that figure had increased to over 25 percent as a result of massive efforts by the Freedmen's Bureau and private benevolent associations. Southern blacks confounded their most severe critics and proved to be highly educable, at times to a degree embarrassing to local whites. Blacks trained in bureau-association schools provided most of the dedicated teachers for black schools when the majority of Yankee instructors returned home after 1870. The closing of the bureau schools did not mean an abrupt cessation to black education in the South; there was, instead, a relatively smooth period of transition in which most of the bureau schools were absorbed into the public school systems of each Southern state. The reorganization and general improvement of these systems for the education of both races on a tuition-free basis undoubtedly proved to be the most outstanding and durable achievement of the Radical state governments between 1868 and 1877. By the latter year the Southern public school systems were far stronger than their antebellum counterparts.

Public education of Southern blacks on an integrated basis was less successful. The temporary integration of one-third of the public schools of New Orleans and the University of South Carolina failed to achieve lasting results. The Radical governments, which had supported and encouraged school mixing, collapsed after removal of federal troops in 1877, and integrated institutions were either quickly segregated or closed. Failure to include a mixed school clause in the Civil Rights Act of 1875 meant that blacks did not even have the recourse of applying to the federal courts to delay the segregation process.

Two significant developments did emerge from the early efforts of education reformers. The initial impetus given black education by Northern benevolent groups was later reflected in the philanthropic assistance furnished by the Peabody Fund, the John F. Slater Fund, and other philanthropies, whose administrators worked diligently to upgrade black education, albeit on a segregated basis. Second, although the idealism of the political Reconstructionists fell short of their immediate goals in the realm of public education, precedents were established for integrated schools, and the constitutional revisions achieved by national leaders through the Fourteenth and Fifteenth amendments laid the groundwork for subsequent successful assaults on segregated education.

Bibliographical Essay

MANUSCRIPT COLLECTIONS

Since the preceding narrative has not concentrated on any individual, there is no single collection of personal papers and letters that is preeminent. The Charles Sumner Papers at the Houghton Library, Harvard University, were helpful in determining reactions of the general public to progressive stages of Sumner's civil rights bill. These papers consist almost entirely of letters to Sumner. Most of the important papers of his authorship were published during or after his lifetime. Neither the Benjamin F. Butler Papers nor the William E. Chandler Papers provide insights or information on the political maneuverings behind the civil rights bill. There are no papers extant of Stephen M. Kellogg, who amended Sumner's bill to remove the school clause. Unfortunately, I was unable to unearth any collected papers of the most fascinating figure of the integration crisis, Thomas W. Conway, although much of his correspondence was printed in the annual reports of the Louisiana state superintendent of education. The Jabez L. M. Curry Papers, on microfilm at the Library of Congress, contain correspondence between Barnas Sears and Robert Winthrop which shed light on Sears's attitudes and policies regarding the Peabody Fund and school integration.

An invaluable source of material on the Freedmen's Bureau, benevolent associations, and Yankee teachers is the vast manuscript collection of the Educational Division, Bureau of Refugees, Freedmen and Abandoned Lands, located at the National Archives. This source contains thousands of letters from teachers to bureau officials and sponsoring societies, letters from Oliver Otis Howard and John W. Alvord, as well as the unprinted "Synopsis of School Reports."

The Department of Archives and Manuscripts of Louisiana State University possesses an abundance of material relating to school problems in Louisiana during Reconstruction. David F. Boyd's diary, found in the Boyd Collection, and Boyd's unpublished essay "Some ideas on Education: The True Solution of the Question of Color in Our Schools, Colleges, and Universities, etc., etc.," provide many insights of LSU's president on the integration question. The Robert M. Lusher Papers includes Lusher's autobiography, written in 1889, which presents typical anti-Radical views against mixed schools. The State Department of Education miscellaneous records, archives, and minutes of the state board of education (on microfilm) give additional information on the integration turmoil in Louisiana.

The struggle for mixed schools in New Orleans was illuminated by the Radical views of Ephraim S. Stoddard's diary in the Howard-Tilton Library, Tulane University. This contains his "Notes on the Mixed School Imbroglio." The William O. Rogers Correspondence and the informative New Orleans School Board Minutes, 1869–1877, both found at the Orleans Parish School Board Office, proved invaluable.

The South Caroliniana Collection of the University of South Carolina provided innumerable materials relating to integration of that institution. Among these were the Faculty Minutes, Trustee's Minutes, Euphradian Society Minutes, University Manuscripts and the Fisk P. Brewer Papers. The Brewer Papers contain a fascinating memoir, "South Carolina University, 1876," written by Brewer, which gives a reasonably objective account of how integration worked at the university.

PRINTED CORRESPONDENCE, DIARIES, MEMOIRS,
& TRAVELERS' ACCOUNTS

Only a few individuals mentioned in this manuscript were prominent enough to have their autobiographies and correspondence published. Oliver Otis Howard's *Autobiography of Oliver Otis Howard*, 2 vols. (New York: Baker and Taylor Co., 1907), Charles Sumner's *The Works of Charles Sumner*, 15 vols. (Boston: Lee and Shepard, 1870–1873), and a reprint of the same papers entitled *Charles Sumner: His Complete Works*, 20 vols. (Boston: Lee and Shepard, 1900), are among this group. Louis R. Wilson, ed., *Selected Papers of Cornelia Phillips Spencer* (Chapel Hill: University of North Carolina Press, 1953), presents informative although ultra-conservative opinions of the University of North Carolina during Reconstruction.

Many experiences of the Yankee teachers who instructed in bureau-association schools were preserved for future generations with contemporary or subsequent publication of their letters, diaries, and memoirs. Among the more enlightening are Mary Ames, *From a New England Woman's Diary in Dixie in 1865* (Springfield, Mass.: Plimpton Press, 1906); Ray A. Billington, ed., "A Social Experiment: The Port Royal Journal of Charlotte L. Forten, 1862–1863," *Journal of Negro History* 35 (1950): 233–64; Sallie Holley, *A Life for Liberty*, ed. John White Chadwick (New York: G. P. Putnam's Sons, 1899); Edward L. Pierce, "The Freedmen at Port Royal," *Atlantic Monthly* 12 (1863): 291–315; Laura M. Towne, *Letters and Diary of Laura M. Towne*, ed. Rupert S. Holland (Cambridge, Mass.: Riverside Press, 1912); Susan Walker, "Journal of Miss Susan Walker," *Quarterly Publication of the Historical and Philosophical Society of Ohio* 7 (1912). The problems of teachers Lucy and Sarah Chase are recounted in a collection of their letters, *Dear Ones at Home: Letters from Contraband Camps*, ed. Henry L. Swint (Nashville: Vanderbilt University Press, 1966). Charles Stearns, *The Black Man of the South and the Rebels* (New York: American News Co., 1872), presents opinions and experiences of a Massachusetts abolitionist who taught freedmen in Georgia and was a firm advocate of federally enforced school integration. Albert T. Morgan, *Yazoo: or, on the Picket Line of Freedom in the South* (Washington: Rufus H. Darby Press, 1884), describes the life of two carpetbaggers from Wisconsin who settled near Yazoo City, Mississippi. There are several brief but perceptive sections relating to freedmen's education and the Morgan brothers' assistance in building a black school.

Yankee journalist Edward King, *The Southern States of North America* (London: Blackie and Son, 1875), and Charles Nordhoff, *The Cotton States in the Spring and Summer of 1875* (New York: D. Appleton, 1876), reported relatively objective accounts of the condition of the former Confederacy by 1875 including pertinent views on the various school crises. A highly subjective report of Reconstruction in South Carolina which includes a devastating picture of the integrated university is *The Prostrate State: South Carolina under Negro Government* (New York: D. Appleton, 1874), by James S. Pike. The bias and racist overtones of this Maine-born journalist are clearly revealed in Robert F. Durden's *James Shepherd Pike: Republicanism and the American Negro, 1850–1882* (Durham, N.C.: Duke University Press, 1957).

FEDERAL DOCUMENTS & PUBLICATIONS

The *Report of the Commissioner of Education* (Washington: Government Printing Office) printed annually after 1867, gives much solid information on the strengths and weaknesses of public school systems in the several states. Largely compiled from reports of state superintendents, this is a particularly helpful reference when those state reports are unavailable. John W. Alvord, superintendent of Freedmen's Bureau Education Division, issued a *Semi-Annual Report on Schools for Freedmen* (Washington: Government Printing Office) from 1866 to 1870. Prepared in January and July, these reports contain invaluable sources of information on the trials and tribulations of bureau-association schools and teachers. Also giving insights into early (1865–1866) problems of the bureau schools is "Reports of the Assistant Commissioners of the Freedmen's Bureau," *Senate Executive Document No. 27*, 39th Cong., 1st sess. The "Report of Carl Schurz on the States of South Carolina, Georgia, Alabama, Mississippi and Louisiana," *Senate Executive Document No. 2*, 39th Cong., 1st sess., is a good source for Southern views on black education. The "Report of the Joint Select Committee Appointed to Inquire into the Condition Affairs in the Late Insurrectionary States . . . ," *House Reports, No. 22*, 42d Cong., 2d sess., commonly known as the "KKK Reports," indicates the prevalence of violence against black schools and Yankee teachers, although the veracity of much of the testimony is doubtful. An even more valuable record of Southern attitudes and reactions to black schooling is found in "Report of the Joint Committee on Reconstruction," *House Reports, No. 30*, pt. 2, 39th Cong., 1st sess.

Perhaps the most-used reference in this manuscript is Benjamin Perley Poore, comp., *The Federal and State Constitutions, Colonial Charters and Other Organic Laws of the United States*, 2 vols. (Washington: Government Printing Office, 1878). This invaluable aid provides a ready reference on school integration clauses or the lack of them in state constitutions to 1878. The standard sources for congressional debates and proceedings, the *Congressional Globe* (to 1873) and *Congressional Record* (after 1873) were used extensively. The "Biographical Directory of the American Congress, 1774–1961," *House Documents*, 85th Cong., 2d sess., No. 442, enables the researcher to locate biographical information on all congressmen serving through 1961, thus eliminating the necessity of checking innumerable editions of the *Congressional Directory*.

STATE DOCUMENTS & PUBLICATIONS

A great many state statutes and codes of the Reconstruction period were consulted for this study and are too numerous to mention individually. A major problem exists in locating state laws of a century ago, and the scholar must usually consult the law library of the appropriate state university or the excellent legal collection of the Library of Congress. Proceedings of certain state constitutional conventions proved helpful in examining proposals and arguments for school integration. Among the more valuable records were the *Journal* of North Carolina's constitutional convention of 1868; the *Proceedings* of South Carolina's 1868 convention; the *Journal, Debates and Proceedings* and *Documents* of Virginia's 1867–1868 convention, and the *Debates and Proceedings* of Arkansas's 1868 constitutional convention. What remains of these records has been reproduced on microfilm by the Library of Congress in the collection known as the Records of the States of the United States. Unfortunately, the only states to preserve the actual debates were Arkansas, North and South Carolina, and Virginia. For the remainder, only the journals survive, providing only the slightest indication of what transpired, especially with reference to mixed schools.

The most important state publications consulted, however, were the reports of Radical superintendents of education in the South for the years 1868–1877. Many of these were published, in whole or in part, in the annual *Report* of the United States Commissioner of Education. Of the various superintendents' reports examined, the most informative and revealing on mixed schools were the *Annual Report of the State Superintendent of Public Education . . . to the General Assembly of Louisiana* (New Orleans: n.p.), 1866–1877, and the *Reports and Resolutions of the General Assembly of South Carolina* (Columbia: J. W. Denny), 1869–1877, the latter incorporating annual reports of the state superintendent of education for the years indicated. The Library of Congress has virtually complete sets of both these reports; LSU does not have a complete set of the Louisiana *Reports* in its Louisiana Collection, although the South Caroliniana Library of the University of South Carolina has a complete set of the *Reports and Resolutions of the General Assembly,* which embody the superintendent's annual report.

CONTEMPORARY PERIODICALS & NEWSPAPERS

Many of the benevolent associations active in freedmen's education from 1865 to 1870 published journals of news and comment which contain many letters from teachers as well as outspoken editorial comments on integration, segregation, and the Southern way of life. It is difficult to locate complete files of these publications although the Library of Congress has a relatively good collection. Among the most helpful journals were the *American Freedman,* published by the AFUC and edited by Lyman Abbott; the *American Missionary,* published by the American Missionary Association; and the *Freedmen's Record,* organ of the New England Freedmen's Aid Society. *De Bow's Review,* new series, is a good source of unredeemed, anti-Radical opinion during Reconstruction with many condemnations of black education and Northern teachers. Among Northern periodicals the *Nation* consistently applauded black schools, integration, and Radical reorganization of public schools while decrying Southern opposition to these objectives. A leading and vocal exponent of remaking Southern schools along New England lines was the National Teachers' Association's (later the NEA) *Journal of Proceedings and Lec-*

tures, especially valuable for the period 1865–1866. An informative although somewhat statistic-laden survey of black education in all states from the colonial period through 1868 may be found in "Legal Status of the Colored Population in Respect to Schools and Education in the Different States," *American Journal of Education* 19 (1870): 301–400.

Files of over forty newspapers, mainly Southern, were examined for the period 1865–1877. These collections are badly scattered and most libraries do not have complete sets; the Library of Congress and especially the library of the University of Texas have the best general collections of Southern papers for the Reconstruction era. The South Caroliniana Library of the University of South Carolina was an excellent source for newspapers published in Columbia and therefore frequent commentators on integration at the local university. Among Southern papers the Conservative point of view was best expressed by the *Atlanta Constitution* and *Augusta Daily Constitutionalist* in Georgia; the *New Orleans Bulletin, Democrat, Times,* and *Picayune* in Louisiana; the *Jackson Clarion* in Mississippi; the *Wilmington Daily Journal* in North Carolina; the *Charleston Courier* (after 1873 the *News and Courier*), *Columbia Daily Phoenix, Weekly Gleaner,* and *Daily Register* in South Carolina; the *Memphis Daily Appeal* and *Nashville Republican* in Tennessee; the *Austin Democratic Statesman* and *Galveston Daily News* in Texas; and the *Richmond Daily Dispatch, Enquirer* (published previously, from 1867 to 1870, under the name *Daily Enquirer and Examiner*), and *Times* in Virginia.

Even reasonably complete files of Southern Radical newspapers (most of them supported by Radical governments through state printing) are almost impossible to find; therefore fragmentary collections of many libraries had to be examined. Three Radical journals were used extensively for favorable comments on black education and school integration: the *Columbia* (S.C.) *Daily Union Herald,* the *New Orleans Republican,* and the black-owned *Washington New National Era.* The latter was a constant and invaluable source of black views and reactions to educational problems throughout the South and nation.

Yankee papers that closely followed educational trends and problems in the former Confederacy include the *Chicago Inter-Ocean* and the *New York Herald, Tribune,* and *Times.* The *Times* was usually a strong supporter of integration, although after 1874 it modified its position on the school clause of Sumner's civil rights bill, thus reflecting changing attitudes of the Grant administration of which the *Times* was a barometer. The *Tribune* gave better coverage of the Reconstruction constitutional conventions than most Southern papers.

A number of pertinent scholarly articles have appeared in this century dealing with educational efforts of the federal government and benevolent associations. Among the more enlightening are William T. Alderson, Jr., "The Freedmen's Bureau and Negro Education in Virginia," *North Carolina Historical Review* 30 (1952): 64–90; John W. Blassingame, "The Union Army as an Educational Institution for Negroes, 1862–1865," *Journal of Negro Education* 34 (1965): 152–59; Ira V. Brown, "Lyman Abbott and Freedmen's Aid, 1865–1869," *Journal of Southern History* 15 (1949): 23–38; Martin Abbott, "The Freedmen's Bureau and Negro Schooling in South Carolina," *South Carolina Historical Magazine* 57 (1956): 65–81; Luther P. Jackson, "The Educational Efforts of the Freedmen's Bureau and the Freedmen's Aid Societies in South Carolina, 1862–72," *Journal of Negro History* 8 (1923): 1–40; Julius H. Parmelee, "Freedmen's Aid Societies, 1861–1871," United States Department of Interior, Bureau of Education, *Bulletin*, No. 38, 1916, pp. 268–301, surveys the associations during a ten-year period. Henry L. Swint imputes strong economic motivation to the Northern-led black education movement in "Northern Interest in the Shoeless Southerner," *Journal of Southern History* 16 (1950): 457–71.

Louis R. Harlan in "Desegregation in New Orleans Public Schools during Reconstruction," *American Historical Review* 67 (1961): 663–75, has thoroughly analyzed integration of New Orleans schools and draws favorable conclusions. Eugene Lowrance, "Color in the New Orleans Schools," *Harper's Weekly* 19 (1875): 147–48, gives contemporary views of a positive nature about New Orleans's mixed schools, while T. Harry Williams in "The Louisiana Unification Movement of 1873," *Journal of Southern History* 11 (1945): 349–69, shows how a political rapproachement between Conservative whites and blacks might have perpetuated mixed schools in Louisiana if unification had succeeded. Black dissatisfaction with schools in Louisiana is given as a major reason for the freedmen's switch to the Democratic ticket in 1876 by Teddy B. Tunnell, Jr., in "The Negro, the Republican Party and the Election of 1876 in Louisiana," *Louisiana History* 7 (1966): 101–16. The efforts of Peabody Fund trustees and general agent Barnas Sears to continue public school segregation and oppose integration in the South are treated by William P. Vaughn in "Partners in Segregation: Barnas Sears and the Peabody Fund," *Civil War History* 10 (1964): 260–74. Earle H. West in "The Peabody Fund and Negro Education, 1867–1880," *History of Education Quarterly* 6 (Summer 1966): 3–21, rationalizes Sears's anti-integration policies by explaining that he permitted temporary discrimination in order to achieve long-range justice. North Carolina public education and the threat of integration is discussed in Daniel J. Whitener's "Public Education in North Carolina during Reconstruction, 1865–76," in *Essays in Southern History Presented to Joseph Gregoire de Roulhac Hamilton, ed. Fletcher M. Green* (Chapel Hill. University of North Carolina Press, 1949), pp. 67–90.

Senator Charles Sumner's efforts to pass a civil rights bill with a school desegregation clause have attracted wide attention from historians. Among the more informative contributions are Alfred H. Kelly, "The Congressional Controversy over School Segregation, 1867–1875," *American Historical Review* 64 (1959): 537–63; James M. McPherson, "Abolitionists and the Civil Rights Act of 1875," *Journal of American History* 52 (1965): 493–510; L. E. Murphy, "The Civil Rights Law of 1875," *Journal of Negro History* 12 (1927): 110–27; and William P. Vaughn, "Separate and Unequal: The Civil Rights Act of 1875 and Defeat of the School Integration Clause," *Southwestern Social Science Quarterly* 48 (1967): 146–54.

MONOGRAPHS

A number of state histories dealing with the Reconstruction era were published in the period 1890–1930, most of them following the school historiography popularized by William A. Dunning which viewed Reconstruction as the rape of the South. Other than as factual references, most of these are of little value to the modern scholar. Typical of these state historians are Ella Lonn, *Reconstruction in Louisiana after 1868* (New York: G. P. Putnam's Sons, 1918); Thomas S. Staples, *Reconstruction in Arkansas, 1862–1874* (New York: Columbia University, 1923); James W. Garner, *Reconstruction in Mississippi* (New York: Macmillan, 1901); Walter L. Fleming, *Civil War and Reconstruction in Alabama* (New York: Columbia University Press, 1905); and John S. Reynolds, *Reconstruction in South Carolina, 1865–1877* (Columbia, S.C.: State Co., 1905). A revisionist work giving a more objective account of Reconstruction in the Palmetto State is Francis B. Simkins and Robert H. Woody, *South Carolina during Reconstruction* (Chapel Hill: University of North Carolina Press, 1932). It is the general area of state Reconstruction studies that offers the most promising opportunity to future scholars.

The growth and development of public school systems in the South has been covered extensively, but these volumes are usually written from the educator's point of view with emphasis on enrollment statistics, curriculum development, and teacher education. Among the more informative general works are Charles W. Dabney, *Universal Education in the South*, 2 vols. (Chapel Hill: University of North Carolina Press, 1936);

Edgar W. Knight, *The Influence of Reconstruction on Education in the South* (New York: Teachers College, Columbia University, 1913). Knight's emphasis on the educational progress made in Southern states during the three-year period before Radical Reconstruction is challenged by Robert E. Potter, *The Stream of American Education* (New York: American Book Co., 1967), pp. 337–38. The more scholarly public school histories include George G. Bush, *History of Education in Florida* (Washington: Government Printing Office, 1889); Cornelius J. Heatwole, *A History of Education in Virginia* (New York: Macmillan, 1916); Edgar W. Knight, *Public School Education in North Carolina* (Boston: Houghton Mifflin, 1916); and Dorothy Orr, *A History of Education in Georgia* (Chapel Hill: University of North Carolina Press, 1950). Thomas H. Harris in *The Story of Public Education in Louisiana* (New Orleans: by author, 1924) includes a prejudiced and highly critical account of integration in Louisiana during Reconstruction, based largely on hearsay evidence.

The most recent general survey of the Freedmen's Bureau is George R. Bentley, *A History of the Freedmen's Bureau* (Philadelphia: University of Pennsylvania Press, 1955), which supplements but does not supersede Paul S. Peirce's earlier work, *The Freedmen's Bureau* (Iowa City: State University of Iowa, 1904). Federal and benevolent association educational activities which preceded the bureau's work are recounted by Willie Lee Rose in *Rehearsal for Reconstruction: The Port Royal Experiment* (Indianapolis: Bobbs Merrill, 1964). The labors of Yankee teachers in behalf of black education with emphasis on the animosity they generated is ably discussed in Henry L. Swint's *The Northern Teacher in the South, 1862–1870* (Nashville: Vanderbilt University Press, 1941). Among the new studies of the bureau on the state level, Martin Abbott's *The Freedmen's Bureau in South Carolina* (Chapel Hill: University of North Carolina, 1967) contains a chapter on education which is highly critical of the New England-oriented curriculum used in most bureau schools. Howard A. White, *The Freedmen's Bureau in Louisiana* (Baton Rouge: Louisiana State University Press, 1970), gives an objective assessment of bureau schools in that state.

Two standard monographs on the educational activities of the Peabody Fund are J. L. M. Curry, *A Brief Sketch of George Peabody, and a History of the Peabody Education Fund through Thirty Years* (Cambridge, Mass.: Harvard University Press, 1898), and Hoy Taylor, *An Interpretation of the Early Administration of the Peabody Education Fund* (Nashville: George Peabody College for Teachers, 1933).

The standard survey of black education before the Civil War is still Carter G. Woodson, *The Education of the Negro prior to 1861* (New York:

G. P. Putnam's Sons, 1915). Racial discrimination against blacks in many areas including public schools is recounted by Gilbert T. Stephenson in *Race Distinctions in American Law* (New York: D. Appleton, 1910). A general study of black education and discrimination is Henry A. Bullock's *A History of Negro Education in the South from 1619 to the Present* (Cambridge: Harvard University Press, 1967). Unfortunately, Bullock's chapters relating to the Reconstruction period are both inaccurate and incomplete, especially concerning integration. An older but more scholarly treatment of black education is Horace M. Bond, *The Education of the Negro in the American Social Order* (New York: Prentice-Hall, 1934). School problems among blacks in our national capital are discussed in *The History of Schools for Negroes in the District of Columbia, 1807–1947* (M.A. thesis, Catholic University of America, 1949) by Lillian G. Dabney. Worthwhile black studies providing background material for educational topics include Vernon Lane Wharton, *The Negro in Mississippi, 1865–1890* (Chapel Hill: University of North Carolina Press, 1947); Alrutheus A. Taylor, *The Negro in Tennessee, 1865–1880* (Washington: Associated Publishers, 1941) and *The Negro in South Carolina during the Reconstruction* (Washington: Association for the Study of Negro Life and History, 1924); and George B. Tindall, *South Carolina Negroes, 1877–1900* (Columbia: University of South Carolina Press, 1952). A monograph dealing with South Carolina blacks during Reconstruction is Joel Williamson, *After Slavery: The Negro in South Carolina during Reconstruction, 1861–1877* (Chapel Hill: University of North Carolina Press, 1965). This work, containing an informative chapter on education, largely replaces Taylor's monograph on the same subject. An inclusive and reasonably accurate survey of black education after the Civil War appears in the chapter entitled "Black Mind, Black Spirit," in Robert Cruden's *The Negro in Reconstruction* (Englewood Cliffs, N.J.: Prentice-Hall, 1969).

Integration or the threat of it in Southern higher education is discussed in several monographs dealing with colleges and universities. By far the most informative is Daniel W. Hollis, *University of South Carolina*: vol. 1–*South Carolina College*; vol. 2–*College to University* (Columbia; University of South Carolina Press, 1951–1956). In *College to University* Hollis clearly sees the 1873–1877 integration of the University of South Carolina as a tragedy detrimental to both state and institution. Other studies touching on college integration are John H. Reynolds and David Y. Thomas, *History of the University of Arkansas* (Fayetteville: University of Arkansas, 1910); Kemp P. Battle, *History of the University of North Carolina*, 2 vols. (Raleigh: Edwards and Broughton Printing Co., 1907–1912); and Walter L. Fleming, *Louisiana State University, 1860–1896* (Baton Rouge: Louisiana State University Press, 1936).

BIOGRAPHIES & GENERAL WORKS

John A. Carpenter, *Sword and Olive Branch: Oliver Otis Howard* (Pittsburgh: University of Pittsburgh Press, 1964), is a sympathetic study, giving suitable coverage to Howard's career as Freedmen's Bureau commissioner. Carpenter's presentation is completely refuted by William S. McFeely, *Yankee Stepfather: General O. O. Howard and the Freedmen* (New Haven: Yale University Press, 1968). McFeely concludes that the commitment of Howard and the bureau in assisting the freedmen was less than complete and that Howard was too willing to compromise on key issues. The author's implication that bureau schools taught blacks to be passive about their rights is arresting but is not substantiated. Otherwise, this book contains only a few vague references to freedmen's education and bureau schools. Otto H. Olsen, *Carpetbagger's Crusade: The Life of Albion Winegar Tourgée* (Baltimore: Johns Hopkins Press, 1965), presents a detailed account of the North Carolina constitutional convention of 1868 and Radical unwillingness to support mixed schools. Richard S. West, *Lincoln's Scapegoat General: A Life of Benjamin F. Butler, 1818–1893* (Boston: Houghton Mifflin, 1965), is a scholarly treatment of Butler's life which sheds some light on the general's motivations regarding Sumner's civil rights bill. David Donald's *Charles Sumner and the Rights of Man* (New York: Alfred A. Knopf, 1970) is the definitive study of Sumner's later career, although it reveals no new insights into the struggle over the civil rights bill. Moorfield Storey, *Charles Sumner* (Boston: Houghton Mifflin, 1900), and other older works are of little help in treating Sumner and federally enforced school integration. Jessie P. Rice, *J. L. M. Curry, Southerner, Statesman and Educator* (New York: King's Crown Press, 1949), provides insights on the early administration of the Peabody Fund and Curry's predecessor as general agent, Barnas Sears.

A large number of revisionist surveys of Reconstruction have been published in the last twenty years, but only a handful do more than mention black education and ensuing problems. Of these general works, John Hope Franklin's study, *Reconstruction after the Civil War* (Chicago: University of Chicago Press, 1961), gives the best coverage to black schools and integration. Rembert W. Patrick, *The Reconstruction of the Nation* (New York: Oxford University Press, 1967), presents some treatment of education in relation to the general Reconstruction spectrum. E. Merton Coulter, *The South during Reconstruction, 1865–1877* (Baton

Rouge: Louisiana State University Press, 1947), discusses in detail the role of the Freedmen's Bureau and benevolent associations in black education as well as presenting numerous opinions of white Southerners on the subject. Coulter, however, paints a bleak picture in failing to acknowledge the beneficial aspects of black schooling, Yankee benevolence, and the Freedmen's Bureau. C. Vann Woodward, *The Strange Career of Jim Crow*, 2d ed. (New York: Oxford University Press, 1957), admits that school segregation in the South was the general practice during Reconstruction rather than developing after 1890 (as with other forms of racial segregation), but he does not discuss the subject at any length.

MISCELLANEOUS MATERIALS

Among the numerous theses and dissertations consulted for this study, fifteen warrant reference. Richard B. Drake, "The American Missionary Association and the Southern Negro, 1861–1898" (Ph.D. diss., Emory University, 1957), is definitive concerning the role of the AMA in black education after 1860. Two intensive studies that illumine the educational activities of the Freedmen's Bureau in Virginia are William T. Alderson, "The Freedmen's Bureau in Virginia" (M.A. thesis, Vanderbilt University, 1949), and by the same author, "The Influence of Military Rule and the Freedmen's Bureau on Reconstruction in Virginia, 1865–1870" (Ph.D. diss., Vanderbilt University, 1952). Educational efforts of the bureau in Tennessee received careful attention by Paul D. Phillips in "A History of the Freedmen's Bureau in Tennessee" (Ph.D. diss., Vanderbilt University, 1964). Francis E. Bonar, "The Civil Rights Act of 1875" (M.A. thesis, Ohio State University, 1940), proved helpful in providing background information for state civil rights legislation of the pre–1875 period. Although researched almost entirely from the *Congressional Globe*, a detailed discussion of the Perce bill is presented by Herbert C. Roberts, "The Sentiment of Congress toward the Education of Negroes from 1860– 1890" (M.A. thesis, Fisk University, 1933). Guy H. Wheeler, Jr., "The History of Education in Texas during the Reconstruction Period" (M.A. thesis, North Texas State University, 1953), gave insights to the confusion in education prevailing in Texas from 1868 to 1874. Roger A. Fischer's "The Segregation Struggle in Louisiana, 1850–1890" (Ph.D. diss., Tulane University, 1967) contains two chapters on school integration in Louisiana (one dealing with New Orleans, the other with rural Louisiana), but the entire manuscript is marred by a strong racist bias. Howard Turner, "Robert M. Lusher, Louisiana Educator" (Ph.D. diss., Louisiana State University, 1944), was an excellent source of background material on Lusher, the pre- and post-Reconstruction superintendent of education in Louisiana. Maxine Sherman, "The Development of Public Secondary Education in New Orleans, 1840–1877" (M.A. thesis, Tulane University, 1939), provided additional information on Reconstruction school problems in New Orleans as did Esther B. Klein's study, "The Contributions of William O. Rogers to Education in New Orleans" (M.A. thesis, Tulane University, 1942). Germaine M. Reed, "David Boyd, Southern Educator" (Ph.D. diss., Louisiana State University, 1970), provides insights into LSU's struggle during Reconstruction and Boyd's changing views on mixed schools. Ruth L. Stubblefield, "The Education of the Negro in Tennessee during the Reconstruction" (M.A. thesis, Fisk University, 1943), is worth consulting as a survey and especially for material concerning black higher education in Tennessee. Richard T. Williams, "History of Public Education and Charitable Institutions in South Carolina during the Reconstruction" (M.A. thesis, Atlanta University, 1933), discussed the attempted integration of the South Carolina school for the deaf, dumb, and blind. An excellent survey of school problems in Louisiana for both the Civil War and Reconstruction eras is found in Leon O. Beasley, "A History of Education in Louisiana during the Reconstruction Period, 1862–1877" (Ph.D. diss., Louisiana State University, 1957).

Several miscellaneous published works provided invaluable assistance and information. The *Dictionary of American Biography*, 20 vols. (New York: Charles Scribner's Sons, 1928–1937), supplied biographical data on several contemporary figures for whom biographies do not exist. After years of searching, I was at last able to locate biographical information on Thomas W. Conway in *Appleton's Annual Cyclopedia and Register of Important Events for the Year 1887*, new series, 12: 578. The chapter treating Barnas Sears and the Peabody Fund could not have been written without consulting *Proceedings of the Board of Trustees of the Peabody Fund*, 1 [1868–1873], 2 [1874–1881] (Cambridge: printed by order of the trustees, 1875–1881). Although published over sixty years ago, a valuable collection of documents with innumerable references to black education, Yankee teachers, and mixed schools is Walter L. Fleming, *A Documentary History of Reconstruction, Political, Military, Social, Religious, Educational and Industrial, 1865 to the Present Time*, 2 vols. (Cleveland: A. H. Clark, 1906–1907).

Index

Abbott, Lyman, 19, 20, 27
Adams, H. E., 96
AFUC. *See* American Freedmen's
Union Commission
Aiken, William, 142
Alabama, 4; more favorable to black
education, 41; situation worsens
(1869), 47; public education in, 52;
school integration in, 57; civil
rights laws in, 124
Alcorn, James L., 61
Alcorn University (Miss.), 106
Alexandria, Va., school in, 17
Allen University (S.C.), 23
Alvord, John W.: education superintendent of Freedmen's Bureau, 5,
11; believes blacks love books, 15;
resigns, 16; requests military protection, 32; concerned over boarding of teachers, 35; lauds Southern
whites, 37; reports improved outlook toward black schools, 38;
reports opposition, 45; mentioned,
13, 83. *See also* Freedmen's Bureau
AMA. *See* American Missionary
Association
American Freedman, 20, 27
American Freedmen's Union Commission (AFUC): contrasted with
AMA, 5; black leaders, 14; breaks
up (1869), 16; money problems,
16–17; integrated schools, 20; teachers, 29; mentioned, 7 n, 19
American Missionary Association
(AMA): works for religious groups,
4; contrasted with AFUC, 5; first
black school under Union authority,
5; teachers, 29; mentioned, 6, 16,
19
American Tract Society, 28
Anthony, Susan B., 125
Antoine, Caesar C., 93
Arkansas, 4; schools in, 18; harassment of teachers, 35; assists black
education, 41–42; public education

in, 53; school integration in, 57–59;
public higher education in, 103;
civil rights laws in, 124
Arkansas Agriculture, Mechanical,
and Normal College, 103
Arkansas Gazette, 58
Arkansas Industrial University, 103
Arkansas Journal of Education, 144 n
Artesia (Miss.), contributes money
for schools, 42
Ashley, Samuel S., 22, 62
Association for Aid to the Freedmen
(1862), 6
Association for the Aid of Freedmen
and the Missionary Association, 3
Atlanta Constitution, 96, 127, 130, 138,
139
Atlanta University, 23, 103
Augusta, Ga., schools in, 19; men-
tioned, 33
Avery Institute, 65 n

Babbitt, Benjamin B., 113, 114
Banks, Nathaniel P., 7–8, 78
Barnwell, Robert W., 117
Bayne, Thomas, 72
Beaufort, S.C., school opened by
Peck, 6
Beauregard, Pierre G. T., 93
Belknap, W. W., 22
Biddle Memorial Institute (N.C.), 23
Bingham, John A., 120, 122
Bird, John T., 121
Bishop, Albert Webb, 103
Blackburn, Jasper, 90
Blaine, James G., 134
Blair, Austin, 121
Boothby, Charles W., 87, 93, 94,
96–97
Boseman, Benjamin A., 109
Bossier Parish (La.), violence in, 48
Boutwell, George, 138
Bowley, James A., 68
Boyd, David F., 81, 92, 104, 105–6,
132

Bradford, Edward A., 142
Bradley, John M., 58
Bradley, Justice Joseph P., 140 n
Brewer, Fisk P., 107, 113
Browley, James A., 110
Brown, William G., 87, 92–93, 96, 99, 152
Buckingham, William A., 154
Buckley, Charles W., 13
Bureau-association schools, 5–23
Burwell, William M., 150
Butler, Benjamin, black educational program, 8; on the Hereford amendment, 122; on mixed schools, 123; promotes Sumner's bill, 133–35; favors Kellogg amendment, 137; praises civil rights bill (1875), 139–40; mentioned, 153, 154
Byas, Benjamin, 65

Cain, Lawrence, 113
Cain, Richard, 69–70, 136
Camden, S.C., attitude toward teachers in, 37
Campbell, Hugh J., 81
Canton, Miss., contributes money for schools, 42
Cardoza, Thomas W., 62
Cardozo, Francis L., 65, 66, 109, 113
Cardozo, J. N., 65 n
Carpenter, Matthew, 128
Carraway, John, 57
Cessna, John, 134
Chamberlain, Daniel H., 69, 110, 117
Charleston, S.C.: schools for freedmen, 2, 8–9; municipal schools, 52
Charleston (S.C.) *News and Courier,* 69, 112, 138, 139
Chase, Lucy, 14
Chase, Salmon P., 5, 6 n
Chicago Inter-Ocean, 139
Child, Lydia M., *The Freedmen's Book,* 28
Citadel (Charleston, S.C.), 108
civil rights legislation, 119–40; act of 1866, 124; act of 1875, 158
Claflin College (Orangeburg, S.C.), 108
Clanton, James H., 30–31
classrooms, 26
Close, May, 34, 35
Colby, William M., 39
Cole, M. C., 92
Colfax, Schuyler, 126
Columbia County, Ga., schools in, 19

Columbia (S.C.) *Phoenix,* 115
Columbus, Ga., aggression against schools (1866), 44
Columbus, Miss., whites donate to rebuild schoolhouse, 42
Combash, William T., 60–61
Committee of Education (1862), 6
Congress: passes act to assist education of blacks, 10; legislative attempts to integrate, 119–40. *See also* civil rights legislation
Conkling, Roscoe, 127
Connecticut, outlaws segregation, 56
Conservative party: opposes mixed schools, ix, 63, 64; in Texas, 71; in Virginia, 72–73; in Louisiana, 87, 89, 93–94, 152; in South Carolina, 117
Constitutional conventions (1867–1868), 55–73
Conway, Thomas W.: biography, 78–79; elected Louisiana superintendent of education, 79; sponsors mixed-school legislation, 80–86; continues integration policy, 90–91; scandal involves, 92; wants university in public school system, 104; favors Sumner's bill, 125; fights Peabody Fund schools, 149–52, 154–55
Corinth, Miss.: schools at, 7; contributes money for schools, 42
Corwin, H. C., 113
cost: of schools, 12; of tuition, 15, 32
Cox, Samuel, 135 n
Crum, William D., 115
Cunningham, Edward S., 104
curriculum, 30, 31 n
Curry, Jabez L. M., 40, 157

Daily Union Herald (S.C.), 112
Darrall, Chester B., 89, 93
Davis, Edmund J., 71
De Bow, James, 39
De Bow's Review, 31, 33–34, 52, 150
DeGress, Jacob C., 71
Democratic party, 127, 138, 140
Denmark Vesey revolt (1822), 1
Department of Education, U.S., school funding, 21–22
Department of North Carolina and Virginia, educational program, 8
Department of the Gulf, educational system, 7

Illinois, nonintegrated schools in, 55
Indiana, nonintegrated schools in, 55
Iowa, outlaws segregation, 56

Jackson, Miss., contributes money for
  schools, 42
Jackson Clarion, 61
Jervey, W. R., 110
Jillson, Justus K., 65, 68, 69, 109, 110,
  114
John F. Slater Fund, 159
Johnson, Andrew, 78
Johnson, Henry, 125

Kansas: nonintegrated schools in,
  55; civil rights laws in, 123–24
Keeting, Charles W., 98
Kelley, William D., 121, 122
Kellogg, Stephen W., and Kellogg
  Amendment, 135–40
Kellogg, William P., 105
Kimball, John, 75
King, Edward, 60, 71
Kinsman, J. Burnham, 8
Ku Klux Klan, 35, 36

LaBorde, Maximilian, 111
Langston, John M., 42
Lee, Samuel J., 110, 111
Lewis, Barbour, 137
Lewis, John R., 15
Lincoln, Abraham, 6, 74
literacy of black troops, 8
Louisiana: mixed schools in, ix; education of freedmen in, 4; educational work in, 7–8; schools in, 18;
  harassment of teachers, 35;
  aggression against schools (1868),
  45–46; hostility increases (1869),
  47; public education in, 50–51, 53;
  desegregation of schools, 78–102;
  public higher education in, 104–6;
  civil rights laws in, 124; Peabody
  Fund support in, 149–57; mentioned,
  152
Louisiana State Seminary and Military Academy, 104
Louisiana State University, 91, 104–6
Luke, William, 36
Lusher, Robert M., 79, 87, 92, 99,
  149–53
Lynch, John, 136

McCleery, James, 47, 48
McDonald, Mrs. M. E., 94

McEnery, John, 105
McIntyre, George F., 113
McIver, Alexander, 132
McTyeire, Holland N., 40
Mallory, Stephen R., 39
Manly, Ralza M., 17, 20, 32–33, 148
Mann, Horace, 50
Massachusetts, civil rights laws in,
  123
Memphis Appeal, 130
Meridian, Miss., donations for black
  education, 42
Methodists, attitude toward black
  education, 38
Michigan, outlaws segregation, 56
Minnesota, outlaws segregation, 56
Mississippi: helps black education
  (1867), 42; hardens opposition
  against schools, 45; public educa-
  tion in, 53; school integration,
  60–62; public higher education in,
  106; school integration a condition
  of readmission to Union, 119–20;
  the Perce bill, 121–22; civil rights
  laws in, 124; mentioned, 4
Moore, Andrew B., 40
Morgan, Albert T., 42
Morgan, Charles, 42
Morris, Joseph W., 115
Morris Street School, Charleston,
  S.C., 15
Morton, Levi P., 123, 133
Morton, Oliver P., 154
Mosely, William, 73
Moses, Franklin J., Jr., 109, 110, 112

Nation, 139
National Teachers' Association, 29
National Theological Institute, 23
Nat Turner uprising (1831), 1
Neagle, James L., 109
New England Freedmen's Aid So-
  ciety, 1
New England free school, as model
  for South, 28
New National Era (D.C.), 76, 112, 127
New Orleans, La.: schools for blacks
  in, 2; schools in, 18; public schools
  in, 50–51; school integration,
  85–90, 93–102, 158; riots, 94–96
New Orleans Bulletin, 95, 96, 153
New Orleans Democrat, 100
New Orleans Picayune, 80, 86, 92, 94,
  95, 96, 152

Robertson, Thomas J., 110
Rogers, William O., 18, 85, 87, 97, 99–100
Ruffner, William H., 73, 129, 156
Runion, J. M., 67

Saint Augustine's Normal School (N.C.), 23
Saint Martin's School (D.C.), 23
salaries of teachers, 13
Sargent, Aaron A., 131
Savannah (Ga.): schools for blacks in, 2; reporters visit schools in, 41
Savannah (Ga.) Republican, 40
schoolhouses, 26–27
schools: Southern attitudes toward, 38–49; violence against, 44–45, 47–48; involvement with presidential campaign (1868), 46; racially integrated in North, 55. *See also* public education of blacks *and under names of individual schools*; students; teachers
Scott, Cornelius Chapman, 115 n
Scott, Robert K., 67–68, 109
Sears, Barnas, 141, 143–57
Selma, Ala., blacks prefer local white teachers, 40
Seymour, Horatio, 46
Shaw, John A., 50
Shaw, Kate R., 93 n
Sherman, John, 123
Sherman, Julia, 34
Simpkins, Paris, 113
Sloan, R. Gourdin, 112 n
Southard, Milton, 136
South Carolina: 1834 statute, 1–2; leaning toward black education, 41; against active support of black schools, 43; public schools in, 51–52; public education in, 53; school integration, 57, 63–70; public higher education in, 108–18; civil rights laws in, 124
South Carolina College of Agriculture and Mechanics, 108, 117
State Journal (Va.), 130
Stephens, Alexander H., 128
Stewart, Thomas McCants, 115
Stewart, William N., 131
Stoddard, Ephraim S., 83, 87, 90
Storm, John B., 121
Straight University (La.), 104
students, black: love of learning, 14–15; rate of learning, 15; subjects taught, 15; number of, 18–19
Sumner, Charles, 55; champions mixed schools, 75, 76, 119, 120, 122–23; and civil rights, 123, 124–30, 153

teachers: salaries, 13; Yankee vs. Southern, 24; living conditions, 26, 35; danger from disease, 27; attitudes of Northern, 27–30, 34; character of, 30; Southern attitudes toward, 31–37; problems of room and board, 35; violence and harassment, 35–36; cordiality toward, 36–37; Southern white, 37; black, 37; mentioned, 14
Tennessee: instruction of slaves not prohibited, 1; education of freedmen in, 4; hardens opposition against schools, 45; schools burned in, 47; public education in, 53; nonintegrated schools, 70–71; closing of black schools, 71
Texas: harassment of teachers, 35, 36; hostility increases, 47; state system for black education, 53–54; nonintegrated schools in, 71; school integration a condition of readmission to Union, 120
textbooks, 28, 30
Thorpe, Margaret, 36
Thurman, Allen G., 127
Tomlinson, Reuben, 42
Tourgée, Albion W., 63
Towne, Laura M., 28, 30

Union League, 44, 79
University of Arkansas, 103
University of Mississippi, 106
University of North Carolina, 107–8
University of South Carolina, ix, 69, 108–18, 158

violence against schools, 44–45, 47–48
Virginia, schools in, 17; Yankee teachers despised, 32–33; donations of land and labor in, 42; hardens opposition against schools, 45; public education in, 53; school integration, 72–73; 1869 political campaign, 119; school integration a condition of readmission to Union, 119–20; opposition to Sumner, 129